Matthias Raspe

GPU-assisted Diagnosis and Visualization of Medical Volume Data

Matthias Raspe

GPU-assisted Diagnosis and Visualization of Medical Volume Data

Exploiting the performance of modern graphics hardware for interactive computations and visualizations in medical applications

Südwestdeutscher Verlag für Hochschulschriften

Impressum/Imprint (nur für Deutschland/ only for Germany)
Bibliografische Information der Deutschen Nationalbibliothek: Die Deutsche Nationalbibliothek verzeichnet diese Publikation in der Deutschen Nationalbibliografie; detaillierte bibliografische Daten sind im Internet über http://dnb.d-nb.de abrufbar.
Alle in diesem Buch genannten Marken und Produktnamen unterliegen warenzeichen-, marken- oder patentrechtlichem Schutz bzw. sind Warenzeichen oder eingetragene Warenzeichen der jeweiligen Inhaber. Die Wiedergabe von Marken, Produktnamen, Gebrauchsnamen, Handelsnamen, Warenbezeichnungen u.s.w. in diesem Werk berechtigt auch ohne besondere Kennzeichnung nicht zu der Annahme, dass solche Namen im Sinne der Warenzeichen- und Markenschutzgesetzgebung als frei zu betrachten wären und daher von jedermann benutzt werden dürften.

Verlag: Südwestdeutscher Verlag für Hochschulschriften GmbH & Co. KG
Dudweiler Landstr. 99, 66123 Saarbrücken, Deutschland
Telefon +49 681 37 20 271-1, Telefax +49 681 37 20 271-0
Email: info@svh-verlag.de
Zugl.: Koblenz, Universität Koblenz-Landau, Diss., 2009

Herstellung in Deutschland:
Schaltungsdienst Lange o.H.G., Berlin
Books on Demand GmbH, Norderstedt
Reha GmbH, Saarbrücken
Amazon Distribution GmbH, Leipzig
ISBN: 978-3-8381-1958-8

Imprint (only for USA, GB)
Bibliographic information published by the Deutsche Nationalbibliothek: The Deutsche Nationalbibliothek lists this publication in the Deutsche Nationalbibliografie; detailed bibliographic data are available in the Internet at http://dnb.d-nb.de.
Any brand names and product names mentioned in this book are subject to trademark, brand or patent protection and are trademarks or registered trademarks of their respective holders. The use of brand names, product names, common names, trade names, product descriptions etc. even without a particular marking in this works is in no way to be construed to mean that such names may be regarded as unrestricted in respect of trademark and brand protection legislation and could thus be used by anyone.

Publisher: Südwestdeutscher Verlag für Hochschulschriften GmbH & Co. KG
Dudweiler Landstr. 99, 66123 Saarbrücken, Germany
Phone +49 681 37 20 271-1, Fax +49 681 37 20 271-0
Email: info@svh-verlag.de

Printed in the U.S.A.
Printed in the U.K. by (see last page)
ISBN: 978-3-8381-1958-8

Copyright © 2010 by the author and Südwestdeutscher Verlag für Hochschulschriften GmbH & Co. KG and licensors
All rights reserved. Saarbrücken 2010

To my family

PREFACE

Abstract

This thesis focuses on the utilization of modern graphics hardware (GPU) for visualization and computation purposes, especially of volumetric data from medical imaging. The considerable increase in raw computing power in recent years has turned commodity systems into high-performance workstations. In combination with the direct rendering capabilities of graphics hardware, *visual computing* and *computational steering* approaches on large data sets have become feasible. In this regard several example applications and concepts such as the "ray textures" have been developed and are discussed in detail.

As the amount of data to be processed and visualized is steadily increasing, memory and bandwidth limitations require compact representations of the data. While the compression of image data has been investigated extensively in the past, the thesis addresses possibilities of performing computations directly on the compressed data. Therefore, different categories of algorithms are identified and represented in the wavelet domain. By using special variants of the compressed format, efficient implementations of essential image processing algorithms are possible and demonstrate the potential of the approach.

From the technical perspective, the GPU-based framework CASCADA has been developed in the course of this thesis. The introduction of object-oriented concepts to shader programming, as well as a hierarchical representation of computation and/or visualization procedures led to a simplified utilization of graphics hardware while maintaining competitive performance. This is shown with different implementations throughout the contributions, as well as two clinical projects in the field of diagnosis assistance. On the one hand the semi-automatic segmentation of low-resolution MRI data sets of the human liver is evaluated. On the other hand different possibilities in assessing abdominal aortic aneurysms are discussed; both projects make use of graphics hardware. In addition, CASCADA provides extensions towards recent general-purpose programming architectures and a modular design for future developments.

Zusammenfassung

Die Arbeit beschäftigt sich mit dem Einsatz moderner Grafikhardware (GPU) für die Visualisierung und Verarbeitung medizinischer Volumendaten. Die zunehmende Steigerung der Rechenleistung ermöglicht den Einsatz von Standardsystemen für Anwendungsgebiete, die bisher nur speziellen Workstations vorbehalten waren. Zusammen mit dem wesentlichen Vorteil von Grafikhardware Daten direkt anzeigen zu können, sind Verfahren wie visualisierungsgestütztes Berechnen (*visual computing*) oder interaktives Steuern von Berechnungen (*computational steering*) erst möglich geworden. Darauf wird anhand mehrerer Beispielanwendungen und umgesetzten Konzepten wie den "ray textures" im Detail eingegangen.

Da die zu verarbeitenden und darzustellenden Datenmengen stetig ansteigen, ist aufgrund von Speicher- und Bandbreiteneinschränkungen eine kompakte Repräsentation der Daten notwendig. Während die Datenkompression selbst eingehend erforscht wurde, beschäftigt sich die vorliegende Arbeit mit Möglichkeiten, Berechnungen direkt auf den komprimierten Daten durchführen zu können. Dazu wurden verschiedene Algorithmenklassen identifiziert und in die Wavelet-Domäne übertragen. Mit Hilfe von speziellen Varianten der komprimierten Repräsentation ist eine effiziente Umsetzung grundlegender Bildverarbeitungsalgorithmen möglich und zeigt zugleich das Potential dieses Ansatzes auf.

Aus technischer Sicht wurde im Laufe der Arbeit die GPU-basierte Programmierumgebung CASCADA entwickelt. Sowohl die Einführung von objektorientierten Konzepten in die Shaderprogrammierung, als auch eine hierarchische Repräsentation von Berechnungs- und/oder Visualisierungsschritten vereinfacht den Einsatz von Grafikhardware ohne wesentliche Leistungseinbußen. Dies wird anhand verschiedener Implementationen in den jeweiligen Beiträgen und zwei klinischen Projekten im Bereich der Diagnoseunterstützung gezeigt. Hierbei geht es zum einen um die semi-automatische Segmentierung der Leber in niedrig aufgelösten MR-Datensätzen, zum anderen um Möglichkeiten zur Vermessung von abdominalen Aortenaneurysmen; jeweils unterstützt durch Grafikhardware. Darüber hinaus ermöglicht CASCADA auch die Erweiterung hinsichtlich aktueller Architekturen für den universellen Einsatz von Grafikhardware, sowie künftige Entwicklungen durch ein modulares Design.

Acknowledgements

There are many people I would like to thank. First of all I would like to say thanks to my supervisor Prof. Dr. Stefan Müller for mentoring my work, for providing many advices, and for his steady patience with my rather laborious style of working. Also, I would like to thank Prof. Dr. Bernhard Preim for offering to review this thesis as well as invaluable comments and discussions. Many thanks to Dr. med. Ralph Wickenhöfer for being a great mentor and inspiring partner and friend during our long collaboration in medical projects.

Furthermore, I would like to thank my former colleagues, Dr. Markus Geimer and Dr. Thorsten Grosch, for lots of inspirations and advice since my very first computer graphics experiences. Also, thanks to Prof. Dr. Dirk Reiners for many hints and shared knowledge in the exciting world of real-time computer graphics and OpenSG wizardry! I would like to thank my colleagues in the computer graphics working group as well for many discussions and for being just a great team: Jakob, Niklas, Stefan, Ulrich, Martin and Oliver; also thanks to Angelika and Brigitte for organizing everything around. Finally, thanks to my fellow PhD candidates, especially Silvia, Daniela, Friedemann, Marius, Johannes, Frank and Wolfram, for spending time during conferences, meetings, etc.

Of course, many students have contributed great ideas, have worked many hours on CASCADA's quirks – and have simply made teaching and coaching worth all the efforts. Among many others, I thank Nils, Stefanie, Andreas, Christian, Stephan, Thomas, Diana, the project teams of MedVis 1+2, MedGPU, and especially Guido for his extraordinary work and persistence to convince me of design patterns... Furthermore, I would like to thank the people at MeVis Research for many interesting sessions and inspiring discussions, also during our study trips to Bremen: Felix, Alexander, Christian, Jan, Christian, and many more. Also, to many people at LOCALITE and Fraunhofer FIT, especially Daniel, Martin, Sven, Dietlind, and Gernoth: thank you! I would like to thank the people at the MTI Mittelrhein as exciting interdisciplinary group; special thanks go to Prof. Dr. Dietrich Holz, Dr. Axel Koch, and Prof. Dr. Karin Gruber.

Although it was only a short time in Uppsala, Sweden, in late 2006 I enjoyed every single day at the "Centrum för bildanalys". I am very thankful to Prof. Ewert Bengtsson for giving me the chance to stay at the CBA, as well as Ingela for being a great and understanding supervisor during the collaborative project together with Joel from the Uppsala University Hospital. Also to all the CBA guys for the awesome time in Sweden: Erik, Kristin, Lena, Hamid, Magnus, and many more – tack så mycket och hej så länge!

Thanks to many people from university for years of friendship, especially Eva, Christian, Rodja, Oliver and Matthias. For the great time since high-school and all the unforgettable occasions together, thanks to my closest friends Andreas, Stefan and Sascha! In addition, thanks to Alexandra for spending many years together and learning many lessons in life.

I am very thankful to my family, especially my mother and brother for enriching my life and being there all the time. Finally, thank you Stefanie for being such a wonderful woman, giving strength, joy and comfort – not only during the exhausting time of writing this thesis.

Matthias Raspe

Contents

Preface	iii
Introduction	**1**
Motivation	3
Contributions	3
Structure	5

I Fundamentals 7

1 Graphics hardware 9
  1.1 Basics 9
      1.1.1 Architecture 9
      1.1.2 Programming languages 12
      1.1.3 Shader Debugging 14
  1.2 GPGPU 16
      1.2.1 From CPU to GPU computing 17
      1.2.2 Operations and algorithms 18
      1.2.3 Data structures 19
      1.2.4 Systems 20
  1.3 Volume visualization 23
      1.3.1 Theoretical background 23
      1.3.2 GPU-based volume rendering 25

2 Medical imaging and processing 31
  2.1 Medical Imaging 31
      2.1.1 Modalities 32
      2.1.2 Communication and Storage 36
      2.1.3 Computer assistance 38
  2.2 Data representation 41
      2.2.1 Grid 42
      2.2.2 Properties 42

2.3 Methods 45
    2.3.1 Preprocessing 45
    2.3.2 Segmentation. 46
    2.3.3 Visualization 47
    2.3.4 Discussion 49
2.4 Summary 50

II Concepts   51

3 Interactive visualization of computations   53
3.1 GPU-based computations 54
    3.1.1 Filtering Video Volumes using the GPU 54
    3.1.2 Tone-mapping Medical Volume Data 60
    3.1.3 Evaluating GPU-based Data Processing 68
3.2 Interaction 73
    3.2.1 Ray Textures 74
    3.2.2 Controlling iterative algorithms. 83
3.3 Conclusion 89

4 Compression computing   93
4.1 Compression domain 95
    4.1.1 Requirements 96
    4.1.2 Methods 97
    4.1.3 Discussion 103
4.2 Wavelet compression. 107
    4.2.1 Haar wavelet transform 107
    4.2.2 Rendering. 109
    4.2.3 Computations 110
4.3 Implementation 114
    4.3.1 Data structures 114
    4.3.2 Compression / Decompression 116
    4.3.3 Rendering. 119
    4.3.4 Computations 121
4.4 Results. 125
    4.4.1 Compression 126
    4.4.2 Rendering. 128
    4.4.3 Computations 128
    4.4.4 Discussion 132
4.5 Conclusion 133

5 Object-oriented GPU programming — 135
- 5.1 Related work — 136
  - 5.1.1 Shader programming — 136
  - 5.1.2 Programming systems — 139
  - 5.1.3 Summary — 141
- 5.2 Object-orientation — 143
  - 5.2.1 Fundamentals — 143
  - 5.2.2 Entities — 144
  - 5.2.3 Communication — 146
- 5.3 Hierarchical representation — 147
  - 5.3.1 Hierarchical rendering components — 148
  - 5.3.2 Case Study — 149
- 5.4 Software engineering aspects — 151
  - 5.4.1 Design patterns — 151
  - 5.4.2 Plugins — 152
  - 5.4.3 Further concepts — 153
- 5.5 Evaluation — 154
  - 5.5.1 Reusability — 154
  - 5.5.2 Performance — 157
- 5.6 Conclusion — 159

III Applications — 161

6 The framework "Cascada" — 163
- 6.1 Motivation — 164
- 6.2 Overview — 165
  - 6.2.1 Structure — 165
  - 6.2.2 System requirements — 165
  - 6.2.3 Extensions — 166
- 6.3 Implementation — 167
  - 6.3.1 General information — 167
  - 6.3.2 Volume representation — 169
  - 6.3.3 Rendering system — 172
  - 6.3.4 Shader handling — 174
  - 6.3.5 Application programming — 176

7 Projects — 179
- 7.1 LiverGPU — 179
  - 7.1.1 Related Work — 180
  - 7.1.2 Prototypes — 182

	7.1.3	Final version 185
	7.2	ARCADE 190
	7.2.1	Medical background 190
	7.2.2	Approaches 194
	7.2.3	Resume 202

8 Conclusion 203
8.1 Summary 203
8.2 Prospects 205
8.2.1 Classification of computations 205
8.2.2 Graphics systems 207
8.2.3 Medical imaging 208

Appendix 211

Publications 212

Bibliography 227

Web-based References 230

INTRODUCTION

During the past years graphics hardware has evolved at an increasingly fast pace. After graphics cards started to become user-programmable around 2001, graphics processing units (GPU) have turned into almost general purpose processors with an extremely high arithmetic intensity (see figure 1). Primarily driven by the entertainment industry, commodity hardware offers computational performance up to orders of magnitude higher than standard processors – even at entry-level prices.

Therefore, graphics hardware has also become of interest for applications in almost every scientific context. In order to meet the requirements of such non-graphics applications, vendors have recently introduced dedicated programming interfaces in order to use the graphics hardware as standard, yet massively parallel processing units. In addition to the increase of raw computing performance, graphics hardware has another advantage: the data to be displayed already resides in video memory and thus can be visualized at almost no additional cost. This is also expressed in the term "visual computing" for research and applications that integrate both visualization and computation on programmable graphics hardware.[1]

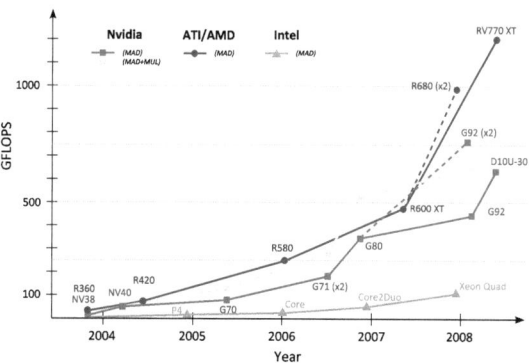

Figure 1: Performance development of GPUs and CPUs in recent years.

A comparable development can be seen in the medical imaging field. Today, a variety of image acquisition systems are available for different kinds of examinations, most of them being non-invasive. In particular, devices based on tomographic reconstruction such as computed tomography (CT) or magnetic resonance imaging (MRI) are capable of acquiring highly detailed images of anatomical structures in a very short time. Consequently, storage, display, and software systems have to keep up with the rapidly growing amount of data being acquired. While the former is no longer an issue due to large archiving systems and

---

[1]As this term, that has been originally introduced by Markus Groß in 1994 [Gro94] is used in different contexts, chapter 3 will discuss the concept in detail.

high disk capacities, visualizing and especially analyzing the large amount of data is a challenging task. Given that medical staff has to examine all of the data for diagnostic reasons, computer guidance and proper visualization is highly desirable. However, as the examiner is responsible for any decision made upon the data, software can only support diagnostics with appropriate quantification of errors and uncertainties. Additionally, advanced algorithms require considerable interaction, tedious parameter setting, and often take too long to compute – especially on the large amounts of data acquired today. This often prevents these functions from actually being used in the clinical practice and workflows on a regular basis.

These two developments – the rapidly increasing performance of graphics hardware and the assessment of large amounts of medical data – lend themselves to be combined. In fact, almost all workstations and software of radiological devices already have many capabilities of visualizing the data. However, direct volume rendering is rarely used for diagnostic procedures: the parameter setting is too complex, no additional (or even loss of) information compared to conventional two-dimensional images, etc. On the other hand, many image processing and analysis methods can benefit from multi-dimensional information (e.g. edge-preserving volumetric filter, analysis of time-varying data), but usually at the cost of higher algorithmic complexity.

This leads to the most recent field of investigation, namely the (additional) utilization of graphics hardware for computations, often referred to as "General Purpose GPU" (GPGPU). Several applications, from tomographic reconstruction to image processing and segmentation, have been implemented in hardware and demonstrate the GPU's superiority for almost all of these algorithms. Nevertheless, using the graphics hardware is not always advantageous. Firstly, creating software for graphics processors required a thorough knowledge of graphics concepts and hardware until the advent of dedicated APIs[2]. There was no alternative to writing programs using graphics interfaces and terminology, let alone being limited by a graphics-centered architecture. The second challenge are the short development cycles of GPUs: a new generation with evolved or new feature sets is introduced approximately every year. As no abstraction level has yet been available across all platforms (i.e., operating systems and graphics hardware), GPU programmers have to get used to new hardware implementations and driver details, to a much greater deal than for standard CPU software. Yet another disadvantage of using the GPU (or any other "external" device) for computations is the fact that its memory is different from the host's memory. Therefore, data to be processed has to be transferred to and from the graphics hardware. As this bandwidth has developed much slower than the raw computation performance, this gap often causes applications to be severely "bandwidth limited". To date, a significant improvement of this situation is not conceivable, at least not for current architectures.

---

[2] API = Application Programmers Interface

Motivation

Based on these introductory aspects, the motivation of this thesis is to integrate the computational and visualization potential of modern graphics hardware for medical applications. Although there are numerous algorithms and techniques for high-quality rendering of medical data, simple two-dimensional views are still the preferred visualization in diagnostic practice nowadays. Apart from the fact that acceptance plays an important role, there is currently not much benefit from three-dimensional visualizations; it is usually regarded as a nice by-product. Therefore, this thesis is going to present approaches towards a combination of three-dimensional visualization into common workflows to demonstrate its advantages.

Furthermore, the rapid increase of GPU performance in recent years enables the use of more complex algorithms as well as the processing of very large datasets. As such large amounts of data can be acquired today, processing and analyzing all of this data is still a computationally demanding task. Graphics hardware can thus come to the rescue, if programming such devices can be further generalized and made accessible for non-graphics experts. While recent developments already indicate this trend, the available techniques and interfaces are at a rather low, hardware-oriented level. In contrast, the framework developed and described in this thesis can be regarded as an additional layer, abstracting from the individual realizations, say software or hardware implementations. Above that, the concept of working directly on compressed data would be beneficial in several aspects, especially for graphics hardware with its limited memory resources.

Contributions

In order to give an overview of the main contributions of this thesis from a more technical point of view, they will be outlined in the following list:

Integration of computation and visualization This thesis will discuss progress in both computer graphics and medical imaging in order to develop a flexible GPU-based framework for the processing and visualization of volumetric (medical) data. Related work in this field, as well as recent developments in GPU computing interfaces provide techniques and functionality at a very low, hardware-centered level. The focus of this contribution is in contrast rather problem-oriented. Building upon basic components which can be implemented using either graphics or GPGPU interfaces, or even software implementations, more complex procedures such as image filtering, segmentation, or other functionality can be realized. As mentioned above, the graphics hardware allows an integrated visualization of the (intermediate) results, with negligible run-time overhead. While this enables to display intermediate results – in particular for iterative algorithms – it also makes it possible to really *interact* with the data and algorithms applied thereon.

Reduction of memory bottleneck In addition to developing such a framework with software engineering concepts in mind, two other areas will be addressed. Firstly, using the graphics hardware as an additional computing device requires data to be transferred from the host to the graphics memory, which can become critical for large volumetric data. Therefore, approaches towards reducing the amount of data by compression techniques are going to be developed in the course of this thesis. While this reduces the total amount of data to be transferred, processing and visualizing the data requires decompression and thus imposes a considerable algorithm and memory footprint. In order to tackle this issue, strategies for the *direct processing of compressed data* will be developed and discussed. The second approach to reduce the transfer costs is to keep the GPU as busy as possible. By providing means for concatenating single programs to complete procedures or workflows, this can be regarded as a lazy evaluation approach: only the data that is actually needed on the other device will be transferred.

Establish object-oriented concepts for GPU framework The developed system is based upon the idea to perform as many operations of a whole workflow as possible on the GPU in order to compensate for the expensive data transfer. Therefore, the framework CASCADA employs a hierarchical approach to represent computations at different levels of granularity. From a theoretical point of view, main *concepts from software engineering* such as object-oriented programming and design patterns will be applied to GPU programming. It will be shown that the run-time overhead introduced by these concepts is relatively small, especially in consideration of the benefits for implementation and maintenance. In addition, different projects and a description of the software system itself make up the practical part of the thesis.

Assessment of computations for GPU implementations Although the implementation of algorithms on graphics hardware is advantageous for many applications, not all procedures benefit from a GPU implementation. There are several factors that might hamper the performance: for example, algorithm structure, size of data, or number of computations per data element. Providing decision criteria would allow the system to *manage the utilization of the GPU*, ideally automatically; also in the context of working on compressed data. This involves an evaluation of the individual algorithms that will be applied, as well as the infrastructure that is currently available. In the course of this thesis, approaches towards such a classification will be discussed theoretically, based on the results and findings of the contributions from part two.

Structure

The thesis is comprised of three parts. The contents of each part are shortly described in the following list:

PART I: FUNDAMENTALS The first part provides basics from both the technical and medical field. The chapter on graphics hardware provides an in-depth discussion of architectures, programming languages, and (volume) visualization. Medical imaging and image processing methods will be presented in the second chapter with a focus on topics that are relevant for this thesis, as well as references to related work and applications.

PART II: CONCEPTS Building upon the theoretical basis from part one, the second part will develop different concepts including reviews of relevant work and an evaluation of the results. Firstly, the integration of visualization and processing will be discussed with references to the term "visual computing". As such an integration involves a considerable amount of communication between the CPU and GPU, these issues will be covered in-depth in the context of working with compressed data in the second chapter. Finally, the third chapter introduces object-orientation for GPU programming with an elaboration of relevant entities, abstraction layers, and other aspects of software engineering.

PART III: APPLICATIONS The third part introduces the GPU-based framework CASCADA which has been developed during the course of this thesis. This part will rather present the implementation of the theoretical concepts and important features and components than provide an exhaustive documentation of the software itself. Subsequently, different applications and projects (partly) realized with CASCADA are presented; again, with a focus on important techniques and solutions. The contributions of this thesis are finally summarized and discussed in the context of latest developments. In addition, a classification approach will be outlined to decide whether a hardware implementation is beneficial at all. Considering the rapid changes and advances in this field of research, some prospects in the field of visual computing and the medical imaging conclude this chapter.

Part I

Fundamentals

CHAPTER 1

GRAPHICS HARDWARE

As graphics hardware plays a key role in this thesis, it will be introduced in this chapter. Firstly, its architecture and programming possibilities are going to be outlined, with references to historical developments. As the performance of programmable graphics hardware has started to soar during the past years, it has become interesting for non-graphics applications to exploit the computational power as well. This general purpose use of graphics processing units ("GPGPU") is an active field of research of its own and will be the focus of the second section. In the subsequent sections relevant concepts of visualizing volumetric data, i.e., three-dimensional grids/arrays of values, are going to be outlined. Some references and discussions of further concepts for real-time volume rendering will conclude this chapter.

1.1 Basics

Using parallel hardware for accelerating computations on large amounts of input data has become the de-facto standard in computer graphics for several decades. Since then, the "graphics processing unit" (GPU) has turned into an extremely powerful processor, especially with the introduction of programmable stages. This increasing flexibility has attracted many non-graphics applications – a trend that has led lately to dedicated streaming systems. Although this simplifies the access to the high computational performance by means of generalized programming languages, the underlying hardware is still based on computer graphics considerations and evolutions.

Therefore, this section will provide an overview of graphics hardware, with a focus on the topics relevant for this thesis. Starting from an architectural point of view, recent changes and additions to the graphics pipeline are presented. Subsequently, programming languages and related concepts will be shortly introduced. Finally, information on shader development and debugging will conclude this chapter. All of these topics will provide references to relevant literature.

1.1.1 Architecture

In principle, there are two basic rendering methods for image synthesis: rasterization and ray tracing. While the former has undergone tremendous developments and technical advancements – primarily due to the graphics hardware fueled by the large game and entertainment industry – the latter is a simple, yet very powerful method. Nevertheless, there are lots of extensions and variations to the original ray tracing algorithm, as well as intensive research for accelerating ray tracing to reach interactive performance on commodity systems. In comparison, rasterization requires very complex algorithms for convincing and competitive results, but achieves real-time rendering performance at multi-million pixel resolutions easily; however, at the cost of inaccuracies and many workarounds. Ray tracing, on the other hand, can simulate much more advanced effects at an (almost) arbitrary level of physical correctness[1]. This comes at the price of rather slow rendering performance – even at moderate image sizes and/or scene complexity. Approaches towards dedicated ray tracing hardware have not been successful, while current advancements indicate a trend towards hybrid solutions or highly optimized software implementations. As ray tracing in general is beyond the scope of this thesis, the reader is referred to according literature.

Every GPU is basically a (massively parallel) hardware implementation of the graphics pipeline, illustrated in figure 1.1. The model can be further divided into the vertex process-

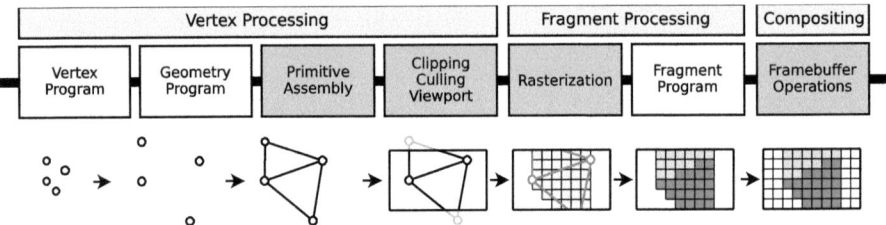

Figure 1.1: The graphics pipeline with programmable (yellow) and fixed or configurable (blue) stages. (Illustration based on Engel et al. [EHK+06].)

ing, fragment processing, and compositing stage.[2] This separation is also reflected in the different hardware units contained in the processor. While the fixed-function pipeline has provided several *configurable* entities from the very beginning, *programmable* stages have been introduced approximately eight years ago. Since then, the pipeline became much more programmable, as is indicated for the current generation by the yellow steps in figure 1.1. Historically, vertex processors have been introduced first, whereas the fragment processor was the much more powerful unit, especially for complex computational tasks. Although this separation is alleviated by the shift to the unified shader model (i.e., all shader types use the same processing units, leading to better hardware utilization, load-balancing, etc.), the

---

[1] Of course, this is still an approximation due to the discrete representation in computers, as well as inherent physical limitations introduced by the ray model for light simulation.
[2] DirectX uses the term "pixel shader" instead of "fragment shader" in Cg or OpenGL. In this thesis, the latter will be used because it describes the functionality more precisely: as a "pixel candidate" the term does not imply further processing steps or settings such as multi-sampling, blending, etc.

1.1. BASICS

fragment processor has been the predominant stage for several years. Another evidence is the number of parallel fragment processors compared to vertex units in earlier GPU generations.

As the exact delineation of different GPU generations varies in literature, and is in addition subject to frequent changes and updates due to recent developments, the evolution of shader programming and the notion of "Shader Model" (SM) can be used as a good indicator. The following table summarizes this evolution and is based on the discussion by Akenine-Möller et al. [AMHH08].

Generation	Year	Shader Model	Features
First	2001	DX 8.0/SM 1.1	programmable vertex shaders, very limited fragment shaders
Second	2002	DX 9.0/SM 2.x	Further programmability of both vertex and fragment shaders (e.g. flow control), introduction of Cg/HLSL and GLSL
Third	2004	DX 9.0c/SM 3.0	Extensions to existing shader types (e.g., vertex textures, increased limits)
Fourth	2007	DX 10.0/SM 4.0	Introduction of geometry shaders, further extensions (e.g., integer textures, bitwise operations), concept of unified shaders

Table 1.1: Historical outline of the programmable graphics hardware

While most of the developments have clearly improved preceding generations and simplified implementations, several very important features have been introduced with the latest generation. Geometry shaders enabled for the first time the creation or deletion of data within the pipeline. This allows in combination with immediate feedback mechanisms (i.e., "transform feedback" in OpenGL) the implementation of advanced algorithms such as displacement mapping, subdivision surfaces, isosurface construction, etc. in hardware.

Nevertheless, there are still fundamental limitations of graphics hardware from the programming point of view. Although most of them are going to be alleviated or removed by the upcoming streaming approaches (e.g., Nvidia CUDA), many existing implementations or the continued support of older graphics hardware face several problems:

- Random write-access ("scattering") is a key feature of many algorithms (see section 1.2.2), but is not supported by fragment shaders. Although there exist implementations using vertex shaders or multi-pass approaches for such operations, these are far from efficient and flexible to use.

- Using the same texture for reading from and writing to is not possible in any shader. This can be overcome by a technique referred to as "ping-pong textures", where the input is duplicated beforehand and the two textures are used alternatingly. Again, this is neither intuitive nor memory efficient, and can become critical for large input textures (double memory footprint).

- While the representation of image data as textures is reasonable from a graphics point of view, using textures as storage for general data – as is also common for graphics applications – is hampered by the limited texture types (dimensions), formats, sizes, etc. In addition, using textures as target for offscreen computations has been further limited in that only few formats and types are supported.

The current advances already provide several solutions for these limitations, but usually face the challenging trade-off between functionality and performance. Graphics hardware has become extremely powerful because of its focused application and the removal of data dependencies enabling the parallel streaming concept. With further developments in the direction of generalized programming systems in tight combination with graphics concepts for immediate and efficient visualization, the graphics hardware is likely to remain highly relevant in the foreseeable future.

1.1.2 Programming languages

Graphics programming has evolved a lot since the introduction of programmable pipeline stages. While custom shader programs had to be written in assembly language in the first years of shader programming, high-level shading languages have improved this tedious and error-prone situation. Especially these dedicated languages have initiated the use of graphics hardware for non-graphics purposes, although an in-depth knowledge of graphics concepts was still required; the term "shading language" itself reflects this quite well. In addition, multiple platforms and APIs have become available with systems such as Nvidia's Cg [FK03] so that one shading language could be used for both OpenGL and DirectX applications.

This section is going to shortly introduce the characteristics of high-level shading languages and some syntactic details. The focus will be on the OpenGL Shading Language (GLSL) [Ros05], as this is the preferred language throughout the thesis and is – in addition to Cg – commonly used in the GPGPU community. While section 1.2 introduces programming concepts for GPGPU applications, chapter 5 will provide a more detailed discussion of other shader programming environments and languages. Further information can be found in many other references as well: language details in the according specifications and programming books [FK03, Ros05]; a general and up-to-date overview in Akenine-Möller et al. [AMHH08]; other languages in the GPGPU context in the extensive surveys by Owens et al. [OLG$^+$07, OHL$^+$08].

OpenGL Shading Language

Initially developed by 3Dlabs in 2001, the OpenGL Shading Language (GLSL, also "GLslang") has become part of the OpenGL standard in 2003 via extensions, and a core component since OpenGL 2.0. As practically all high-level shading languages, GLSL is based on the programming language C with several additions for graphical data types and operations, access to OpenGL states etc. However, some features of the C language are not supported, most notably pointers, recursive constructs, type casts, or arbitrary data types.

1.1. BASICS

GLSL program objects are assembled from strings that define the different shader programs, i.e., vertex and fragment shaders.[3] In contrast to other approaches, the program code is compiled within the graphics driver. While this simplifies the programming workflow on the one hand, as no additional external tool is required, the hardware manufacturer is responsible for providing an up-to-date compiler on the other hand. This can lead to different behaviour and results, depending on the driver's feature set and quality.

As mentioned above, in addition to (most of the) standard data types found in C programs there are graphics oriented vector and matrix types in GLSL, for example: `vec4`, `mat3`, or `bvec2`, for a vector of four floats, a 3×3 matrix of floats, and a vector of two booleans, respectively. Accessing the vector components can be done by array indices or – very common and efficient in shader programs – field positions (`x`, `y`, `z`, `w` etc.). Additional features such as swizzling or masking (i.e., replicating/changing field components for read or write access), as well as component-wise arithmetic operations and comparisons, or geometrical computations (e.g., scalar products) are natively supported and are thus extremely efficient.

Depending on the type of shader program, different sets of operations are available. For example, the vertex shader can only read from vertex input data and textures, but cannot access the frame buffer or neighboring elements. Fragment shaders, on the other hand, are optimized for texture fetches and can thus operate on multiple textures (for read and write operations), thereby using advanced texture filtering and mip-mapping. Communication between the different shaders, and between shaders and application is provided by classifiers that specify the handling of the parameters: while `uniform` elements are constant for all input data, `attribute`s define individual properties of the input; `varying` variables are used for inter-shader communication, usually interpolated during rasterization. Due to the general concept of parallelism, there are several limitations for all types of shaders to ensure data independency.

Cg

Nvidia's "C for graphics" has been the first widely available and multi-target shading language.[4] That is, Cg programs can be compiled for different graphics APIs and hardware platforms/generations by specifying hardware profiles. This allows an improved matching of the program's functionality with the according hardware capabilities, and thus the identification of potential incompatibilities already at compile-time.

While GLSL programs are compiled and assembled within the graphics driver, Cg uses an external compiler that can be executed during run-time or as separate building step (fig 1.2). The latter approach allows further, low-level optimization in the assembly code, which is still common practice for games and other highly optimized shaders. However, the increasing complexity and growing number of shader programs used in one application renders this impractical, especially taking Cg's powerful error class system into account. This allows

---
[3] As for other languages, geometry shaders are considered optional in the current shader generation.
[4] Microsoft has also developed Cg, but provides their own language (HLSL) which is practically identical with Cg. It is, however, limited to the DirectX API and will not be considered here separately.

the identification and handling of both conventional and profile-dependent errors during compilation at application run-time.

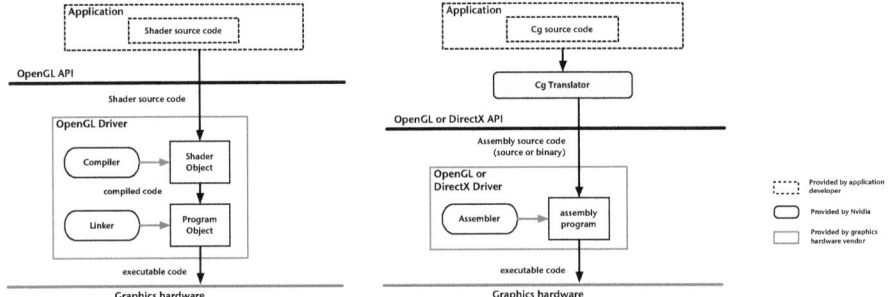

Figure 1.2: Comparison of the system environment for GLSL (left) and Cg (right). (Illustration based on [Ros05])

In addition to these differences, Cg provides the higher level concept of *interfaces* adopted from Java or C# – however, without the full potential of these object-oriented languages. By using interfaces in shader programs, the code structure can be improved by "outsourcing" custom type declarations. In combination with the advanced include mechanisms in recent Cg versions, this allows a very clean and modular programming style.

Finally, a large amount of profiles enables the transition to other APIs. Therefore, the Cg program is compiled using profiles such as `gp4fp` or `vs_4_0` for OpenGL fragment programs or Direct3D 10 vertex shader, respectively. Due to the differences of the shading languages, however, suboptimal code and side-effects might be introduced, so that lots of tests are needed to ensure consistent results and behaviour among the different platforms in practice.

CgFX/glFX

Yet another concept of shader programming is the combination of multiple shaders into an *effect*. This introduces another level of abstraction in that the collaboration of the shaders in different contexts is specified. There are varying approaches for the graphics APIs, with "glFX"[5] being the latest one. These systems are used predominantly for graphics effects, and thus play a minor role in GPGPU applications. Nevertheless, further information and the relation between effect systems and other approaches will be addressed in chapter 5.

1.1.3 Shader Debugging

Tools for developing shaders have been available for quite a long time, with various systems and environments by different vendors and graphics APIs. An extensive discussion of available shader development tools would be out of scope of this chapter, however. In addition,

---

[5]see http://www.khronos.org, last visit Feb 18 2009

1.1. BASICS

such a discussion would become outdated very quickly due to the dynamic developments in this area. Some of the subsequently presented debugging tools incorporate development functionality, but further information can also be found at the websites of the different shader languages introduced before. References to according tools can be found in the plethora of literature on shader programming as well. The book by Akenine-Möller et al. [AMHH08] is an excellent and up-to-date starting point.

The focus in this section is on the analysis and debugging of shaders. As the context of this thesis (and the developed framework CASCADA) is the utilization of graphics hardware especially for non-graphics applications, debugging tools will be discussed from this point of view. Several of these methods and tools have been used for working with and assessing shader programs in the course of this thesis and related projects; additional information can be found in chapters 3, 6, and 5. Nevertheless, most concepts apply to both GPGPU and standard shader programming.

In general, the execution of shader programs on dedicated hardware (i.e., the GPU) does not allow direct access to low-level information such as memory addresses, internal states, etc., as is possible for CPU implementations. Thus, there are basically two approaches to still provide tools for GPU programming: *software emulation*, and *shader code instrumentation*.

The former approach is rather obvious and known from other applications, such as programming portable systems, game consoles, future hardware, etc. However, architectural properties are hard to simulate: first and foremost the massively parallel layout of GPUs. As Owens et al. [OLG+07] and Strengert et al. [SKE07] postulate in their review of debugging tools, debug code can only be executed on the GPU to allow an efficient workflow and powerful means for debugging. Consequently, emulation approaches are not considered here.

Shader code instrumentation, on the other hand, uses the actual hardware for computing the results. Depending on the type or complexity of these computations, the data to be analyzed has to be read without introducing side effects, considerable performance overhead, numerical issues, etc. While being advantageous with respect to emulation approaches, code instrumentation is technically a very challenging task.

Selected debugging methods

"printf-style"   This very simple yet effective approach uses the fragment shader for displaying the variable or result in question. As the name implies, this requires the manipulation of shader code, similar to its counterpart for software implementations. However, due to the separation of the GPU into different processing stages with diverse capabilities, this approach is very limited in practice. Debugging implementations that consist of multiple passes, or the inspection of geometry shader functionality is not possible. Nevertheless, the direct visualization of (non-graphical) data is useful in many cases and a common technique in GPGPU programming, which has been adapted in most debugging toolsets.

gDEBugger The debugging and profiling system "gDEBugger" for the OpenGL API has been developed by Graphic Remedy since 2004 [6]. Their commercial tool is available for virtually all platforms and allows to monitor the application's activity and behaviour, including additional shader debugging functionality for all types of shaders. Therefore, shader code and dependent information such as OpenGL states, variable values, etc. can be edited and visualized. Several logging mechanisms, viewers for texture data or input buffers provide additional information during run-time or as external log files.

glslDevil In addition to the different commercial solutions, Strengert et al. [SKE07] have proposed a flexible non-commercial system for debugging GLSL shader programs called "glslDevil". Although breakpoints are currently not supported, their system provides powerful tools for inspecting shader entities or stepping through loops. As the preceding system, glslDevil supports all types of shaders and makes explicit use of code instrumentation. Therefore, the shader code's syntactic structure is analyzed to automatically manipulate the code and integrate performance-neutral debug information.

Summary

The preceding section provided a short overview of shader development and debugging. This is still an active field of research, as the graphics hardware is evolving fast and, especially for GPGPU programming, the paradigm seems to shift towards generic approaches such as CUDA. Above that, implementing advanced tools for different platforms, APIs, and operating systems is a challenging and tedious task.

1.2 GPGPU

After introducing the concepts of graphics hardware for traditional computer graphics applications, this section discusses "general purpose" uses of GPUs, GPGPU in short. Different scientific communities have developed approaches for using graphics hardware for non-graphics applications. This is mainly due to the huge performance increase of graphics processors, in combination with more flexible programming languages during the last years. Recently, dedicated APIs have been proposed by major vendors of (graphics) hardware that abstract completely from the underlying hardware; see also chapter 5 for a discussion of programming languages.

In the following sections introductory information about GPGPU will be given. Firstly, analogies between traditional computer graphics (as outlined in section 1.1) and GPGPU approaches will be presented, with references to current advances. Secondly, the building blocks of implementations – algorithms and data structures – will be outlined in the sub-

---

[6] http://www.gremedy.com, last visit Feb 14 2009

1.2. GPGPU

sequent paragraphs. Dedicated APIs and streaming architectures are the focus of the third section, and will be summarized with a short discussion in the remainder of the section.

1.2.1 From CPU to GPU computing

Implementing programs on the graphics hardware requires other structures and concepts than CPU implementations. Although current programming languages and streaming APIs allow an almost similar programming style, the underlying hardware is still optimized for graphics-like program layout (i.e., parallel and independent streams of data). Additionally, thorough knowledge of computer graphics concepts is needed to implement GPGPU programs efficiently. In Owens et al. [OHL+08] the different approaches for writing graphics programs, GPGPU programs using graphics APIs, and new streaming concepts, respectively, are compared and discussed.

GPU programming

Before dedicated streaming architectures have been introduced, Harris [Har05] identified analogies between software implementations and their GPU counterpart, as summarized in table 1.2. Although the new streaming APIs do not require these graphics structures anymore, it helps to understand the underlying concepts and effects. In addition, the framework developed in the course of this thesis is based on graphics concepts for most of its functionality, as dedicated systems have not been available during development. However, CASCADA 2 already supports CUDA, which will be both introduced later.

CPU	GPU	Description
Arrays	Textures	Data is usually transferred as vertex arrays or textures to the GPU.
Inner Loop	Shader program	A kernel (or operation) is applied to multiple elements of the input stream in parallel on the GPU. Software implementations usually consist of a loop iterating over all elements.
Feedback	Render-to-Texture	Algorithms are usually a concatenation of multiple small computations. Offscreen textures and sequential passes implement the data connection. General APIs such as CUDA provide unified memories for flexible read/write access.
Invocation	Rasterization	Operations on data are performed by executing the according shader program with the data as input. As the fragment processor is primarily used, fragments are created by rasterizing primitives, with correct data at the vertices for texture access etc.

Table 1.2: CPU–GPU analogies

Streaming programming

Although these concepts can be applied to practically all algorithms, structuring complex computations "along the graphics pipeline" is not very intuitive and requires in-depth knowledge of computer graphics systems. Therefore, modern APIs provide dedicated computing modes that allow the CPU-like usage of graphics hardware. As most of these applications are in the field of visual computing (see also chapter 3), a tight and efficient connection to rendering facilities is still available.

1.2.2 Operations and algorithms

GPGPU applications are usually built from fundamental algorithms and common operations similar to the development of general software. These operations are referred to with common terms in stream computing, and thus should be shortly outlined in the following list. Further information can be found in the cited literature, as well as in Owens et al. [OLG+07, OHL+08] for a broader overview.

Gather Reading data from an array by randomly indexing (i.e., `v = d[a]`). This resembles a texture fetch in GPU programming.

Scatter Writing data to an array at arbitrary position (i.e., `d[a] = v`). Fragment processors do not support scattering, in contrast to vertex and geometry programs.

Map The application of a function to every stream element, executing GPU programs on primitives.

Reduce Reduction of the stream by performing "unifying" operations (e.g., averaging); see figure 1.3 for an example. Related to reduction is *filtering*, where a subset of a stream is computed.

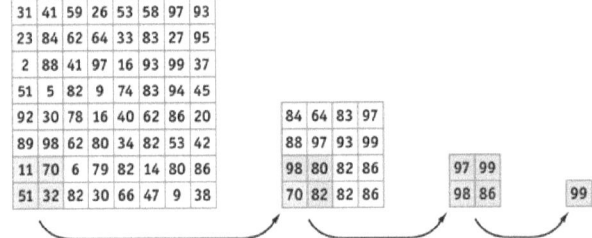

Figure 1.3: Reduce operation for determining the maximum. In every iteration, four adjacent elements are compared, with the largest value being written to the output position. (Image courtesy of Harris [Har05])

Scan Scanning, also known as "parallel-prefix-sum" computes the sum for every element in the stream over the preceding elements (e.g., summed area tables, histograms).

Sort Sorting algorithms usually based on sorting networks (i.e., non-recursive structure), for example bitonic merge sort.

Search Algorithms similar to sequential software implementations, but usually performed in parallel. Examples are binary search or *k*-nearest-neighbor, as in Zhou et al. [ZHWG08].

1.2.3 Data structures

After outlining common algorithms and procedures, this section will shortly introduce typical approaches for GPU data structures and libraries providing such functionality. As the architecture of graphics hardware is considerably different from CPUs, an adaptation of standard approaches is required for optimal performance. In general, data structures are regular arrangements of similar objects in order to optimize access to and processing of data elements with respect to computational and memory efficiency. Depending on different criteria (number of elements, insertion/deletion, access pattern, etc.) sequential structures such as arrays or stacks, tree-based structures, or hash tables are typically used.

For GPU implementations, two-dimensional texture memory is still the "first-class citizen" for storing data. This is mainly due to the fact that memory, caches, etc. are highly optimized for parallel, two-dimensional access patterns. Above that, other dimensions are less flexible because of driver limitations (e.g., maximum texture size) or write access. Although this situation is less critical for streaming APIs that provide even more flexibility and replace the notion of texture by arbitrary memory buffers, an understanding of the graphics concepts is beneficial for reasonable performance.

During the past years, numerous data structures have been implemented on graphics hardware. In the following list, the most important approaches will be outlined, with a focus on structures that are used in CASCADA (see chapter 6). Also, some of the concepts will be addressed in chapter 5 in the context of object-oriented GPU programming. An extensive discussion of different approaches is given in Owens et al. [OLG+07]. Lefohn et al. [LKS+06] provide a thorough comparison and classification of various techniques.

Arrays Continuous multidimensional memory as preferred data structure in GPGPU applications, with 2D textures being the natural choice for GPU architectures. Address translators (Lefohn et al. [LKS+06]) or other layouts (Harris et al. [HBSL03]) allow the implementation of practically all applications.

Adaptive structures Generalized arrays for implementing data structures such as quadtrees or *k*-d trees (Zhou et al. [ZHWG08]). See see chapter 4 for further examples (e.g., mip-mapping based approaches).

Other Data structures that do not support random access, such as stacks, sets, or queues. Although there exist some implementations of stacks and hash maps, they are clearly not as efficient as data-parallel structures and are still subject of active research.

Although the different data structures already cover a wide range of applications, their reuse and maintainability has become a challenging task. Designs too general usually lead to suboptimal performance and the integration into existing systems usually requires considerable code changes. Therefore, libraries provide an abstraction and help reducing the additional implementation efforts. An early approach is the "Glift" system proposed by Lefohn et al. [LKS+06].

While Glift has been implemented using graphics API and the Cg shading language, the success of streaming systems such as CUDA is also due to an early available toolset. The "CUDA Data Parallel Primitives Library"[7], CUDPP in short, is a library of data-parallel algorithm primitives, as presented in the preceding section. It was initially developed in the context of Harris et al. [HSO07], and runs on processors that support CUDA. As for Glift, CUDPP strives to provide optimal performance and modularity, and is designed for working on GPU data originating from GPU computations and data transferred from the host application.

1.2.4 Systems

In the preceding paragraphs, streaming approaches and dedicated GPGPU architectures have been mentioned. Since its introduction in early 2007, Nvidia's CUDA has become the de-facto standard for stream computing. Alternatives such as OpenCL or Brook+ have been released just recently, so that further developments are hard to project. Nevertheless, these generalized architectures will play a key role in the near future of high-performance visual computing and thus should be outlined shortly in the following sections.

CUDA

The "Compute Unified Device Architecture" is a technology by Nvidia that generalizes the use of graphics hardware for non-graphics purposes. It has many concepts with BrookGPU in common, which has been developed by Buck et al. [BFH+04, Buc05]; see also section 5.1.2 for further information. Furthermore, in chapter 6 the integration of CUDA in the framework CASCADA will be described, so that only a short overview of CUDA's concepts is provided in this section.

The novel concept of CUDA is its abstraction model in order to exploit parallel structures. A hierarchy of threads, shared memory, and synchronization mechanisms allow a combination of data and thread parallelism, as well as task parallelism. This concept can be regarded as a "divide-and-conquer" approach: the problem is divided into sub-tasks to be processed independently, and further into cooperative sub-tasks to be solved in parallel. From a technical point of view, CUDA implementations scale to an (almost) arbitrary number of processors, also across multiple graphics boards or computation units: the underlying run-time system manages the setup and communication.

CUDA is realized as an extension of the C/C++ programming language, i.e., functions are directly written in the C/C++ code using dedicated specifiers and other keywords. Therefore, an additional compilation step is required to separate the CUDA-specific, *device* code from

---

[7]http://www.gpgpu.org/developer/cudpp (last visit January 19 2009)

1.2. GPGPU

standard application code executed on the *host*. The `nvcc` compiler forwards the standard code to the system's compiler (`gcc`, Intel compiler, etc.). The device code will be executed on the GPU and is controlled by the host, thus being similar to graphics-based approaches. While the application code can use the full range of the C++ language, the device code (i.e., the kernels) are limited to a streaming variant of C. This is again akin to the traditional GPGPU approach which will be addressed in chapter 5.

In addition to the separation of device and host, the following terms are commonly used during CUDA development:

Kernel Simple functions or complete programs implementing the operation to be performed on the data.

Thread Addressable unit managed by the processors on the graphics hardware that contain the kernels.

Block Organizational unit containing fixed number of concurrent threads. Cooperation and communication is realized by barriers and shared access to memory within the block.

Grid Highest level of the hierarchy built from thread blocks.

Each of the components are executed in parallel and thus exploit the massively parallel structure of the hardware. This leads to the very high number of threads being executed in the order of thousands to tens of thousands. Therefore, certain restrictions have to be maintained, e.g., recursion is not supported, as the memory overhead for the stacks would become too large. Finally, *configurations* define the layout of blocks in the grid.

Due to a large amount of implementations and examples, the number of CUDA users is rapidly increasing, with applications from practically all kinds of fields with high computational requirements. This demand, on the other hand, supports the advances and development of the underlying hardware, drivers, libraries, and the software itself.

Brook+

At the time of writing, CUDA can be used only on Nvidia hardware. Nvidia's main competitor AMD has extended the BrookGPU since 2007 in the course of the AMD Stream Computing development [Bro07]. This further development led to Brook+ featuring an enhanced compiler, support for multiple GPUs, etc.

As depicted in figure 1.4, the system consists of the source-to-source compiler `brcc`, and the run-time library `brt` executing precompiled kernel functions.

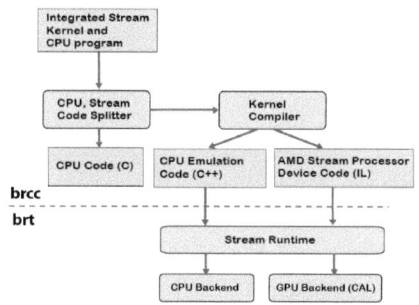

Figure 1.4: Brook+ architecture

Although there are already some applications and demos available that utilize AMD/ATI streaming hardware, the development seems to be way behind CUDA. However, such progresses strongly correlate with the available hardware, where ATI's consumer and workstation systems outperform Nvidia's equivalents by both computational performance and energy efficiency.[8]

OpenCL

While the aforementioned systems are vendor-specific, a large group of practically all industry-leading companies and several research institutions has worked on the open standard "OpenCL" (Open Computing Language [Khr]) for parallel programming of heterogeneous systems. That is, it is supposed to provide a uniform programming environment for developing efficient and portable code for high-performance computing on servers, desktop systems, and handheld devices. In addition, the processors can be a set of different types such as multi-core CPUs, GPUs, Cell architectures, etc. The first specification has been released in December 2008, thus resulting in only few implementation examples available at the time of writing. Furthermore, OpenCL is going to be a main concept of the upcoming release of Apple's operating system Max OS X.

The architecture is similar to other approaches in that there is one host and one or multiple OpenCL devices. Each device is comprised of one or many computing units, that consist of one or multiple processing elements. The kernels that are assigned by the host are either OpenCL kernels, written in OpenCL C, or native kernels. As for other GPGPU approaches, OpenCL is a subset of the C language with extensions for parallel computing, which is also translated by the (integrated) OpenCL compiler and executed at run-time. Aside from standard, SIMD-like[9] types, OpenCL also supports advanced vector types (e.g., `float8` or `int16`), and proposes further types `double` or `quad`[10], as well as combinations (e.g., complex numbers).

As for other GPGPU concepts, the efficient combination with standard shaders is inherently provided by direct access to OpenGL objects such as textures or offscreen buffers, as well as interfaces to Nvidia's CUDA.

The preceding section has shortly introduced the use of graphics hardware for general purpose computations. This field of research has evolved very fast, not only due to the rapid development of GPUs. Clear advances such as the increasing flexibility of programming languages and dedicated streaming approaches, and the combination of high-performance computing and visualization have led to powerful applications. This topic will be addressed in detail in chapter 3, and is the general motivation of the developed framework CASCADA. The fundamentals of visualizations, especially for volume data, will be presented in the following section.

---

[8]This has become an important issue with modern GPUs requiring dedicated power supplies.
[9]SIMD = single instruction, multiple data
[10]128-bit floating point

1.3 Volume visualization

As volumetric data plays an essential role in this thesis, basic principles and current techniques for rendering volume data will be introduced in this section. The notion of *scientific visualization* for displaying large amounts of data from complex computations and acquisitions goes back to McCormick in 1987. These visualizations have been performed by means of computer graphics from the very beginning, as the data has geometric meaning in most cases. While only dedicated, special purpose systems were capable of performing the extensive computations back then, commodity graphics hardware has exceeded the performance of these expensive machines by far during the last years.

The volume data that should be visualized is usually of various origin, format, and complexity: numerical simulations, geological measurements, video sequences, or data from medical imaging are some common examples. As the focus of this thesis is the processing and visualization of medical volume data, the subsequent sections and chapters are usually limited to this kind of data. However, lots of the methods presented in this section are applicable to other data as well. Especially in chapter 3, some remarks on extending approaches to other volume data will be given in the context of visual computing.

The following sections will introduce fundamental concepts for rendering volume data and interacting with it. As an extensive and thorough discussion of volume visualization would be beyond the scope of this work, the interested reader is referred to the wealth of (introductory) literature available. The book by Engel et al. [EHK+06] provides a broad overview and several starting points. In particular, the articles by Engel et al. [EE02] and Ikits et al. [IKLH04] present excellent and concise introductions. The coverage here follows the *volume rendering pipeline* depicted in figure 1.5, with an emphasis on steps that are relevant for concepts and discussions throughout the thesis.

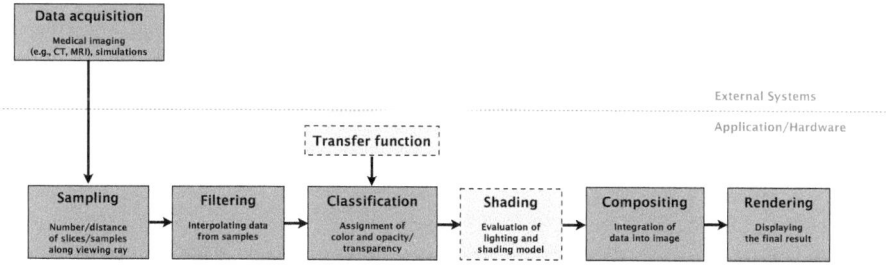

Figure 1.5: The volume rendering pipeline containing common processing steps (dark gray) and optional stages (light gray). The acquisition of data is usually accomplished by external systems, with medical imaging being extensively described in section 2.1.

1.3.1 Theoretical background

As mentioned before, volume data can be generated by simulations, be the result of three-dimensional imaging techniques such as CT scans, etc. Data in general computer graphics is denoted as three-dimensional and objects usually consists of a set of points (with or without topological information) or mathematical formulae that describe a *surface* in three-dimensional space. Volume data is also made up of a set of 3D data, but resembles a *solid* structure, with information given at every (discrete) position within the object's boundary. See section 2.2 for further information on the data representation.

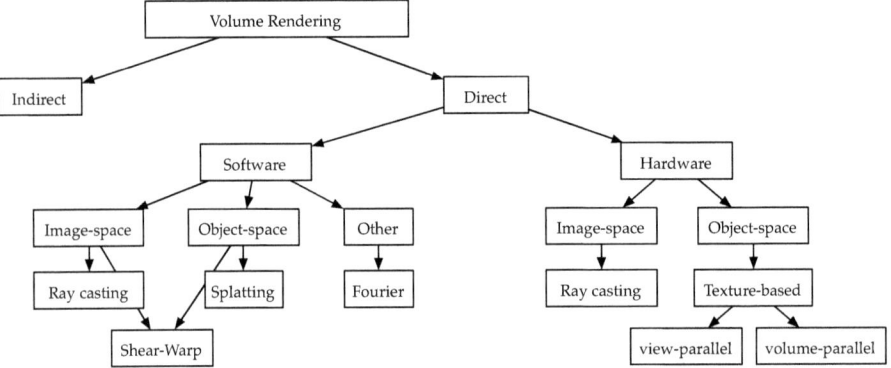

Figure 1.6: Overview of common volume rendering methods.

In general, there exist two basic ways to visualize such data: by extracting a surface for standard rendering, or by displaying an "accumulation" of the complete data. The former is referred to as *indirect* method, while the latter is denoted *direct volume rendering*, as classified in figure 1.6. The extraction of such a surface representation from the volume data is usually done by specifying a threshold, referred to as *iso-value*. All positions with a value (close to or) equal to this threshold are converted to an intermediate surface representation, that can then be rendered using standard methods. The seminal method for constructing surfaces is the Marching Cubes algorithm by Lorensen and Cline [LC87], that has been extended and improved since then in various contributions.[11] However, an extensive discussion of indirect methods would be beyond the scope of this thesis, as the focus is mainly on direct rendering methods.

Due to the fact that computational performance has increased considerably during the past, direct volume rendering methods have become widely available and much more flexible than in the first years of volume visualization. Based on the mathematical concepts of light transport, the so-called *emission-absorption model* is a reasonable approximation of the general formulation, and thus the most preferred method in real-time volume rendering. The basic idea is depicted in figure 1.7.

---

[11]In the context of GPU implementations, the marching cubes method has been implemented using geometry shaders (see section 1.1) as well. Although the performance exceeds that of software implementations by far – mainly due to parallelism – it can be only considered as proof of concept.

1.3. VOLUME VISUALIZATION

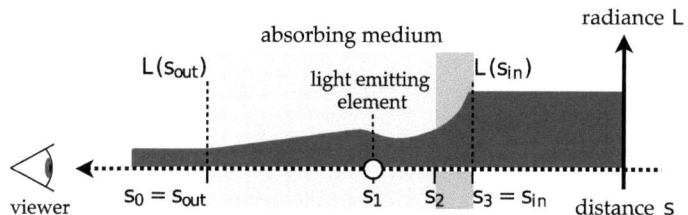

Figure 1.7: Concept of direct volume rendering using the emission-absorption model: The initial radiance L is absorbed differently along the optical path, with a light-emitting element contributing to the visible radiance at s_{out}. (Illustration based on [Pal08])

In its general form, the volume rendering integral is given by:

$$L(s_{out}) = L(s_{in})e^{-\int_{s_{in}}^{s_{out}} \kappa(t)dt} + \int_{s_{in}}^{s_{out}} q(s)e^{-\int_{s}^{s_{out}} \kappa(t)dt} ds \qquad (1.3.1)$$

and computes the radiance at the exit point $L(s_{out})$ as the sum of the (background) radiance entering the volume $L(s_{in})$, attenuated along the optical path depending on the material's absorption coefficient κ, and the integrated contribution of the (light emitting) source terms q attenuated by the medium along the remaining path (i.e., starting from s instead of s_{in}). In the context of volume rendering the absorption integral is often substituted by the optical depth τ to further introduce the more intuitive term "transparency". See according references for further details.

1.3.2 GPU-based volume rendering

In addition to the two rendering methods, i.e., direct and indirect rendering, the aforementioned concepts can be implemented in software or using programmable graphics hardware. Implementations using the graphics hardware can be further divided into fixed-function approaches relying on considerable collaboration with the host application, and (almost) purely GPU-based implementations. While the former are still relevant for limited hardware (e.g., on mobile devices), the focus here will be on implementations exploiting modern programmable graphics hardware. The following paragraphs are organized in the order of the volume rendering pipeline from figure 1.5 and discuss different limitations and characteristics, in addition to referring to state-of-the-art techniques.

Sampling and filtering

Rendering volume data requires the computation of the volume integral from equation 1.3.1. As there exists no analytical solution for this integral in practice, and due to the discrete nature of data representation and computations, numerical approximations are needed. This leads to the following equation:

$$L(s_{out}) \approx \sum_{i=0}^{n} c_i \alpha_i \prod_{j=i+1}^{n} (1 - \alpha_j) \qquad (1.3.2)$$

where n denotes the number of samples used for approximation, c_i the emitted (colored) radiance at the current position, and α_i the opacity, respectively.[12] The colors are defined by assigning optical properties to the volume data at position i by means of a transfer function, as will be described later.

Hence, the volume has to be sampled and integrated along the observer's viewing direction. If special purpose methods, such as Fourier-based volume rendering, are omitted due to their marginal relevance in practical applications, basically two approaches remain (see figure 1.6). First, so-called *object-space* methods process the volume in its domain, and thereby contribute to the resulting image. On the other hand, *image-space* techniques start from the image to be created, and assemble its content by sampling the volume, as will be discussed below. Note the resemblance to methods for surface rendering: scanline conversion resembles an object-space, and ray tracing an image-space algorithm, respectively.

Both methods have the sampling process in common, i.e., the volume data is sampled at different locations in order to approximate the volume integral (equation 1.3.2). Sampling a three-dimensional scalar field addresses mainly two issues: the number of samples, and the discrete structure of the data. As is obvious from the discrete equation, an infinitesimally small distance between two samples converges to the continous integral. However, the data itself is already discrete, and the Nyquist-Shannon theorem limits the number of samples needed to represent the signal: twice the maximum frequency, i.e., two samples per voxel are sufficient to reconstruct the signal. Below this sampling distance the result is subject to artefacts due to undersampling. Therefore, there are techniques to reduce errors by adjusting the sampling rate or position; see [EHK[+]06] for further details.

The second issue is the fact that the positions for sampling the volume data are in most cases not exactly at the voxels' centers. Therefore, the value at the sample's position has to be computed by applying a reconstruction filter. This can be accomplished by taking the value of the closest position (nearest neighbor), a linear interpolation of the neighboring voxels, or a higher-order reconstruction filter. While the two former techniques are available as hardware implementations with most graphics hardware, more advanced filter kernels or reconstruction of non-standard formats (e.g., compressed data as in chapter 4) require custom shader programs.

Texture-based volume rendering This method has been the most common direct volume rendering approach and resembles an object-space method. Although there exist again two approaches, only the view-parallel method will be taken into account here, as it has displaced the volume-aligned in practice due to superior visual quality, simpler code, and less memory consumption. The concepts of both methods are depicted in figure 1.8. In order to sample the volume data, a stack of parallel polygons is created. For the view-aligned approach, these polygons are parallel to the viewing plane, that is, each polygon is computed by clipping its plane with the volume's boundaries (usually a cuboid). The distance of the slices then resembles the sampling distance. The sampling itself is performed by the rasterized polygons

---

[12]Note that the colors have to be weighted with the according opacity, as non-associated colors are assumed.

1.3. VOLUME VISUALIZATION

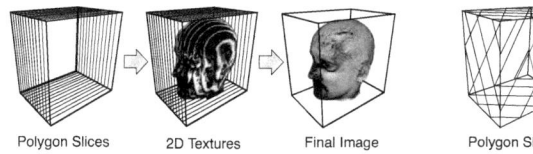

(a) Texture based volume rendering using volume aligned polygons, requiring three 2D texture stacks.

(b) Texture based volume rendering using view aligned polygons and a single 3D texture.

Figure 1.8: Texture-based volume rendering using volume aligned (a) or view aligned (b) polygons. Note the superior quality for the view aligned method. (Images courtesy of [EHK⁺06])

where each fragment samples the volume data that has been assigned as texture to the proxy geometry before. As mentioned above, filtering is needed for reconstructing values at the fragment positions and usually depends on the data format and layout, desired visual quality, and performance. As shown in figure 1.6, texture-based volume rendering is only resonable as hardware implementation, because it exploits several graphics hardware concepts to achieve useful performance.

Ray casting As its equivalent for rendering surfaces, ray casting is an image-space method. This technique was introduced long before graphics hardware has been widely available (e.g., Levoy [Lev90]). The term "ray casting" refers to the process of creating primary rays from the viewpoint only.[13] First implementations were pure software approaches that required highly optimized data structures to achieve tolerable performance. However, they were still far from real-time except for very small data sets or coarse renderings. GPU implementations usually follow the concept proposed by Krüger and Westermann [KW03a] that represents a full GPU-based solution, as the rays' creation is also performed on the graphics hardware. In

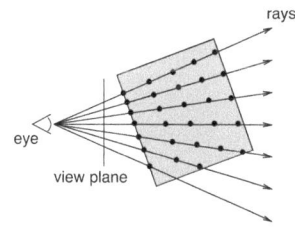
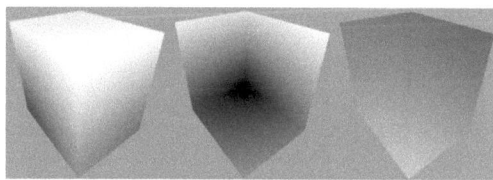

(a) Concept of ray casting.

(b) GPU ray generation using color-coded textures.

Figure 1.9: Ray casting principles: sampling the volume using viewing rays (a), and textures for GPU-based ray generation (b).

general, the idea behind ray casting is to generate rays starting from the viewpoint through the viewing plane, and sample the volume data along each ray at certain intervals from its

---

[13]There exist other terms such as volume ray tracing or ray marching that emphasize the process of sampling along the ray, contrary to standard ray tracing where only intersections with geometry are evaluated.

entry to exit position with respect to the volume's boundary (see figure 1.9(a)). Note that also other criteria or optimization strategies such as empty space skipping can be applied here. GPU-based ray generation, as depicted in figure 1.9(b), renders the front and back faces of the boundary geometry. The fragment position in volume coordinates is then stored in RGB-textures, resulting in the typical color encoding. The ray vectors are finally constructed from the fragment pairs in the textures.

Sampling is performed similar to the texture-based approaches, but without explicit proxy geometry: the volume texture is accessed directly within the shader program. This allows both the use of hardware filtering, or custom reconstruction. In contrast to texture-based rendering, ray casting is more flexible with respect to sampling strategies:

- rays can be adaptively created, manipulated, etc., as will be shown in section 3.2.1
- the integration of optimizations such as empty space skipping or jittering is much easier (see [EHK+06] and [Pal08] for details)
- iso-surface rendering is as simple as using the sampled fragment if the value is within the threshold, or discarding it otherwise.

However, hierarchical data structures such as octrees require additional steps to adjust to the different resolution levels, as is discussed in Guthe et al. [GWGS02], for example. Due to its advantages in general, GPU-based ray casting is used in the framework developed in the course of this thesis. Hence, subsequent discussions and techniques will put an emphasis on this volume rendering method.

Classification

After the volume data has been sampled, the values have to be assigned visual properties. This classification process is usually done by so-called *transfer functions*, as indicated in figure 1.5. Depending on the type of input data, the transfer function maps input values to optical information, that is, usually color and opacity. Therefore, one-dimensional RGBA textures resemble the lookup tables for standard approaches. This allows an efficient and straightforward integration of optical properties, but is in practice limited with respect to delineating structures for visual inspection of complex data.

Transfer functions have been a research topic for several years, as they provide powerful means to visualize complex data. However, one-dimensional lookup textures are limited in that they assign the same input value equal visual properties – without taking other information into account. Therefore, structures of a certain density cannot be separated from samples that have the same value due to interpolation (e.g., at the boundary of dense structures to air, see figure 1.10(a)). In order to overcome this situation, multi-dimensional transfer functions have been introduced. Instead of a simple, one-dimensional function, two or more input parameters are assigned visual properties. Typical examples for additional parameters are gradient magnitude information, temperature, multiple MRI modalities (see section 2.1), etc.

1.3. VOLUME VISUALIZATION

Furthermore, the additional computational complexity of multi-dimensional transfer functions becomes a considerable user interaction challenge. While for one-dimensional classification a function editor is rather intuitive, two-dimensional transfer functions already require higher-order manipulation tools (e.g., polygonal widgets). Higher dimensional interaction is practically not feasible without simplifications, special input metaphors and/or devices, etc. In figure 1.10 transfer functions of different dimension are applied to a CT volume data set, with custom mean-value coordinate interpolation for arbitrary polygon widgets. Note the clear separation of the structures' boundaries using the 2D transfer function.

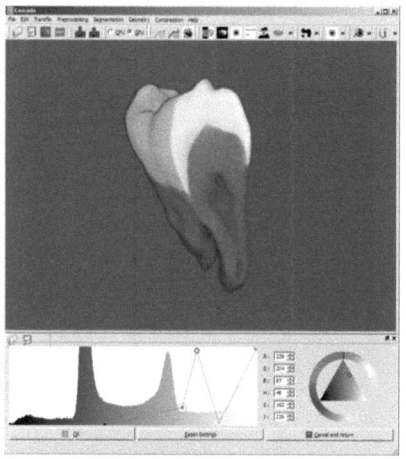
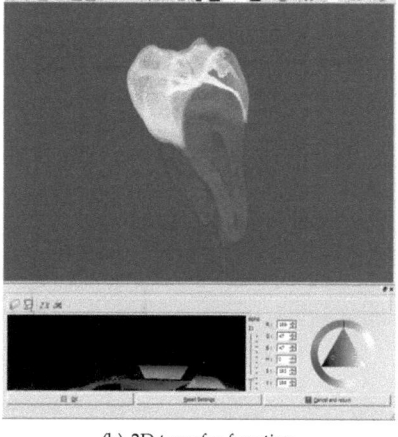

(a) 1D transfer function (b) 2D transfer function

Figure 1.10: Direct volume renderings of the same data set in CASCADA, using (a) one- and (b) two-dimensional transfer functions, respectively.

Rezk-Salama et al. [RSKK06] propose in their work the use of high-level interaction semantics. Therefore, a large amount of transfer function settings for medical data sets have been analyzed to extract representative information. Using their system, the user can control the visualization by adjusting parameters related to anatomical details (e.g., transparency of vessels or bones) instead of gray levels etc.

Compositing and rendering

The integration for the final image is usually denoted as compositing step. Here, the samples from the preceding step are assembled, taking their visual properties into account. Independent from the volume rendering technique used for visualization, this process is based on the second part of equations 1.3.1 and 1.3.2, respectively. In order to implement this computation efficiently, different approaches are possible, with graphics hardware acceleration playing an important role in most implementations today. While texture-based approaches mainly rely on alpha blending capabilities of graphics hardware, ray casting approaches accumulate the classified samples manually. Although the former provide high performance even on older GPUs, the focus here will be on ray casting methods due to their superior visual quality and flexibility. Equation 1.3.3 summarizes the blending operation for back-to-front rendering mode, where C denotes the color, and α the opacity, respectively.

$$C_{dst} = C_{src}\alpha_{src} + C_{dst}(1 - \alpha_{src}) \qquad (1.3.3)$$

The integration step for the ray casting method is either performed using multi-pass techniques, or – especially on newer hardware – by single-pass programs. The latter consist of a loop that iterates along the ray and calculates the contribution to the integral at the current position. This also allows the natural integration of further concepts, such as early ray termination or adaptive sampling; see Engel et al. [EHK+06] for details.

However, the complex architecture of graphics hardware might introduce side-effects that hamper the overall performance, as discussed by Leung et al. [LNM06]. For example, fragments at object boundaries do not have to be integrated for the whole ray, whereas neighboring fragments might require full evaluation. The organization of fragments in groups (fragments "in flight") thus introduces a performance dependency. In contrast, multi-pass algorithms inherently separate the "slower" fragments from those already finished by the information update between rendering passes. Due to the additional overhead from state changes, CPU-GPU communication, etc., the performance savings are often more than outweighed, however.

The presentation of important concepts of the volume rendering pipeline could be extended with many further techniques, but would be beyond the scope of the thesis. For more detailed information on the fundamentals and a wide coverage of further approaches, see Engel et al. [EHK+06].

CHAPTER 2

MEDICAL IMAGING AND PROCESSING

Today, practically all medical procedures rely on image data that has been acquired beforehand: from ECG[1] ablations or ultrasound slices to multidimensional MRI data – the information is usually represented digitally and undergoes several processing steps. In order to discuss different approaches in the course of this thesis for medical applications, this chapter starts with an overview of medical imaging. Therefore, relevant imaging methods and modalities are presented, followed by considerations on workflows in clinical practice. The concept of computer assistance with a focus on diagnostics (in contrast to therapy, surgery, etc.) will be addressed in the subsequent section.

As an integral part of computer diagnosis is the processing of acquired data, background on image processing is provided in the second part of this chapter. The first section provides basic information and definitions for representing and manipulating image data. While many algorithms process the data in their raw representation, compressing the data becomes also increasingly important due to the huge amounts of data being acquired. Thus, the concept of compression computing introduced in chapter 4 is motivated. Subsequently, important methods in image processing, segmentation, as well as visualization applications are going to be summarized. A short discussion concludes this chapter.

2.1 Medical Imaging

In order to examine a patient, there is a variety of methods for acquiring information. Depending on the exigence, i.e., an emergency situation or some less severe illness, the medical staff collects information based on the patient's descriptions. This anamnesis is then the basis for further examinations, that might involve the control of internal body functions, testing the musculoskeletal system, analysis of blood or other liquids, etc. However, especially for trauma patients these procedures are usually not possible as immediate action is required. Therefore, medical imaging techniques are used for getting an overview of the situation and initiate further procedures.

The focus in this work will be on data from medical imaging, more precisely on radiological imaging. An in-depth coverage of all imaging techniques would be beyond the scope,

---
[1]ECG = Electrocardiogram

thus the following paragraphs only outline the principles of morphological and functional imaging. The interested reader is referred to the large amount of literature, with books by Dhawan et al. [DHK07] or Suetens [Sue02] being excellent starting points.

2.1.1 Modalities

In medical imaging, the term *modality* describes the type of data or equipment that acquires information of the subject to be examined. As is common for all digital sampling processes, the data is an approximation of the real signal due to limited spatial resolution, bit depth, etc. In addition, the data has to be stored in a reasonable format that provides optimal quality with respect to file size. Although storage is practically infinitely available today, data has to be transferred on a regular basis as well; these issues will be addressed in the subsequent section.

The variety of modalities in use today can be separated into *morphological* and *functional* imaging. While the former describes the anatomical relation (e.g., shape, size, vascularity) of different organs or structures, functional imaging focuses – as the name implies – on the structures' functions, metabolic activity, behaviour, etc.

Morphological imaging

Radiography/Angiography   *Radiography* is the use of X-rays to image the internal structure of objects. As X-ray imaging creates a projected image, the attenuations of the different materials along the ray are summed. Modern radiographical imaging uses digital detectors instead of film, mainly because of their superior flexibility and better contrast ratio. *Fluoroscopy* is a variant of radiography, where the image is displayed immediately through the use of image intensifiers. It requires less radiation and therefore allows the continuous screening during interventions (see also section 7.2), for example.

Angiography is a dedicated imaging method to visualize the lumen of vascular structures. Therefore, contrast agent is administered through the use of catheters or other injection devices resulting in enhanced structures. The image, referred to as angiogram, is then created at time intervals of optimal uptake. Optionally, a contrasted angiogram is subtracted from an image without contrast agent, which is referred to as *Digital Substraction Angiography* (DSA) for depicting only the contrasted areas.

Computed tomography   As already mentioned in the preceding paragraph, X-ray imaging does not allow the exact determination of structures along the ray, i.e., the third spatial dimension due to the summation process. By taking multiple radiographies from different angles, *computed tomography* can reconstruct three-dimensional data.

Since the first CT devices, the technical setup has been optimized in numerous ways leading to different generations of CT scanning systems, which in turn results in a wide clinical use of third-generation devices today. Another great improvement regarding acquisition times and spatial resolution – especially in axial direction – has been accomplished by *Multi-Slice CT*. Here, multiple rows of detectors enable the acquisition of several slices

2.1. MEDICAL IMAGING

at once. Current devices consist of 64-256 rows, whereas one of the latest systems features 320 slices. Most of the scanners in use today have a spiral configuration, i.e., the table with the patient is moved continuously, thus further reducing scanning time – despite the more complex reconstruction algorithms. Finally, so-called *Dual Source CT*s contain two X-ray sources that are arranged at offset angles. These are run either at different energy levels resulting in different imaging properties available at one time, or at the same level for further reducing the acquisition time by a factor of two if fast imaging is crucial (e.g., for high-quality imaging of the coronary arteries).

Aside from the relatively moderate costs for device purchase and maintenance, computed tomography has several disadvantages. Most importantly, the radiation exposure is rather high, especially if detailed images are required or large portions of the body are examined. For example, the effective dose of a thoracic CT is approximately 400 times higher than an overview X-ray image of the same region [Wet07]. As CT imaging has become relatively cheap per examination, scans require a critical consideration to prevent nonessential exposure. In addition, many diagnostic problems involve vascular structures that require the application of contrast agents due to the low discrimination to other tissue in X-ray based modalities. Therefore, CTA[2] imaging is considered as an invasive method and requires additional precautions (agent intolerances, additional stress for the cardiovascular system, etc.).

As CT data is the basis for one of the projects presented in chapter 7, additional information such as imaging details or specific data properties will be provided in the according section. Further information on the value ranges and different processing and viewing options will be given in section 3.1.2 as well.

Magnetic resonance imaging Magnetic resonance imaging (MRI)[3] has been used and improved extensively since its invention in the late 1970s. As the details of the imaging process and the different uses are more complex than for CT, the following discussion will be limited to main differences and applications with respect to CT. Several authors, such as Wetzke [Wet07], Suetens [Sue02], or Preim and Bartz [PB07] provide an in-depth review of the imaging process.

In contrast to computed tomography, magnetic resonance imaging does not use X-radiation and thus does not impose any ionizing exposure dose on the patient. Instead of measuring the varying attenuation of rays by different structures, MRI uses specific properties of tissue in external magnetic fields. As this imaging process requires a sufficient amount of protons (i.e., water and/or fat) for a measurable signal to be generated, not all structures of the human body can be depicted: for most parts of the lung or the cortical bone, for instance, MRI is not suited. Computed tomography, on the other hand, cannot discriminate

---

[2]short for CT Angiography
[3]Originally, the term "nuclear magnetic resonance" (NMR) was used and describes the basic principle more precisely. However, due to the negative associations with the word "nuclear" especially in the public, the more neutral MRI has replaced the old term soon.

different types of soft tissue (e.g., brain matter) due to the identical attenuation of X-rays. As MRI allows a very detailed differentiation of these structures, it is an ideal complement in radiological imaging, as can be seen in figure 2.1.

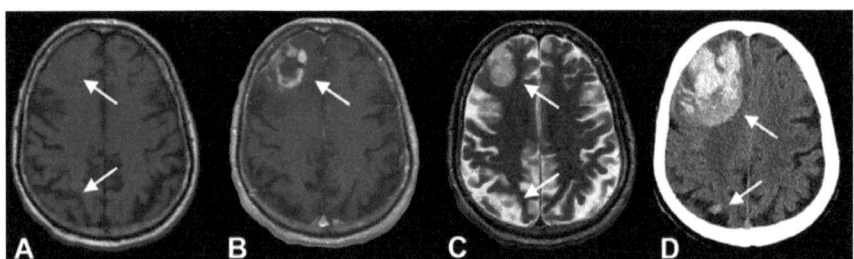

Figure 2.1: Comparison of MRI sequences: T_1-weighted (A), contrasted T_1-weighted (B), T_2-weighted (C); and a later CT-scan (D), clearly showing the differences to MR images. The images depict brain tissue with severe hemorrhage in the parts of the right hemisphere (arrows).

However, there are also several disadvantages with magnetic resonance imaging. Firstly, MRI is a very expensive technique, especially for high-field devices with more than 1.5 Tesla. To achieve a good signal-noise-ratio, the external magnetic field has to be extremely homogenous and strong – which can only be achieved by using superconducting magnets. This results in turn in extremely high installation and maintenance costs. Secondly, the very high magnetic field intensities require precaution with respect to metallic structures. Therefore, pacemakers and cochlea implants are currently a strict contraindication, prostheses or other implanted parts such as surgical clips or stent-grafts (see section 7.2) should be subject to further consideration. Depending on the type and location of the object, injuries can be caused by mobilization, thermal induction, and/or failure of electronic components. Finally, MRI scanning has acquisition times in the order of several minutes and is thus much slower than CT. This results in artefacts, especially from breathing, heart motion, or general pulsation.

Ultrasonography Another modality to examine preferably soft structures of the body is *ultrasound*. Due to the very inexpensive and mobile devices, this method has become the de-facto standard for initial diagnoses, follow-up routines, and for monitoring pregnancy. There are neither contraindications nor negative effects known in practice, although ultrasound is not suited for bone structures and (large) regions of air. In contrast to intraoperative MRI, where only few devices are available worldwide, ultrasound is used during interventions on a regular basis, also due to its real-time capabilities. As it is not relevant for projects discussed in this thesis, further information can be found in according literature, such as Wetzke [Wet07] or Suetens [Sue02].

2.1. MEDICAL IMAGING

Functional imaging

In contrast to morphological imaging, functional modalities acquire information about processes and functions of anatomical structures for diagnostic purposes. Except for functional MRI, this involves the use of radionuclides and is therefore often referred to as nuclear imaging. These methods are only addressed in section 3.1.2 and summarized in the following paragraphs.

Functional MRI This variant of MRI is a rather new technique based on changes of blood flow and oxygen contentration due to neural acitivity, and is therefore currently used only for cerebral imaging. *Functional MRI* (fMRI) is basically a collection of multiple scans measuring the aforementioned parameters, while the scanned patient is performing certain tasks such as finger tapping or reacting to visual patterns. This set of MRI volume data then contains both the anatomy (i.e., morphological imaging) and differences in oxygen concentration (functional imaging) over time for each voxel. As the acquisition times for such experiments are rather long, motion artefacts hamper the analysis of this complex data, and lead to a low signal-noise-ratio and spatial resolution. However, fMRI is an active field of research and is already used on a regular basis for planning intricate neurosurgical interventions for tumor patients.

Although not directly a functional imaging modality on its own, *diffusion tensor imaging* (DTI) is another variant of MRI that is often used in combination with functional MRI. In DTI, a series of diffusion gradients is applied to the subject and therefore computes a tensor for each voxel. This tensor describes the anisotropy (i.e., principal direction) of water diffusion in the tissue. When used for brain imaging, so-called fiber tracts are computed by tracing the different directions locally, resulting in a coarse approximation of fiber morphology. This is of great help for neurosurgery, as paths can be found to avoid the impairment of essential structures, as described for example in Rieder et al. [RRRP08].

Nuclear imaging In order to assess the activity of structures in question, as well as their (coarse) spatial location, radionuclides are used by means of tracer molecules. These radiopharmaceutical substances accumulate in certain organs or pathological structures (e.g., melanoma) due to increased metabolism, vascularization, etc., and therefore give rise to measurable concentration changes. The main field of applications are thus oncology, neuroimaging, or regarding perfusion processes.

Scintigraphy is the most basic nuclear imaging method and can be compared to X-ray. Except for the fact that radiation is not caused by an external source but from radioactive decay, a gamma camera is used to detect the emitted radiation of the marked substances. While this process results in planar projections of the examined structure, *Single-Photon Emission Computed Tomography* (SPECT) uses tomographic reconstruction for three-dimensional imaging. However, the spatial resolution of SPECT data is very low[4] due to the filtering of radiation for correct reconstruction. Therefore, advanced filtering and visualization methods

---
[4]Currently no more than 128×128 pixels per slice

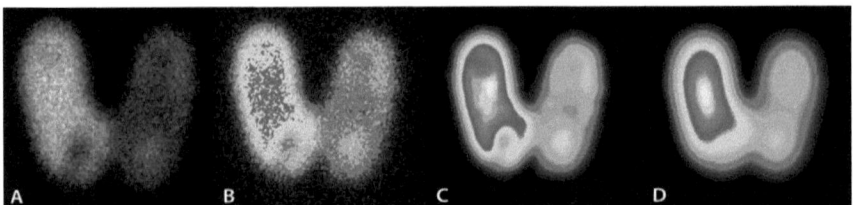

Figure 2.2: Different visualizations of a scintigram of the thyroid gland. Original data (A), color-encoded version (B), color-encoding with noise removal at different levels (C, D). While noise is removed successfully, important structures are lost in the last version. (Image courtesy of M. Hoffmann)

are used for enhancing image structures without losing important information, as depicted in figure 2.2.

Finally, another commonly used method in nuclear imaging is the *Positron Emission Tomography* (PET). Although the measured data is also located by means of tomographic reconstruction algorithms, the detected signals are caused by annihilation events that occur due to the radioactive decay. However, the resulting resolution is significantly lower than CT, but still better than for SPECT. Another disadvantage of PET systems are the higher costs due to the more complex devices and the expensive supply of special radionuclides.

2.1.2 Communication and Storage

The different imaging modalities outlined above can be regarded as a single procedure in clinical practice, but usually involve several departments and/or the coordination with external medical staff (e.g., family physician). Optimizing these workflows is also an active field of research, as not only the situation for the patient is improved, but also costs can be reduced.

Most of the aforementioned imaging devices are comprised of different entities. Firstly, the acquisition device itself is usually controlled by specialized hardware and software systems close to the device. Secondly, the examination of the acquired data is performed on workstations with dedicated display systems, analysis software, etc. This can be performed either immediately after the imaging procedure, or – as is common in most cases – a considerable time later. Therefore, the original data has to be stored and should be available (almost) independently from the original device or workstation. This requires means for archiving the data with all relevant meta-information (e.g., annotations, different modalities), as well as a standard for communication among different departments, clinics, etc. As several projects in the course of this thesis work with clinical data, interfaces to these facilities have been integrated and adapted; see chapter 7 for details.

2.1. MEDICAL IMAGING

DICOM

The representation and exchange of practically all kinds of data in medical practice is defined by the worldwide standard DICOM (Digital Imaging and Communications in Medicine)[5]. Starting in the early 1980s, different institutions have proposed common protocols and interfaces to work with images of all kinds of modalities independent of the acquisition device and its software. This collaboration of manufacturers as well as clinicians and software developers resulted in a global network of working groups that define new or revise existing specifications on a regular basis. The DICOM standard in its current structure has been proposed 1993, starting with 9 parts and approximately 750 pages. In 2008 it contained 18 parts and covered as much as 3800 pages – with additional supplements, drafts and correction proposals being continuously worked on. Therefore, only a short overview of important features can be provided here. The interested reader is referred to literature such as Preim and Bartz [PB07] or Kramme [Kra02], or to the standard itself.

DICOM is comprised of various *services* that inherently specify distributed operations across a network. These represent basic functionality such as `Store` for sending/saving image data, `Query/Retrieve` for database communication, or `Print` for X-ray printouts. The standard also defines a *file format* (denoted as "offline media" in part 10), as well as the DICOMDIR file, which provides additional information about multiple files or directories. Furthermore, DICOM data is organized hierarchically: one patient can have one or more studies; per study several series are possible; and each series can contain multiple images. DICOM data objects are basically a collection of attributes that are grouped in the data set. Each of these groups contains tags that denote the individual attributes, e.g., patient ID, modality, or pixel spacing. Although only one attribute can be used to specify pixel data per object, this can contain multiple frames or multi-dimensional data. However, one object usually represents a two-dimensional image, that is, volume data is in general comprised of multiple files for the consecutive slices. Finally, compressed pixel data is also supported, with different compression formats available, such as JPEG (incl. lossless), JPEG 2000, or RLE.[6]

PACS

While the DICOM standard specifies the individual operations as well as the file format, PACS (Picture Archiving and Communication Systems) denote computers or networks that are explicitly used for storing, retrieving, distributing, and presenting the images. These systems do not only handle images of various modalities, but also additional information such as annotations or filter operations, which are encoded using the DICOM standard. Originally, PACS were introduced to reduce (or replace) the amount of hard-copies, i.e., print-outs or X-ray films. Today, the second, more important objective is the availability of data independent of its location by means of networks. This allows off-site viewing ("teleradiology"), either asynchronously or during collaborative sessions.

---

[5]Official website at http://dicom.nema.org/ (last visit Feb 23 2009)
[6]See chapter 4 for more information on compression techniques and references.

PACS are usually designed in a traditional server–client fashion, where the client can be a stand-alone application or based on web technology. In addition, the server usually has to interface several infrastructures, that often exist already, such as HIS (hospital information system) or RIS (radiology information system). When taking external clinics/facilities or multiple (referring) doctors in own practice into account, this integration becomes rather challenging due to the individual workflows, policies, or applications used at the different sites.

2.1.3 Computer assistance

As outlined at the beginning of this section, medical imaging technology has evolved a lot during the past decades. Especially the high image quality of modern CT and MRI devices led to new or clearly improved medical procedures. In addition, most of the techniques have become faster and widely available. This results in a steady increase of the amount of data that is acquired and consequently has to be diagnosed. Today, the number of images produced by CT scanners, for example, easily exceed a few hundred per examination. Other modalities often provide additional information which result in multiple dimensions for the image data (e.g., fMRI/DTI studies). Reviewing all of this data in clinical practice is very demanding and limited – even for highly trained personnel.

Therefore, supporting diagnosis by means of software is an active field of research and a large segment in the health care market. Most manufacturers of medical imaging devices usually provide several applications or modules for this *computer assistance* in addition to standard functionality (e.g., tomographic reconstruction, viewers or archives). In general, these systems strive to provide assistance in that the huge amount of data is processed and presented in a "compressed" way, that is, with (only) relevant information for the current problem being highlighted, extracted, etc. However, there are differences in the terms used for such systems, as well as the range of features varies considerably. The following paragraphs address the terminology of these systems first, while validation strategies are discussed in the second part of this section. As this thesis emphasizes the utilization of graphics hardware for the processing and visualization of volume data acquired using radiological imaging methods, other applications of computer guidance such as "computer assisted surgery" (CAS) or "computer-based training" (CBT) will not be addressed here.

Terminology

Literature varies in denoting support systems for diagnosis, but two levels of software assistance are commonly used: computer-assisted/-aided *detection* and *diagnosis*.[7] While the former is used for systems that indicate regions of interest (e.g., potentially pathological tissue), the latter performs different analysis steps to provide a classification, quantification,

---

[7] Although the short form "CAD" has been already used for engineering and product design software for many years, the acronym is also an established term in the medical context.

2.1. MEDICAL IMAGING

etc., and is therefore often based on preceding detection. Several authors or companies have introduced additional letters for distinguishing the different levels of computer assistance:

CADe *Detection* of regions of interest based on different criteria

CADx *Diagnosis* by providing additional data for detected/marked regions

CADq *Quantification* of selected structures using measurement tools etc.

Apart from such differentiations and terms, all assisting systems have in common that they do not replace the diagnosis itself. That is, the *decision* still has to be performed by a clinician, which is very unlikely to change in the foreseeable future due to ethical and legal reasons. However, supporting the doctor's decision is very important, especially taking the aforementioned increase in the amount of medical images into account.

Another advantage of using software for assistance is to reduce varying results on the same data. While an *intra*-observer variability can be tolerated in most cases, *inter*-observer differences are often critical in diagnosis, especially for follow-up routines. This situation changes for the worse if the expert level of the different people examining the data varies considerably. As will be outlined in section 7.2, software guidance can reduce this variability for aortic aneurysm evaluation and accelerate the manual process by semi-automatic steps.

Validation and performance measurement

Software assistance has become an integral part of medical imaging today. Lots of procedures rely on measurement tools, display systems, or other functionality for further assessment and diagnostic guidance. As most of these tasks have been performed without the help of software before, computer assistance has to prove being beneficial – ideally in terms of costs, workflow, *and* accuracy. Regarding the latter aspect, such systems have to be evaluated and compared against a *gold standard*, that is, the traditional approach to the problem in most cases. Some solutions, however, have become possible only because of utilizing software; these procedures are in general harder to assess.

Bowyer [Bow00] addresses in his article different types of challenges in validating medical image analysis, as well as common pitfalls in evaluating their performance. Although an extensive discussion of the various considerations would lead too far here, fundamental information on metrics and terms is still going to be provided, especially in the context of segmentation of volume data. Further information can be also found in Udupa et al [ULZ$^+$06] and Preim and Bartz [PB07], for example.

In general, an objective information about the "reality" is assumed to be available and is thus usually referred to as *ground truth*. This can be a binary clinical diagnosis (e.g., presence or absence of malignant tissue), a known quantity from phantoms[8], or a collection of manual segmentations by clinicians. These examples are of different complexity levels: the first resembles a detection problem, whereas the other quantify the examined structures.

---

[8]Phantoms are crafted devices or artificial models that simulate real objects and allow the exact measurements of sizes, volumes, etc. According examples would be a hose containing a known amout of contrast agent for vessel segmentation, or a synthetic data set, respectively

Detection performance An evaluation of detection problems often uses terms that refer to the diagnostic notions: *true positives (TP)*, *false positives (FP)*, *true negatives (TN)*, and *false negatives (FN)*. While positive/negative indicates the decision of the algorithm, true is used if the algorithm matches the actual result; figure 2.3 depicts the different combinations:

		Algorithm Detection	
		abnormality present	abnormality not present
Truth of Clinical Situation	abnormality present	true positive	false negative
	abnormality not present	false positive	true negative

Figure 2.3: Definition of true/false positives and negatives (Image after [Bow00]).

There are some metrics derived from these relations and commonly used in different contexts. *Sensitivity* specifies the rate of correctly detecting an existing abnormality, whereas *specificity* refers to the rate of correctly detecting the absence of an abnormality as such.[9] Each term is used as a fraction or percentage value; a perfect algorithm would result in 1 for both values (or 100%, respectively). Equation 2.1.1 summarizes the definition of both terms as ratio of the total number of the basic results. In addition, the values are only meaningful if used in combination; otherwise there would exist trivial solutions.

$$\text{Sensitivity} = \frac{|\text{TPs}|}{|\text{TPs}| + |\text{FNs}|} \qquad \text{Specificity} = \frac{|\text{TNs}|}{|\text{TNs}| + |\text{FPs}|} \qquad (2.1.1)$$

Quantification performance While the aforementioned measures assess the performance of detection algorithms by means of binary values, software that computes additional information such as lengths, volumes, etc. requires other metrics. Depending on the details of the algorithm, either distance measures such as the mean symmetric average, Hausdorff or Euclidean distance, or volume measures are appropriate. The latter typically assess the quality of a segmented region S with respect to a ground truth GT by taking the intersection of both volumes into account. This leads to the following metrics that have been used, for example, in Priese et al. [PSW05] or Sturm et al. [Stu04]:

$$\text{Coverability Rate} = \frac{|S \cap GT|}{|GT|} \qquad \text{Error Rate} = \frac{|S \setminus GT|}{|S|} \qquad (2.1.2)$$

Originally used for assessing information retrieval, the *Dice coefficient* is another common value for measuring the similarity of two sets, as in equation 2.1.3 for two sets R and S. Here, the ratio of the sets' intersection and their sum is computed, that is, a single value suffices for denoting the quality of the overlap. As the sets are taken into account regardless of their spatial relation, there are cases where suboptimal segmentations would still result in a high coefficient.

$$\text{Dice coefficient} = \frac{2 \cdot |R \cap S|}{|R| + |S|} \qquad (2.1.3)$$

---

[9]Depending on the scientific discipline, these metrics are also called *precision* and *recall*.

2.2. DATA REPRESENTATION

The aforementioned metrics have been used in this thesis mainly for assessing the results of the GPU-based segmentation of low-resolution liver data sets presented in section 7.1. Further information on different testing methods, as well as a thorough discussion of estimating the performance in practice can be found in the article by Bowyer [Bow00].

2.2 Data representation

The data that is acquired by the different imaging modalities is the very basis for subsequent steps, such as diagnostic review, image processing, visualization, etc. As many examples and applications in this thesis are based on medical data, an overview of the fundamentals will be provided in the following paragraphs. In addition, the focus of this work is on processing and visualization of *volumetric* data, i.e., three-dimensional information. The discussion will thus be limited to modalities that typically acquire 3D data, such as imaging methods based on tomographic reconstruction. Nevertheless, references to other dimensions will be given where appropriate or concepts apply to other representations as well (e.g., sequence of ultrasound images as volume). More information on image and volume representation can be found in literature such as Schroeder et al. [SML04] or Preim and Bartz [PB07].

Three-dimensional image data from medical imaging is usually comprised of consecutive two-dimensional slices. In order to properly describe the orientation and axes, the DICOM standard[10] defines the LPS standard that is depicted in figure 2.4. A right-handed coordinate system is used, with the longitudinal axis (i.e., along the patient) defined as z-axis.

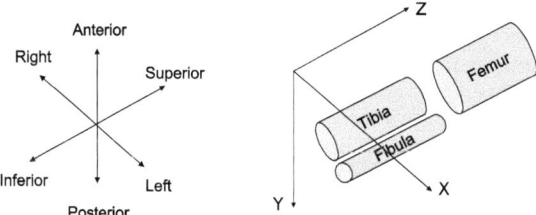

Figure 2.4: The DICOM standard LPS coordinate system (Image based on ITK/VTK documentation).

Image data can be represented in a variety of forms, with different applications and disciplines preferring one representation over the other. In the following sections, general aspects of image data will be described in a non-formal fashion. For more fundamental and formal details, the reader is referred to according literature such as Jähne [Jäh97] or Sonka et al. [SHB99], as well as Bender and Brill [BB03], Schroeder et al. [SML04] or Engel et al. [EHK+06] for an implementation-oriented introduction.

---

[10] As introduced later, the DICOM standard contains numerous meta-information. Here, the DICOM Plane Attribute Descriptions C.7.6.2.1.1 specify the image position orientation.

2.2.1 Grid

In order to represent and describe discrete image data, one can use different properties or categories. Images consist of an (ordered) collection of similar elements that represent a sampling of a continuous signal. These *pixels*[11] satisfy a spatial relation, depending on the type of ordering, usually referred to as "topology". For medical imaging, processing and visualization applications the most common types are cartesian or regular grids. While the former are comprised of equidistant samples in all dimensions (e.g., square pixels in 2D), the latter represent data with different spatial resolutions. Often the term *anisotropy* is used in this context, whereas cartesian data is referred to as *isotropic*, respectively.

In addition, there exist two different representations of regular image data that can be considered equivalent in practice. *Pixels* are samples of finite size (defined by the image's *resolution*), with the samples' position at the center of the pixels. *Grids* represent the image's information at the grid points, with the image resolution specifying the distance of the individual grid points in each dimension. As can be seen in figure 2.5, each representation can be transformed into the other by translating the position of the samples by half the resolution.

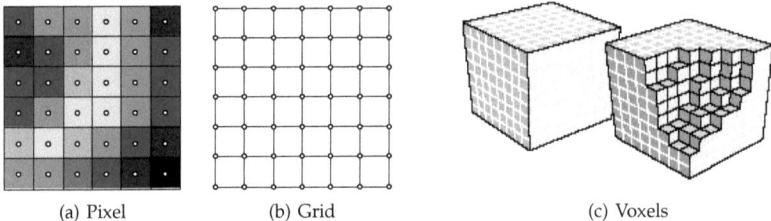

(a) Pixel (b) Grid (c) Voxels

Figure 2.5: Layout of image data. In (a) the individual elements are addressed within the center of the pixels; for grids (b) the data is stored at grid points. The concept of pixels extends to three-dimensions (c) analogously denoted as "voxels" (Image (c) courtesy of [EHK+06])

After this short introduction about the layout of the image data, several categories were identified and will be used to outline characteristics of image data from different points of view. Most of these concepts are the basis for the contributions presented in this thesis on the visualization and processing of three-dimensional image data in diverse settings and application contexts.

2.2.2 Properties

In medical applications the acquired data is usually subject to multiple processing stages, where the first operations are usually performed directly within the acquisition devices, e.g., the CT system. In order to abstract from the different imaging modalities (see section 2.1.1)

---

[11] Artificial term derived from "picture element".

2.2. Data representation

with their individual internal data formats, the following properties emphasize various aspects of data representation in general and its processing.

Dimensionality

The first category uses the dimension of the data as distinctive feature. Although the technical representation of the data in memory is in general independent from the logical dimension (i.e., usually contiguous chunks of linear memory), regarding the data as images, volumes and the like is a natural choice. Also, the dimension here is defined by the *logical layout* of the data in contrast to the data type. That is, dimension is considered to be the degree of the higher-level representation of the whole data set. For example, a single image of a DTI data set where each pixel consists of a 7-dimensional vector[12] will have the same dimension as data from a two-dimensional CT reconstruction with only scalar values per pixel: both are two-dimensional images. Following the terms for image data in computer graphics [Ope00] (i.e., textures) the *external format* describes the arrangement or dimension properties. The *internal format* refers to the internal representation, respectively, and resembles the attribute data in VTK [SML04], for example.

At the beginning of this section, different representations of image data have been introduced. There exist other structures that are usually inspired by theoretical considerations (e.g., the hexagonal layout for its single neighborhood type), but will not be considered here. In addition, the dimension is not limited to spatial coordinates only: depending on the usage of the data, each axis can be regarded as an arbitrary base vector of time, pressure, single wavelength, etc. Within the scope of this work, mixed types that are comprised of usually two dimensions (e.g., flat-3D textures by Harris et al. [HBSL03]) are used extensively in CASCADA, and will be described in detail in chapter 6.

Domain

Apart from the dimension is the data's domain a typical property. Depending on the acquisition of the information, data can be in different native representations, with the spatial layout (for element access, etc.) as a grid of pixels/voxels being the most common type. There exist several transformations from one domain to the other, for example the Fourier transform between spatial and frequency domain.

Spatial domain Data in the spatial domain is defined by samples that are arranged in a grid of (equidistant) elements, with functions that access and/or manipulate the data are defined in the same domain.

Range domain Here, the elements' *values* are taken into account, regardless of (or in combination with) their position. For example, the bilateral filter (for details, see Tomasi and Manduchi [TM98]) works in both spatial and value domain.

---

[12] As introduced in section 2.1.1, DTI contains anisotropic diffusion data of brain tissue. This information results in six values per voxel (symmetric tensor) plus an optional scalar value specifiying the confidence in some applications.

Frequency domain Spatial information is converted into frequencies of different wavelengths and amplitudes, with the Fourier transform being the most often used transform. Details can be found in Jähne [Jäh97] or Sonka et al. [SHB99].

Temporal domain Here, the data resembles (spatially fixed) samples at different time steps leading to temporal representation. Based on theoretical work such as Jähne [Jäh93], several analogies to the spatial domain can be identified. For example, Langs and Biedermann [LB07] have extended edge-preserving filter to the time dimension, i.e., applying 3D bilateral filter kernels to a volume of video frames, instead of 2D kernels on the individual images.

Compression domain Computations in this domain, as discussed in detail in chapter 4, are inspired by the fact that certain representations simplify operations that are more complex in other domains. The term "compression domain" is often used for volume rendering only, and describes visualization techniques that exploit the compact representation.

Hierarchies

A common technique to accelerate procedures in both computer graphics and image processing is to structure (image) data hierarchically. There exist two basic approaches: *space partitioning*, and *scale-space* (or *pyramidal*) methods, which are shortly outlined in the following description:

Space partitioning This approach imposes an additional structure to the data, in order to locally adapt to features, partition spatial information into different logical levels, etc. The most common realizations for both image processing and graphics applications are tree-like structures (e.g., quad-trees/octrees, k-d-trees; see [AMHH08] for details). These logical structures allow a more efficient representation of the data with respect to interesting information, and consequently an acceleration of computations on this data.

Scale-space methods By means of diffusion processes the image information is blurred controllably. This introduces another dimension, so that for two-dimensional images a whole series of images (i.e., volume) is created. While this concept is quite appealing due to its mathematical basis (see [Jäh97] for details), the considerable overhead due to the additional dimension is challenging in practice. However, there exist efficient and commonly used representations resulting in a pyramidal layout, as depicted in figure 2.6(a). These "mip-maps" have been supported in graphics processors for several hardware generations already. While these pyramids are ideally created by recursively applying Gaussian filter kernels, and are therefore usually referred to as *Gaussian pyramids*, yet another representation is used for multiple applications. By recursively subtracting subsequent levels in scale-space, the so-called *Laplacian pyramid* (see figure 2.6(c)) is created and corresponds to the differential scale-space. This representation is an essential part of the Wavelet transform as used for compression, and is further addressed in sections 4.1.2 and 4.2.

2.3. METHODS

(a) Mip-Mapping (b) Gaussian pyramid (c) Laplacian pyramid

Figure 2.6: Pyramidal layout of an image representation at multiple scales (a); Gaussian (b) and Laplacian (c) pyramids of a two-dimensional image, with coarser levels being magnified to the original resolution. (Images courtesy of Gamasutra and Wolfram Research, respectively)

2.3 Methods

Many algorithms and discussions throughout this thesis are in the field of image processing, segmentation, and visualization. Therefore, a common basis for terms and procedures is required and will be established in this section. On the other hand, there is a wealth of scientific literature available on each topic alone, so that this introduction cannot cover all methods thoroughly. In addition, other subjects such as image registration or computer vision are not going to be addressed, but can be found in most of the references cited below.

2.3.1 Preprocessing

As will be discussed in several contributions in this thesis, acquired image data contains noise and imaging artefacts. There are usually several reasons for these deteriorations, but limitations of the acquisition device (e.g., spatial resolution, inhomogenities, physical properties) and moving objects (e.g., heart motion, indirect movements during surgery) are the most common issues. Hence, image data is usually processed to improve the signal-to-noise ratio, that is, to emphasize the image's information content for subsequent purposes.

For the different properties of image data outlined in section 2.2.2, as well as for further criteria (e.g., texture information) there exists a large number of methods. While the different approaches presented in chapters 3, 4, and 7 introduce most of the algorithms and refer to related work and seminal literature, a coarse classification should introduce processing algorithms here.

Several authors such as Sonka et al. [SHB99], Jähne [Jäh97], or Preim and Bartz [PB07] use different criteria for categorizing image processing algorithms, but there are common features. In general, algorithms have one set of data X as input and another set of data as output Y, and perform a mapping from one set to the other. The input data can range from a single data element or an image to a whole set of multiple volumes. Likewise, the output can be one or multiple data elements, images, etc. Let x be a single element from the input set X, and the function f the mapping (i.e., algorithm including parameters) into the output set Y. Then the following categories can be defined:[13]

1. $x \to f(x)$: result depends only on source element (e.g., scaling gray values, look-up tables)

2. $x \to f(x, \{x_i\})$: result depends on source and limited set of neighbors (e.g., linear/non-linear filter with constant or adaptive window size)

3. $x \to f(x, X)$: result depends on source element and whole set (e.g., histogram equalization)

4. $x \to f(X)$: result depends on input data set only (e.g., image properties, Fourier transform)

Practically all algorithms and methods presented in the course of this thesis can be assigned to one of the groups. As the focus of this work is on graphics hardware, some of the categories are well suited for GPU implementations. Operations using lots of inter-element communication or scattering approaches, however, are usually not directly portable to hardware for efficient applications. See chapter 1 and section 8.2.1 for additional information and the discussion of using such a classification for performance estimation.

2.3.2 Segmentation

Image segmentation denotes the process of separating objects of interest from other structures and background. This delineation is a fundamental step in image analysis, especially as all further information extraction depends on the outcome of the segmentation. In the medical context, segmentation is required for basic tasks, such as volume or length measurement, as well as for complex three-dimensional model extractions for intervention or advanced therapy planning. However, medical image segmentation is a challenging problem: insufficient discrimination of different tissue (i.e., low contrast), deteriorated image quality from noise or imaging artefacts, or a high variability in shapes (i.e., for applying a-priori knowledge) are some of the complicating issues. Thus, segmentation is still a highly active research field, targeting at different levels of interactivity (see section 2.3.4), for example.

The following list outlines a selection of different categories of segmentation methods with several examples and references; several have been implemented in the CASCADA framework as well. For a more detailed discussion and further references see pertinent literature, as well as the coverage in the contributions in the second part of the thesis.

Thresholding As the simplest segmentation method, thresholding algorithms are typically used in combination with further procedures. Examples are the manual determination of binary or multi-level thresholds, automatic procedures (Otsu's method, see [Jäh97]), or local adaptive thresholding (see Lehmann et al. [LOPR97]).

---
[13]Note that practically all categories are independent of the dimension.

2.3. METHODS

Edge-based Another group of algorithms uses edge information in the images for segmentation purposes. These edges can be computed by dedicated edge operators (e.g., Sobel, Prewitt), or resemble direct or extended gradient information, such as the gradient vector flow (Xu and Prince [XP97]). For easily paramerizable objects (lines, circles, etc.), the Hough transform is another edge-based method; see Sonka et al. [SHB99] for details.

Region-based This group of algorithms represents methods using the information of (connected) regions within the image data for segmentation. A fundamental algorithm is region growing, proposed by Adams and Bischof [AB94], and extended by many others; see section 7.1.1 for further information. Other approaches are hierarchical algorithms (e.g., split and merge, color structure code [Stu04]), the watershed segmentation, etc.

Graph-based Another powerful approach is to represent image information by means of graphs and operations thereon. Usually, these algorithms assign costs to edges in the graph, and algorithms evaluate this information afterwards. A well-known example is the Live-Wire algorithm by Mortensen et al. [MMBU92], or other graph algorithms in combination with distance transforms (e.g., for centerline computation, see also section 7.2.2).

Model-based While most of the aforementioned algorithms use the image information only, model-based methods incorporate additional, high-level knowledge. One common approach are deformable models that strive to fit general models to the specific data set. Therefore, different constraints for the model (and in some approaches also for the image) are considered. Another large group of algorithms are based on level sets that describe the boundary of regions as function over time; see Preim and Bartz [PB07] for an introduction and references.

As the field of image segmentation is exceedingly wide, additional groups can be defined. However, procedures based on statistical or texture information would be beyond the scope of this thesis, and are thus not addressed. Furthermore, atlas-based methods use a very large set of acquired image data as a-priori knowledge for segmentation. This usually involves image registration, which is only addressed shortly at the end of this section. The interested reader is therefore referred to according literature, such as Sonka et al. [SHB99], Lehmann et al. [LOPR97] or Jähne [Jäh97] for segmentation in general, and Maintz and Viergever [MV98] or Fitzpatrick et al. [FHCRM00] for registration, respectively.

2.3.3 Visualization

In section 1.3 the visualization of volumetric data was introduced, preferably using direct rendering methods. While the focus there has been on (GPU-based) volume rendering in general, the role of visualization for medical applications is going to be addressed in this section. This topic is also a highly active field of research, especially due to the widely available and very powerful graphics hardware. Thus, many modern workstations used in radiology today utilize commodity hardware for advanced volume rendering, usually with predefined look-up tables (i.e., transfer functions) for different modalities and/or anatomies.

Nevertheless, most clinicians work with standard, two-dimensional visualizations of the acquired data on a regular basis. In addition, the range of values in the images are interactively adapted to the display's capabilities and diagnostical purpose for optimal information using combined window–level parameters (see also section 3.1.2). These visualizations can either be the native format of the image data (e.g., standard radiographs), or reformatted versions of a tomographically reconstructed data set. This technique denoted as "multi-planar reformation" (MPR) is usually used along the main axes of the reference system (i.e., in axial, sagittal, and coronal direction), or additionally in arbitrary directions. Furthermore, advanced imaging systems allow so-called "curved MPR" visualizations, where three-dimensional curves – instead of a single plane – can be defined for image reformation; see also section 7.2.2 for applications.

This seems to question the relevance of volume visualization in clinical practice. However, several medical applications can be found where volume rendering is advantageous with respect to traditional display techniques. Virtually all approaches outlined in the following list make explicit use of graphics hardware today, so a detailed overview of the rendering methods in general can be found in Engel et al. [EHK$^+$06]. The medical context is emphasized in the state-of-the-art report by Klein et al. [KBF$^+$08], as well as in Preim and Bartz [PB07].

Surface rendering The visualization of surfaces is used extensively for virtual endoscopy or anaplasty applications. This includes the interactive reconstruction process (e.g., GPU-based marching cubes implementations), as well as the integration of the surface data with direct volume rendering. Scharsach et al. [Sch05, SHN$^+$05] proposed several techniques using graphics hardware. In addition, the CASCADA framework presented in chapter 6 includes isosurface rendering based on ray casting.

Emphasized rendering A typical problem of volume rendering is its visual complexity. The large amount of details in direct volume rendering compromises its benefit. Therefore, several authors proposed to attenuate (or completely hide) unimportant structures, whereas regions of interest are enhanced. The structures' importance can be modelled explicitly, e.g., by segmentation and labelling, or implicitly by evaluating the current viewing parameters etc. Among many approaches discussed in Preim and Bartz [PB07], Bruckner [Bru08] were the first to exploit GPU techniques for advanced interactive illustrations, and Viola et al. [VKG04] for importance-driven rendering, respectively.

Multi-modal rendering Although multiple modalities merged into one visualization can be examined using traditional 2D views as well, volume rendering techniques are commonplace for this rather modern application. In combination with additional data, such as fiber tracts and activation areas for DTI/fMRI visualization, for example, the combined rendering of 2D (MRI planes) and 3D information (fiber tracts) are also used for neurosurgical planning, depicted in figure 2.7. See Rieder et al. [RRRP08] for

2.3. Methods

supplemental rendering of widgets, or Preim and Bartz [PB07] for a thorough discussion of tensor imaging and visualization applications.

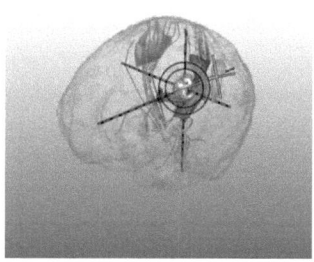 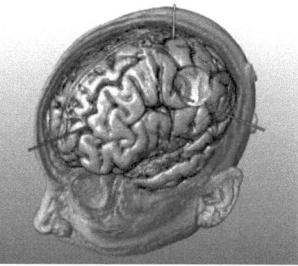

Figure 2.7: Multi-modal volume rendering of combined CT/MRI/fMRI/DTI data set, including additional widgets (left) and enhanced clipping (right). Image from Rieder et al. [RRRP08]

Volume clipping Volume clipping describes the limitation of the whole volume data to a subset, with geometry defining new, interactively changeable boundaries. This is a powerful technique for visual inspection and is thus often used for medical purposes. However, care has to be taken at the clipped boundaries as shading information is needed: usually the gradient is ill-conditioned. Fundamental research can be found in Weiskopf et al. [WEE03] and Engel et al. [EHK$^+$06]. Clipping is supported in practically all volume rendering systems, and has been integrated in CASCADA as well.

Fly-through rendering Moving the viewpoint into the volume data (e.g., for virtual endoscopy) requires some preparation, especially for ray casting. This technique is also denoted as "fly-through rendering", and is covered in detail in Scharsach [Sch05].

2.3.4 Discussion

As already mentioned at the beginning of this section, addressing further methods of medical image analysis would be beyond the scope of this introduction. The three topics covered in the preceding paragraphs – preprocessing, segmentation, and visualization – also represent most of the implemented methods in CASCADA. However, further techniques are the focus of current investigations, especially image registration; see Maintz and Viergever [MV98] or Fitzpatrick et al. [FHCRM00] for an introduction. Graphics hardware is well suited for such algorithms due to their inherent parallelism and arithmetic intensity as shown by Köhn et al. [KDR$^+$06], for example. Furthermore, interfaces such as Nvidia CUDA provide adequate flexibility, with the CascadaCUDA implementation outlined in section 6.3 offering an additional programming abstraction.

2.4 Summary

The preceding sections provided a short overview of medical imaging and processing methods relevant for the remainder of this thesis. However, as both topics make up large research areas of their own, only some aspects have been covered. After addressing medical imaging modalities and the role of computer assistance, the second part of this chapter introduced the technical representation and properties of data. Subsequently, a selection of image processing methods were outlined, as well as references to further reading. As visualization plays an important role in this thesis, additional concepts were presented, based on the concepts from section 1.3.

In the third part of this thesis the GPU programming framework CASCADA will be introduced. As will be shown in several contributions, the utilization of graphics hardware is beneficial for many applications. In order to develop such algorithms and examples, the framework contains basic functionality for handling volume data, preprocess image data, perform segmentation operations, etc. Of course, such a system cannot be directly compared with large libraries or applications for image processing and (volume) visualization such as ITK/VTK [14] or Amira [15].

Another well-known system is MeVisLab [MeV07] that is available for free in a basic version. As this system also provides interfaces to the aforementioned ITK/VTK as well as a powerful user interface, it has been used in several projects in this thesis; see chapter 7. A comparison of MeVisLab with other systems can be found in Bitter et al. [BUW+07], as well as in section 3.1.3 for an evaluation regarding CASCADA.

---

[14]Insight/Visualization Toolkit, Kitware Inc., http://itk.org and http://vtk.org (last visit April 2, 2009)

[15]Amira, Visage Imaging Inc., http://www.amiravis.com (last visit April 4, 2009)

Part II

Concepts

CHAPTER 3

INTERACTIVE VISUALIZATION OF COMPUTATIONS

The integration of visualization and computation has become increasingly important during the last years. As introduced in the preceding chapters, the advances of modern graphics hardware provide enough computational performance and usually push the limit further with each generation. The term "visual computing", that is used today in the context of computer graphics and scientific computing, describes this very well. For example, Nvidia refers to its range of graphics products, dedicated computing hardware and the programming architecture CUDA as visual computing systems. In addition, visual computing has become a research area of its own in recent years due to the ubiquity of high-performance graphics hardware.

Originally, however, *visual computing* has been coined by Groß for integrating computer graphics, visual perception and imaging [Gro94]. This notion comprises both the creation and acquisition/analysis of information based on images. Especially the latter refers to natural as well as artifical concepts, that is, human vision and computer vision. Although several aspects of human vision will be taken into account in this chapter (sections 3.1.1 and 3.1.2), the focus in this thesis is on the combination of computer graphics and visualization techniques on the one hand, and image processing methods on the other hand.

In the course of this chapter, different approaches towards such an integration are proposed and discussed. These concepts, as well as the software engineering aspects described in chapter 5, have led to the development of the GPU-based framework CASCADA, presented in the third part of this thesis. With respect to visual computing, strategies for utilizing graphics hardware for non-graphics tasks are outlined first. The combination of visualization and computations also enables the direct interaction with whatever is rendered: time-consuming, iterative algorithms displaying intermediate results or real-time simulations, where user interaction directly affects entities or rendering parameters.

Interacting with rendering of (mainly) volumetric data is another important facet of what is here referred to as visual computing and will be discussed in the second part of this chapter. Firstly, an approach for the direct manipulation of the ray casting process is presented in order to allow controlling of different parameters on a per-ray level. While this concept is not limited to GPU implementations, the possibilities in the context of visual computing are various. The second interaction technique focuses on the computation aspect. Here, the user influences iterative algorithms by directly manipulating input data, thus providing an additional and direct source of information for the algorithm. This relates to the notion of *computational steering*, as will be discussed below.

3.1 GPU-based computations

Combining expensive computations with the visualization of (intermediate) results is quite obvious, given the various advantages mentioned in the introduction. Although software, i.e., CPU implementations benefit from advances in processor technology as well as implementations on graphics hardware, there is still the need to transfer the data to the display device for any visualization. The fusion of GPU and CPU is a current issue, as several recent developments indicate (e.g., Intel's Larrabee [SCS[+]08], or APIs as the proposed computing language OpenCL [Khr]). However, available hardware, let alone stable drivers, applications or performance details are still on the horizon. In addition, these devices seem to be not as powerful and extensible as their "external" counterparts due to thermal restrictions, compromises in die area, etc. Consequently, implementing algorithms on graphics hardware is still a reasonable choice, especially for computing-intense applications and complex visualization requirements.

3.1.1 Filtering Video Volumes using the GPU

The first application developed in the course of the thesis towards this integration of computing and visualizing procedures on the GPU was presented by Langs and Biedermann [LB07]. It was originally inspired by image processing, more precisely improving video frames by means of denoising algorithms. Video images are very suited for visual computing for two reasons. Firstly, video data is meant to be visualized at the end of the pipeline by its very nature. Above that, graphics hardware has been capable of rapidly processing large amounts of RGB image data ever since, as the predominance of fragment processors indicates (see section 1.1 for details).

Also, denoising videos is an important preprocessing step, especially for video material captured under dim lighting conditions. In the context of medical image processing, noise is a permanent issue, especially when the radiation exposure is limited or the external magnetic field is limited in strength; see section 2.1.1 for information. As this thesis focuses on computations for medical applications, the original contribution is shortened and updated to become more relevant for such applications.

The contribution is organized as follows. After a short introduction, the approach of filtering video sequences of arbitrary lengths by means will be explained. Quality and performance comparisons in the following section, as well as an outlook on improvements and filtering in other domains will conclude the contribution.

3.1. GPU-BASED COMPUTATIONS

Introduction

Data acquired by any type of analog-digital converter, such as CCD and CMOS image sensors or sensors in CT/MRI scanners contains noise. This can be observed in video sequences or images captured in dim lighting conditions and applies to medical imaging as well (e.g., low-dose CT). As a result, further processing such as segmentation becomes difficult for these data sets.

In order to enhance the distorted data, filtering is a common first step in the workflow. Typical examples for such noise filters are the Gaussian or median filter as linear and non-linear filters, respectively. In order to enhance the distorted data, homogeneous regions should be smoothed while maintaining region boundaries, i.e., edge-preserving smoothing. Therefore, the well-known bilateral filter [TM98] will be used here.

The target data sets are video sequences, i.e., a sequence consisting of individual frames. However, the concepts also apply to three-dimensional data in medical applications, especially as such data is acquired as series of two-dimensional slices (e.g., CT scans, ultrasound sequences). Thus, there is the possibility of filtering each frame separately with a two-dimensional kernel for comparison. The video sequence is regarded as a volume and consequently the bilateral filter is applied in all three dimensions. Areas in the video sequence that are not changing or moving from one frame to the next are then homogeneous regions in time. Thus, the parameters of the bilateral filter can be chosen in a way that the influence of each frame is limited and compensates for the lack of denoising with the now available temporal dimension.

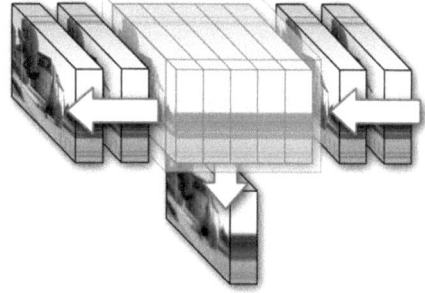

Figure 3.1: Streaming video frames for volume filtering.

Representing video sequences as volumes and operations thereon is no new idea. See Jähne [Jäh93], Hájek [Háj02], or Daniel and Chen [DC03] for related work. However, advanced filtering is rarely used due to its high computational costs. To perform filtering on reasonably sized video sequences in an acceptable amount of time, recent graphic processing units (GPU) found in commodity hardware are therefore utilized. This approach allows for performing high quality volumetric filtering of video sequences at PAL resolution in realtime.

Approach

With respect to the architecture of GPUs, only the fragment processing unit is utilized. The vertex shaders are not used in this approach[1], as is obvious for pure pixel data such as video frames. Following the traditional approach (see section 1.2), a quadrilateral in size of the

---
[1]Geometry shaders have not been available back then.

input data (i.e., video frame resolution) is drawn using the graphics API to initiate data processing. Here, the source video frame is the input data to be processed by the initial shader, i.e., the first render pass. A one-dimensional bilateral filter is then applied to this texture resulting in one filtered pixel value, which is written to the framebuffer (or some equivalent off-screen target). This result is used in subsequent processing steps to realize three-dimensional filtering in the entire application, and can be extended to other dimensions as well.

Bilateral filtering on the GPU As image denoising is a common research topic, various filter types and algorithms have been proposed. Among these approaches anisotropic diffusion and wavelet based filters are well studied and widely used, mainly due to their edge preserving properties (for the latter see also chapter 4). In the context of GPGPU, however, anisotropic diffusion as an iterative solution is less suited for GPU implementations due to the extra communication and setup needed.[2]

Barash has shown in [Bar00] that bilateral filtering resembles anisotropic diffusion by using adaptive smoothing as a link between the two approaches. Therefore, it is possible to implement bilateral filtering as a more GPU-friendly algorithm because of its "local operation" nature, while maintaining their common basis. Thus the bilateral filter could be realized as a GLSL shader program without significant changes to the original algorithm.

The bilateral filter itself was introduced in 1998 by C. Tomasi und R. Manduchi [TM98]. Its basic idea is to combine the domain and the range of an image. The domain describes the spatial location or closeness of two pixels, while the range describes their similarity, or the distance of the pixel values. In traditional filters only a pixel's location in the spatial domain is taken into account, resulting in less influence for more distant pixels, for example; the bilateral filter, however, takes also the similarity into account.

In addition, the bilateral filter is inherently non-linear because of the image's range term, and therefore is not directly separable. In this implementation, however, the separated bilateral filter introduced by Pham and van Vliet[PvV05] is used. As described in their work, it is not a true separation of the original bilateral filter, thus leading to approximated rather than equal results. Nevertheless, for the purpose of filtering video sequences the introduced error (due to truncated sampling in the different directions) is negligible, especially considering the potential increase in performance. In the approach presented here, the source frame is convolved with the separated, two-dimensional bilateral filter, that is, applying the one-dimensional kernel twice. The internal video volume is then built from these filtered slices and finally reused several times for the convolution in the third dimension. The whole procedure is described in more detail in the following section.

Streaming concept Filtering video data in a volumetric manner cannot be done directly for sequences of reasonable lengths, as the entire data usually does not fit in the graphics memory. Therefore, a streaming approach has been implemented to process videos of arbitrary length.

---

[2]This has become less critical due to features such as shared memories on current architectures.

3.1. GPU-BASED COMPUTATIONS

When choosing the parameters for the kernel so that n previous and n subsequent frames are used to filter the current frame, $2n + 1$ frames have to be kept in the graphics memory at one time. In every filtering step the next video frame is loaded to the GPU, which is then processed separately in x and y direction using the separated bilateral filter. This two-dimensionally filtered slice is subsequently added to the video volume, thus replacing the oldest slice in the volume. The last step is to generate the processed video frame by filtering the video volume in z direction. The final video frame is then displayed and/or downloaded into the CPUs memory, to be written to a file or processed further. The whole process is depicted in figure 3.2.

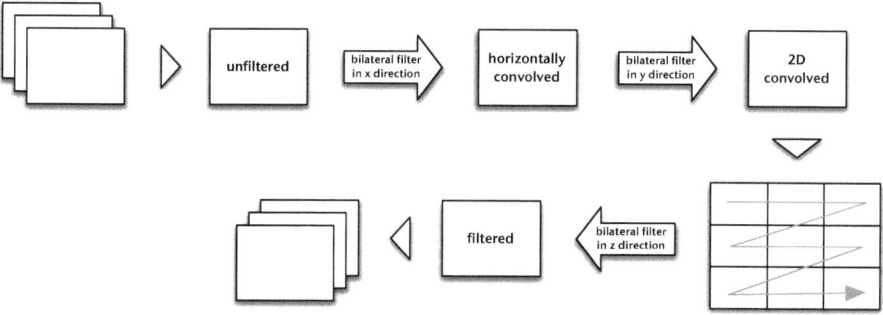

Figure 3.2: Processing steps of the separable bilateral filtering approach

In order to minimize data transfers during copying to and from the GPU and inside the GPU's memory, a ring buffer storage scheme is used for the video volume. Thus, it is possible to constantly add slices to the volume until the maximum number of slices is reached. The texture has to be updated only in a subregion leading to further optimization. Due to limitations of the maximum texture size on the graphics hardware, "flat3D" textures as proposed by Harris et al. [HBSL03] are utilized.

Results

The subsequent paragraphs summarize the results of the approach presented before. In addition to a comparison and evaluation of the different filter kernel dimensions, both volume representations are discussed.

Comparison 3D and 2D filtering In order to assess the quality of the filtering – especially the difference between the 2D and 3D version – a *full reference* comparison has been applied. This method requires both the original (i.e., undistorted) image and the filtered image for comparison. In general, however, the original image is not available, or little information is known about the distortion at the most.[3] Therefore, synthetic noise has been added to a video

---

[3]The former is usually referred to as *no-reference*, the latter as *reduced-reference* comparison.

	outdoor		synthetic	
	SSIM	MSE	SSIM	MSE
unfiltered	0,393	669,6	0,311	626,3
"2D bilateral filter" (GPU-BF 2D)	0,737	135,0	0,720	125,7
"3D bilateral filter" (GPU-BF 3D/flat3D)	0,844	87,3	0,890	73,9
AfterEffects "Remove grain"	0,829	89,7	0,908	68,3
"Neat Video"	0,909	53,9	0,954	48,1

Table 3.1: Quality comparison

sequence without noise (the reference sequence), where the noise is made up of an evenly distributed random value between -50 and 50 added to the R, G, and B channel of every pixel independently. This is motivated by the nature of noise of commodity sensors, especially when used in dim lighting conditions. The video sequences have then been compared with two different measures by performing a frame-by-frame comparison, averaging the measured error values for the entire sequence. The first video sequence that was compared is an outdoor video sequence captured in daylight without noticeable noise. The second video is a synthetic animation showing a typical pre-video countdown, combined with a testbar screen for broadcasting, thus being completely noise free.

The two measures for comparison are the SSIM (Structural Similarity Index Measure) introduced by Wang et al. [WBSS04] and the MSE (Mean squared error). The SSIM is a measure specially designed to compare two images in a perception based manner, whereas the MSE measure is purely mathematically based and straightforward to compute:

$$\text{MSE} = \frac{1}{MN} \sum_{y=1}^{M} \sum_{x=1}^{N} (I_1(x,y) - I_2(x,y))^2 \qquad (3.1.1)$$

However, by its nature the MSE is not capable of measuring the difference from an observer's point of view. Enhancing the contrast, for example, would result in significantly different pixel data while the overall impression is equal (or better). Related to this measure is the (peak) signal-to-noise-ratio (PSNR):

$$\text{PSNR} = 10 \cdot \log_{10}\left(\frac{I_{max}^2}{\text{MSE}}\right) \qquad (3.1.2)$$

This term, commonly used in engineering, describes the ratio between the maximum possible value of the image and the value of noise which affects the fidelity of the original representation. As the numerator in the quotient is constant for all images in this application (8 bit per channel), the MSE is used throughout this work.

After computing an error value for the distorted video sequence in comparison to the original sequence, the distorted video sequence filtered with the 2D and 3D bilateral filter, respectively, can be compared with the reference sequence. The results can be seen in table 3.1. The filter methods used by the commercial programs are not disclosed, thus only a visual comparison of the results has been possible and is shown in figure 3.4(a). As can be seen there is no significant difference of the filter quality between the two very different types of

3.1. GPU-BASED COMPUTATIONS

video sequences: both error metrics indicate the same relationship: the quality of 3D filtering surpasses the quality of the 2D filter.

In addition, the time needed for filtering a single frame has been measured. The application was tested on a commodity Windows PC that featured the following components: Intel CoreDuo 6400 (2.13 GHz), 2 GB RAM, NVIDIA GeForce 8800 GTX 768 MB PCIe 16x. The video sequence "outdoor", used for comparison, has a resolution of 720 × 576 and consists of 1085 frames. The denoted time per frame is an average over all frames of the filtering only, that is, excluding the time needed for reading or writing the video file or loading the data to the GPU. The results are given in figure 3.3.

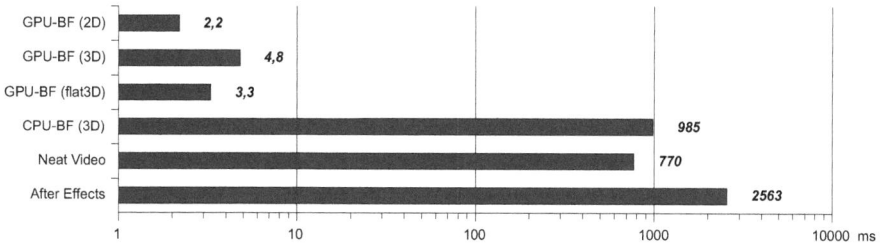

Figure 3.3: Performance comparison (time per frame)

Performance 3D and flat-3D volume The processing time for the implementation using the flat-3D volume storage concept indicated a performance gain of approximately 25% on the aforementioned hardware in contrast to native 3D volume textures, as can be seen in figure 3.3. On previous graphics hardware the difference using the flat volume was even higher, up to a factor of two. This indicates a trend for improved and complete 3D texture processing in graphics hardware and extends to volumetric data sets (e.g., CT scans), as will be discussed further in the course of this thesis. Therefore, if no advanced texture access (e.g., trilinear filtering) is needed, flat volume textures are an appropriate alternative to native 3D textures.[4] Despite the additional overhead for address translation, they offer a considerable performance increase, especially with older graphics hardware.

Conclusion and future work

In this contribution the use of a 3D bilateral filter for noise reduction on video sequences was shown to result in higher quality than frame-by-frame 2D bilateral filtering. In figure 3.4(b) another real world example with comparable performance results is given, which depicts a video frame acquired in a very dark room, lit only indirectly by a projection screen. In this case denoising the captured data is crucial to visual quality and further processing. These concepts apply for practically all noisy image data, especially in the medical context:

---

[4]This implies that the maximum size of 2D textures for the specific hardware meets the application's requirements, of course.

 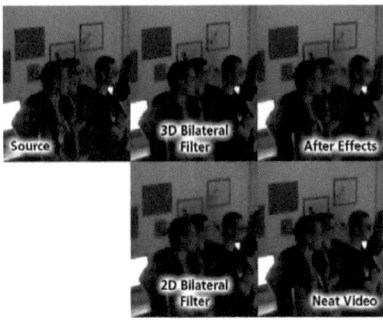

(a) Comparison of different filtering methods for the example video with additional noise

(b) Filtering of video sequence with natural noise due to low lighting.

Figure 3.4: Visual comparison of filtered video data: sequence "outdoor" with additional noise (a) and real world example taken in dim lighting conditions with natural noise (b).

low-dose CT scans show considerable noise, for example. Utilizing modern commodity graphics hardware clearly decreases processing time for this rather costly volumetric filter operation. In order to exploit their capabilities even better, flat volumes offers advantages for three-dimensional data compared to true 3D textures for a wide range of graphics hardware.

Based on this application, it is also possible to perform fast filtering of real 3D data sets to enhance the results of subsequent processing steps. However, the size of the volume is then directly limited by the available memory on the graphics card, so that other approaches like bricking or compression have to be employed. The latter approach will be discussed in detail in chapter 4.

Finally, the dramatic decrease in filtering time by using the GPU has been shown with video data of 8 bit per channel. It would be interesting to see how well the approach extends to data of 16 bit per channel or even other representations, e.g., high dynamic range data. This is going to be addressed in the following section.

3.1.2 Using a GPU-based Framework for Interactive Tone Mapping of Medical Volume Data

The contribution in the preceding section presented the clear advantage of GPU implementations for image processing applications compared to software solutions. While this application can be generalized to other image or volume data, some hardware-centric limitations might hamper an extension to arbitrary data. As already mentioned in the outlook, data of higher bit depth or non-scalar types require a different handling. In addition, the limited bandwidth for transferring the data might become an issue due to the larger amount of data.

The following work presented in Raspe and Müller [RM07] discusses the application of tone-mapping algorithms on medical data. This serves in the context of visual computing as

3.1. GPU-BASED COMPUTATIONS

both an extension of image processing algorithms to non-trivial data, as well as an approach to integrate the computational workload into the visualization process. Although the algorithms are limited to global tone-mapping functions due to reasons discussed later on, the rather complex functions indicate again an advantage of GPU implementations.

Especially data from functional imaging modalities has a much higher dynamic range and requires considerable interaction for proper visualization using the traditional windowing approach. As can be seen in figure 3.5, the details of the data sets are much less visible for linear mapping than for a tone-mapped visualization. Therefore, one approach is the integration of tone mapping algorithms into the visualization pipeline of volume data by exploiting modern graphics hardware. Different tone mapping methods in consideration of miscellaneous medical modalities will be discussed, as well as the role of transfer functions in the context of high dynamic range rendering.

Introduction

As the data acquired and processed with medical imaging systems usually has a higher value range than standard output devices, different approaches can be applied to map the range of values to the display. For medical data, controlling a window of varying width and center that defines a linear mapping within this window is the de-facto standard in examining image data (see section 2.3.3). While this is straightforward to use and allows for fast implementations, its results are limited and often require lots of manual interaction. Depending on the focus of the diagnosis this can become a tedious manual process.

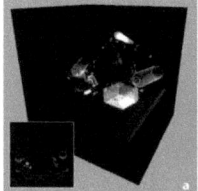
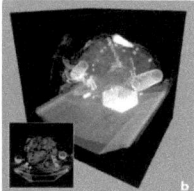

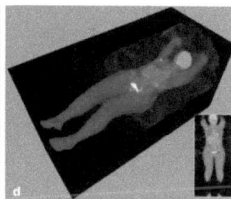

Figure 3.5: Direct volume rendering of high dynamic range volume data: CT data set (a,b), and whole body PET scan (c,d), with insets depicting single slices for reference. While the linear mapping (a, c) reveals only the maxima of the data sets, tone mapping algorithms (b,d) can display the whole dynamic range in real-time.

In the field of computer graphics and computer vision, high dynamic range images are a common approach to represent simulated or captured illumination without introducing errors by band-limiting the signal. These images are stored in data types of a larger numerical range and/or precision, typically 16 or 32 bit integers or floating point. However, displaying such HDR data by mapping the input data linearly to the output device's range is not sufficient, as only the bright areas would be visible (see figure 3.5). To overcome this issue, a lot of research has been done in both the computer graphics and computer vision community. With such a foundation it is quite obvious to apply those techniques to medical data in order to improve the visualization. As each modality in medical image acquisition requires a different interpretation – depending on the protocol even single acquisitions – this topic has to be discussed more thoroughly to avoid a misinterpretation of the results.

The remainder of this contribution is structured as follows: In the next section existing approaches are discussed, with a focus on both GPU implementations and tone mapping algorithms in general. The possible application to different modalities of the different tone mapping algorithms will then be considered. The results of applying the techniques to medical volume data will be described afterwards with a discussion of both performance and visual results, concluding with directions of further investigation.

Related work

In this paragraph existing approaches and techniques are discussed to outline the context of this contribution. Therefore, high dynamic range imaging in both general and medical applications is described first, followed by a more closer look on tone mapping methods.

High dynamic range imaging Mainly initiated by the seminal work of Debevec and Malik [DM97], a lot of research on high dynamic range imaging, i.e., image data with luminance values of multiple orders of magnitude, has been done since then. However, such HDR data is usually displayed on devices with a much lower dynamic range. Although first prototypes of HDR displays are available, so-called tone mapping (or tone reproduction) algorithms still need to be applied to visualize the data adequately. For further reference, Reinhard et al. review various existing approaches and address the whole "pipeline" of high dynamic range imaging in their book [RWPD05].

Basically, tone mapping operators can be categorized into *global* or *local*, some of them with an additional time-dependency. Global operators define some function that maps equal input values to equal output values, thus being computationally inexpensive. These functions can be as simple as a linear function, whereas more advanced operators are more complex and usually incorporate a logarithmic term and other properties of human perception. The results of such tone mapping functions are illustrated in figure 3.6 and show the already high potential of global operators.

In contrast to this "constant" mapping, local operators are able to adapt to changes by considering the neighborhood of each value. While this approach is very powerful, applying such locally varying operators to medical data needs some discussion. Lately, Bartz et al. [BSC+06] have proposed to use tone mapping operators on medical data for improved visual representation. Their algorithm is based on the local operator from Reinhard et al. [RSSF02] with an additional variant for regarding a three-dimensional neighborhood, as is advantageous for most volumetric data. Due to the local nature of the algorithm, the processing time of several seconds for moderately sized volumes is obviously not interactive. They also use datasets of traditional modalities as CT and MRI only, the former providing even a constant mapping (i.e., Hounsfield units) of the measured values. More involved data such PET or non-scalar MRI from functional or diffusion-tensor imaging, that cannot be tone mapped locally without introducing errors, has not been considered or left as future work.

3.1. GPU-BASED COMPUTATIONS

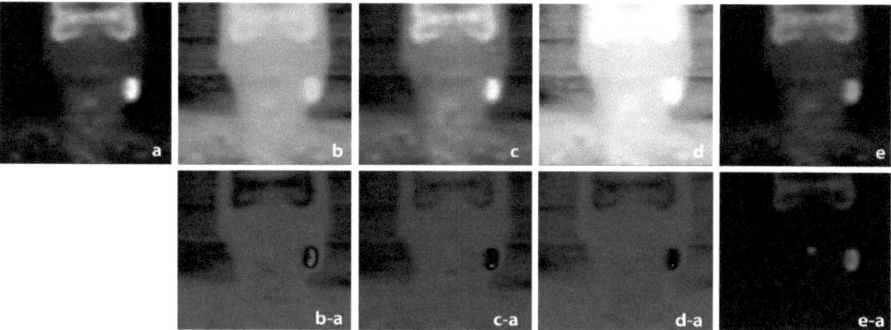

Figure 3.6: Overview of all the tone mapping algorithms implemented, applied to a human head-/neck PET scan (coronal view). The linear mapping (a) is compared to the operators by Reinhard (b), Drago (c) and the logarithmic (d) and exponential (e) methods. The bottom row shows the difference to the linear mapping, with blue colors denoting positive, red colors denoting negative values, respectively.

Finally, plenty of work has been done to implement the techniques on graphics hardware, as image processing is a particularly suitable application for GPUs. In 2003 already, Goodnight et al. [GWWH03] have successfully implemented a time-dependent (i.e., adapting over time, thus mimicking the human visual system) tone mapping system for color images. Due to the much lower performance and more restricted programming of graphics hardware back then, they have not been able to achieve real-time frame rates. Vollrath et al. [VWE05] have proposed a generic, real-time capable framework to implement the volume rendering pipeline on the graphics hardware. Their system implements Reinhard's tone mapping operator successfully, but they do not discuss it in the context of medical data. Another representative work is that of Yuan et al. [YNCP06] who have developed a sophisticated system for visualizing large high dynamic range data volumes at interactive rates. The three- and four-dimensional data is mainly from numerical simulations, geosciences, etc. and is thus processed with special attention for precision issues. However, they have not investigated the applicability of their methods on medical data sets as well.

Medical data For medical diagnosis and, of course, depending on the current problem, there are lots of different imaging modalities available. As discussed in the introductory sections in chapter 2.1, the majority of acquired radiological data is of tomographic nature nowadays. These data usually consist of scalar values, i.e., gray or luminance values within some range defined by the image acquisition system. Due to technical and computational reasons the currently used range for morphological imaging is usually 16 bits, where not all bits have to be used; special DICOM tags specify the exact layout. Functional imaging uses a higher bit depth. The following table lists typically used bit depths and value ranges for the modalities discussed here.

Modality	Bit depth	Typical range
CT	12 (integer)	-1k...3k
MRI	10/12/16 (integer)	0...1-32k
fMRI	16 (integer/float)	-32k...32k
DTI	16/32 (float)	-32k...32k
PET	16 (integer/float)	0...32k

Table 3.2: Typical properties of data in common modalities

Aside from these properties the data differ in their interpretation and thus need consideration for tone mapping alorithms. Computed tomography data, for example, has a fixed relation between the value at some position within the volume and the subject's tissue density at that position. That is, the higher the measured volume the lower the radiographic density, and vice versa – a relation represented by the Hounsfield scale. Here, transforming a CT signal I with some nonlinear global tone mapping function Φ would imply to interpret the data as if the Hounsfield function H had also been transformed, thus leading to the result I_H, that can be used for classification etc.:

$$I_H = H(I) \iff \Phi(I_H) = \Phi(H(I)) \tag{3.1.3}$$

In principle, only positron emission tomography (PET) also allows for a proportional relation between the measured intensity and the corresponding data (usually metabolic acitivity). All other modalities discussed here do not provide a direct mapping between the values and some scale, as even the values of different acquisitions can have different meaning. Based on these considerations it is clear that only global tone mapping provides a reasonable chance to maintain an interpretation of the data. In addition, global tone mapping algorithms are especially suitable for GPUs due to their inherent parallelism.

Tone mapping Tone mapping is an important procedure in high dynamic range imaging. In diagnostic visualizations the data is manually compressed by specifying a window of controllable width and center position. Although this linear interpolation between the minimum and maximum of the output device can also be regarded as the tone mapping function, it cannot achieve proper, data-driven results automatically. In addition, the mapping will result in an information loss if the input range is larger than the output range – which is usually the case for medical data. In order to investigate the results of applying tone mapping algorithms from high dynamic range imaging to medical volume data while not sacrificing the real-time visualization of the system, global operators are practically the only option.

All of the following algorithms require some information about the data itself and some global user definable parameter. First, the so-called *background intensity* I_{avg} has to be estimated. Instead of simply averaging the intensities by computing the arithmetic mean, the geometric average as suggested by Reinhard [RWPD05] is used:

$$I_{avg} = \exp\left(\frac{1}{N}\sum_{i=1}^{N}\log(I_i + \varepsilon)\right) \tag{3.1.4}$$

3.1. GPU-BASED COMPUTATIONS

In addition, the unitless parameter α is known as the *key* and represents the overall light level of the data in an interval of $[0...1]$. Let L be the luminance of the input data, then α can be estimated according to [RWPD05] by: [5]

$$f = \frac{2\log L_{avg} - \log L_{min} - \log L_{max}}{\log L_{max} - \log L_{min}}, \quad \alpha = 0.18 \cdot 4^f \quad (3.1.5)$$

While α can also be controlled by the user, providing a reasonable default value is usually preferable. Some of the following algorithms that have been implemented introduce further parameters that will be discussed accordingly.

Logarithmic and exponential scaling Using the logarithm or an exponential mapping function is straightforward and has its background in Weber-Fechner's law considering the relationship between measured and perceived stimuli. However, these approaches only achieve reasonable results for medium ranged images, i.e., in this context CT or low-valued MRI data. First, the logarithmic function is given: [6]

$$L_o(\vec{x}) = \frac{\log(1 + L_i(\vec{x}))}{\log(1 + L_{i_{max}})} \quad (3.1.6)$$

The exponential function in (3.1.7) maps input luminances to output luminances, where input values close to zero are mapped to zero, infinitely bright values are mapped to 1.0. This implies a renormalization because the output will never cover the full range available. Reinhard [RWPD05] reports that exchanging $L_{i_{max}}$ with $L_{i_{avg}}$ and vice versa yields a different effect, also shown in the corresponding graph in figure 3.7.

$$L_o(\vec{x}) = 1 - \exp\left(-\frac{L_i(\vec{x})}{L_{i_{avg}}}\right) \quad (3.1.7)$$

Extended logarithmic scaling Following the logarithmic behaviour of the human visual system, Drago et al. [DMAC03] have further investigated improvements of logarithmic functions. They proposed to adjust the logarithm's base with the input value and thus achieve a wider range of values to be reasonably mapped. As can be seen in the second term of the following equation, this base is interpolated within the range of 2 and 10:

$$L_o(\vec{x}) = \frac{L_{o_{max}} \cdot 0.01}{\log(1 + L_{i_{max}})} \cdot \frac{\log(1 + L_i(\vec{x}))}{\log\left(2 + 8\left(\frac{L_i(\vec{x})}{L_{i_{max}}}\right)^{\frac{\log(p)}{\log(0.5)}}\right)} \quad (3.1.8)$$

There are two parameters which can be specified by the user: the bias p controls the contrast, with larger values reducing the contrast. Also, the maximum output luminance $L_{o_{max}}$ (in cd/m^2) can be set, with a default value of 100.

---

[5] Note that the logarithms used in the following equations are assumed to be to the base of 10, if not stated otherwise.
[6] For the equations in the following subsections the luminance function's input parameter is used as n-dimensional vector $\vec{x}$, where n denotes the dimension of the data ($n = 3$ for volumetric scalar data)

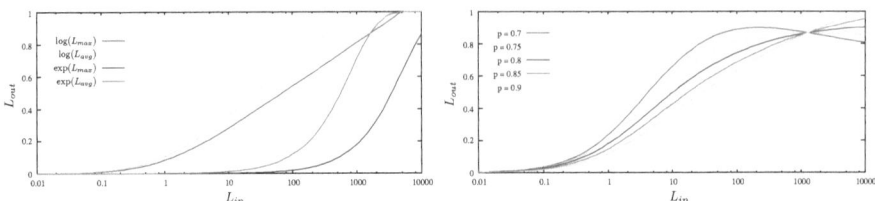

Figure 3.7: Graphs for the default logarithmic/exponential tone mapping curves with varying parameters, and tone mapping after [DMAC03] with varying parameters.

Photoreceptor Model While the assumption that the human visual systems is of logarithmic nature is basically correct, Reinhard and Devlin [RD05] propose that this holds only for a certain range of values. As logarithms produce negative values and have no upper bound, they need to be modified for an adequate model. This leads to the following relation:

$$L_o(\vec{x}) = \frac{L_i(\vec{x})}{L_i(\vec{x}) + \sigma(L_{i_a}(\vec{x}))} \qquad (3.1.9)$$

$$\sigma(L_{i_a}(\vec{x})) = (fL_{i_a}(\vec{x}))^m \qquad (3.1.10)$$

$$k = \frac{L_{i_{max}} - L_{i_{avg}}}{L_{i_{max}} - L_{i_{min}}}, \quad m = 0.3 + 0.7k^{1.4} \qquad (3.1.11)$$

In the equations (7) and (8), the term L_{i_a} denotes the adaptation level and can be set to $L_{i_{avg}}$ in our case, as no temporal or chromatic adaptation is needed. In addition, σ is often regarded as semisaturation constant. The following graphs illustrate the influence of the parameters k and f on the result:

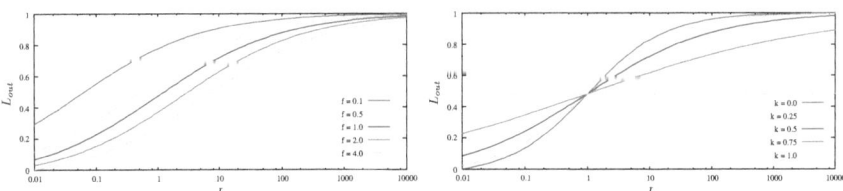

Figure 3.8: Graphs for the tone mapping curves according to [RD05] with varying luminance parameter (top) and key parameter (bottom).

Results and Discussion

Different kinds of datasets have been used, focusing on modalities with a large dynamical range. Therefore, the data sets used here are CT and PET data, with properties specified in the following table. As can be seen from the images, the rendering has been done without using transfer functions. This is mainly due to the different ways of how transfer functions can be used in the context of high dynamic range rendering and is subject to further investigation.

3.1. GPU-BASED COMPUTATIONS

Data set	Resolution	Bit depth	min/max
CT backpack	$512 \times 512 \times 373$	12 (int)	0 / 4072
PET body	$168 \times 168 \times 715$	16 (int)	2 / 32767
PET head	$128 \times 128 \times 83$	16 (int)	0 / 32767

Table 3.3: Properties of the data sets used for this study.

Performance As expected, the higher the dynamic range of values, the larger the improvement over linear mapping. MRI data sets, for example, usually provide values up to approximately 1k and thus do not benefit much from tone mapping. As can be seen in figure 3.6, the implemented algorithms result in quite different renderings, with Drago's algorithm being a good candidate. In addition, with only one parameter this operator is very easy to use.

The algorithms have been implemented directly within the rendering shader programs. Without exhaustive optimization, the performance overhead is negligible for all renderings: even ray casting the whole volume maintains real-time performance on commodity hardware. Adjusting the user parameters as well as the statistical data of the volume data is done via uniform variables that are transferred to the graphics hardware only when updated and thus do not impose a performance penalty.

Usability In comparison to the standard windowing scheme, only little interaction is needed with the approach presented here. While this automatic initialization of the visualization parameters is generally considered positive, radiologists still put an emphasis on the need to manually focus on specific ranges. The parameters for the tone mapping algorithms, however, are hard to relate with the traditional approach. Therefore, a combination of the two techniques by approximating the automatically determined tone mapping function linearly with adequate windowing parameters would be preferable. Also, for multi-modal registration purposes, the visualization of the whole range of values was considered to be useful. The more detailed structures in the tone mapped data (as in figure 3.5b, for example) provide a better visual guidance when specifying landmarks in two modalities with different value ranges, e.g. PET and CT or MRI data.

Conclusion and future work

In this contribution, the advantage of using the GPU for improving the visualization of volume data of higher dynamic range than the output device has been shown. After reviewing several approaches to compress high dynamic range data, their applicability to medical data has been discussed. Global operators offer a good way of transforming the data while being computationally less expensive and inherently amenable to parallel architectures. On the other hand, local operators would introduce an uncertainty into the visual representation impeding diagnostic interpretation. Therefore, some representative global operators in the GPU framework have been implemented.

As the results are promising, there are some options for further investigation. Firstly, applying such operators to other, more specific image modalities such as fMRI/DTI has not been addressed in detail yet. Especially the growing importance of functional imaging with data that does not simply correspond to scalar properties such as luminance or density will lead to more complex algorithms. With the real-time performance at hand, visual approaches such as the "design galleries" by Marks et al. [MAB+97] would improve both the handling of the algorithms' parameters and multiple dimensions.

Another direction of research is the role of the transfer function in the context of high dynamic range imaging. Similar to pre-/post-classification in volume rendering (see section 1.3), one can use the (HDR) transfer function with the original data and apply tone mapping procedures afterwards. Alternatively, the transfer function can be accessed by (low dynamic) values of the volume that has been tone mapped before. The implications are subject to further research, as well as its applicability to different modalities, especially for non-scalar types.

3.1.3 Evaluating the Performance of Processing Medical Volume Data on Graphics Hardware

As discussed in the preceding sections, GPU implementations of complex computations are superior to software algorithms. Also, such computations are not limited to rather simple, image processing filters: in Erdt et al. [ERS08] considerable mathematical operations were implemented, for example. Especially for reasonably large amounts of data and non-standard data types, many applications can benefit from hardware implementations as well, as discussed by Owens et al. [OHL+08] in the context of recent APIs and hardware.

However, the integration of computation and visualization is sensitive to data transfer. With GPUs as external devices (with respect to the CPU and its memory), all data has to be loaded to the graphics memory for further processing. Whereas the computational performance of graphics hardware has grown exponentially during the past years, the memory bandwidth has increased only moderately, as shown in figure 3.9.

As already mentioned in the introduction of this chapter, and as addressed by Buck et al. in [BFH+04, Buc05], the performance of GPU implementations mainly depends on the *arithmetic intensity*. This term describes the ratio of computations and memory accesses, where GPUs perform better the higher the ratio becomes. This suggests on the one hand to hide the memory's latency by reordering programs (i.e., interleaving texture fetches with multiple arithmetic operations). On the other hand, transferring data from the host's memory has to be done as infrequent as possible.

Therefore, the following contribution by Raspe et al. [RLM08] focuses on a comparison of image processing and segmentation algorithms as single operations, as well as a sequence of operations. Whereas GPU implementations for the former can only exceed their software counterpart if the operation is rather complex, concatenating hardware operations to perform a whole workflow clearly outperforms software implementations; even for larger amounts of data. Considering the focus on visual computing, not only the much higher performance

3.1. GPU-BASED COMPUTATIONS

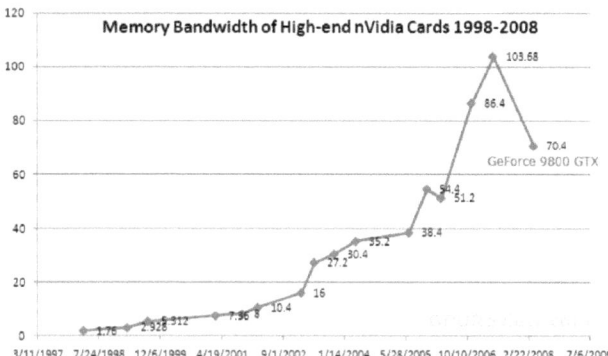

Figure 3.9: The development of GPU's memory bandwidth (in gigabytes per second) over the last decade. (Image courtesy of GPUReview)

of hardware implementations is attractive. The fact that the computation results can be visualized directly, i.e., without introducing any overhead or data transfer, allows for literally interactive applications.

Introduction

With the advances of computer graphics hardware during the last few years, the computational performance of such commodity hardware is able to clearly outperform modern multi-core processors. As shown recently in [OLG+07], many areas are able to benefit from the computing performance of programmable graphics processors (GPU). In medical application, however, visualization tasks are still the primary use for graphics hardware.

While many general purpose applications have been successfully addressed, image processing remains a particularly interesting field due to the architecture of graphics hardware. Being optimized especially for two-dimensional textures, processing such image data is obvious and achieves optimal performance. However, lots of image data is represented three-dimensionally, especially in the medical field. This imposes several issues for applications targeting at graphics hardware. Firstly, the available on-board memory becomes critical for large volume data being easily produced by modern imaging systems. Secondly, 3D textures are limited in flexibility thus preventing their use as target memory. However, the main problem is still the data transfer to and especially from the graphics memory. For certain applications this is not as problematic as it might seem. As shown in Langs and Biedermann [LB07], by using the graphics hardware for filtering large volumes representing video frames a performance gain of several orders of magnitudes with respect to commercial CPU implementations is achievable. Köhn et al. [KDR+06] have implemented image registration algorithms on the GPU and also report a clear performance improvement that has only been flawed by some graphics driver limitations.

In order to evaluate the discussion for processing (medical) volume data, different types of operations will be discussed with respect to their run-time performance as CPU and GPU implementations, respectively. Therefore, the GPU-based framework CASCADA, which is already used in the context of medical segmentation (see chapter 7) regards computation processes at a more abstract level and handles processing and visualization tasks uniformly. The cross-platform system also provides basic functionality for handling (medical) volume data and integrates different visualization techniques and input devices. In chapter 6 both versions of the framework will be described in detail, while CASCADA 1 was used in this contribution.

Material and Methods

The system for (general purpose) GPU programming focuses on processing volume data, mainly from tomographic imaging systems such as CT or MRI. While conceptual and implementation details of the framework will be described in chapters 5 and 6, respectively, the remainder of this section outlines the methods for evaluating and comparing its performance.

In order to provide a measure for the efficiency of the framework, its processing performance has been compared with MeVisLab [MeV07], a widely used software system for efficient medical data processing and visualization. Although CASCADA also provides software implementations of the algorithms, these are not as optimized as established tools in this regard. Most of MeVisLab's core algorithms are based on an image processing library that, in combination with the powerful frontend, allows the flexible and rapid development of applications. At the time of writing, however, the system does not utilize programmable graphics hardware, except for visualization purposes, simple modifications of primarily visual results via shader programs, and some experimental filter implementations.

As mentioned before, an important factor for leveraging the performance of GPUs is the amount of data transfer relative to the processing. Obviously, a much better performance can be achieved by loading the data once to the graphics memory and perform as much computations as possible there. This is also preferable for the simultaneous visualization of the results during computation.

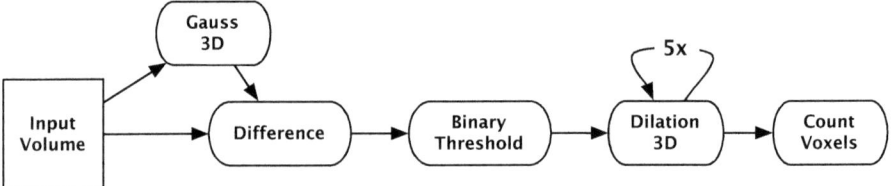

Figure 3.10: Test setup for evaluating the performance of an example pipeline consisting of different types of operations.

Two different scenarios for comparing the systems have been set up. The first one is intended to show the performance at operations with different levels of computational complexity, ranging from simple thresholding to gradient computation in a 3D neighborhood. The second performance benchmark (figure 3.10) aims at mimicking a reasonable procedure

3.1. GPU-BASED COMPUTATIONS

for volume processing, so the focus is on combining different operations while limiting data transfer to the extent needed.

All the experiments were performed on an Intel Core2Duo (2.4 GHz) with 2 GB RAM and an Nvidia Geforce 8800 GTS with 640 MB of VRAM. For MeVisLab the SDK version 1.5.1 available from the website with default settings was used. The algorithms were applied in both applications to the same datasets, depicted in figure 3.11: a $512 \times 512 \times 223$ CT scan and an MRI scan $256 \times 256 \times 256$, both with 16 bit values, available in DICOM and raw format, respectively.

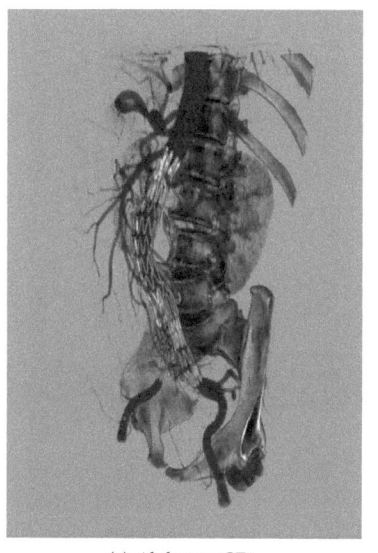
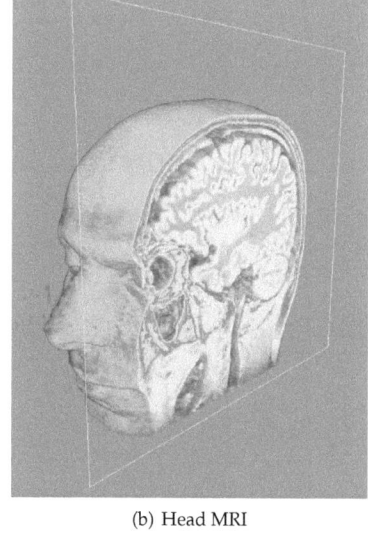

(a) Abdomen CTA (b) Head MRI

Figure 3.11: The datasets used for evaluating the performance of GPU and CPU implementations: a CT scan of the abdomen (a) and a smaller MRI scan of a head (b).

Results

In the following tables all the timings from the aforementioned experiments have been collected. The first table shows some details on the single operations with increasing complexity (no neighborhood, 4/6-neighborhood, and 8/26-neighborhood, respectively). In addition to their behaviour in the different dimensions, the transfer overhead is measured in detail.

The second table gives an overview of reasonable concatenations of varying operations. No additional time for data transfer and/or conversion is measured here, as both systems work in their appropriate format for subsequent execution. In MeVisLab, special caching modules have been integrated to decouple the different processing steps for more comparable measurements.

Operation	MeVisLab	Cascada (all)	Cascada (GPU)
Binary	0.73 / 0.21	1.9 / 0.55	0.038 / 0.011
Gradient 2D	10.1 / 2.9	2.6 / 0.7	0.06 / 0.017
Gradient 3D	14.9 / 3.9	2.6 / 0.72	0.059 / 0.018
Gauss 2D	1.36 / 0.37	2.48 / 0.73	0.061 / 0.017
Gauss 3D	3.65 / 1.01	2.59 / 0.78	0.09 / 0.026

Table 3.4: Computation times in seconds for the two data sets (CT scan/MRI scan). The GPU version excludes data transfer from/to the video memory and is averaged over multiple runs.

Operation	MeVisLab	Cascada (GPU)	⌀ speedup
Gauss+Difference	3.6 / 1.48	0.74 / 0.23	5.5
Binary Threshold	0.7 / 0.23	0.125 / 0.049	5.2
Dilation 3D (5x)	27.12 / 7.6	1.14 / 0.343	23
Count Voxels	1.1 / 0.7	0.33 / 0.078	6
Total	32.9 / 10.8	2.41 / 0.76	14

Table 3.5: Single computation times in seconds for the two data sets (CT scan/MRI scan). The GPU version includes the shader and all setup steps between the stages; the initial upload is omitted here (see table 3.4). Total time does not include data I/O for both platforms

Discussion and Extension

As shown in the results, the GPU is able to clearly outperform CPU implementations for all operations, with speed-up factors of up to 250 – even for non-trivial algorithms. In contrast, including the additional time for the data transfer to and from the GPU reveals the severe impact on the performance: depending on the type and dimensionality of the operation, and the size of the volume the software implementation can surpass the GPU's performance. Aside from several optimizations that are left as future work for the GPU system to tackle this issue, reloading the whole volume in every stage is not very likely. Therefore, the second benchmark has been set up to provide a more realistic scenario where the GPU is still more than one order of magnitude ahead of CPU implementations, and is thus well suited for computationally demanding task of medical data processing.

While the image processing filters presented here have been limited to small 3^2 or 3^3 neighborhoods and rather simple operations, in Erdt et al. [ERS08] more complex settings have been used. In order to implement a segmentation of hepatic vessels, the volume data is preprocessed by using a customized vesselness filter, based on Frangi et al. [FNVV98]. This results in a high response for tubular structures in the data, and thus requires a larger neighborhood for reasonable detection. The authors have used a 7^3 window and compared a CPU solution with a GPU implementation based on CASCADA. Especially for this filter operation the hardware implementation achieves a speed-up of up to 100, even for non-separated filter kernels. In addition, the computation of the Hessian matrix that involves six partial derivatives is still more than one order of magnitude faster than the software version. This results in a total performance gain of a factor of more than 15 if the data transfer is taken into account.

Of course, there is still room for improvement and investigation, aside from just technical optimizations. Software performance is not only measured in raw computing performance, but also in programming effort where a research system as CASCADA has to be compared to other platforms (see chapters 5 and 6 for an extensive discussion). Also, graphics hardware vendors have already started to simplify the use of their hardware by regarding GPUs more as devices than purely graphics oriented hardware, where the technical realization of "visual computing" is subject to change. Regarding the fast development cycles of graphics hardware, the performance advantage will most likely be increasing as can be easily seen from speedups with past hardware generations.

3.2 Interaction

After discussing the possibilities of combining visualization and computations by means of GPU implementations, the following approaches focus on the *interaction* with the data. In particular, interacting directly with processing steps performed on the data will be addressed. Techniques used for direct volume render already provide interactivity by means of editing transfer functions, apply cutting tools, etc. However, the notion of interaction will be extended to computations, especially for the application of iterative segmentation methods.

This idea was originally introduced several years ago, mainly by Ben Shneiderman's *direct manipulation* [Shn83]. This early work investigated fundamental concepts such as the desktop metaphor for office applications or – in general – *information visualization*; see Card et al. [CMS99] for an overview. Later contributions led to the notion of *computational steering* where the interactive control of parameters with (ideally immediate) visual feedback is suggested.

Before the fast evolution of graphics hardware, such interaction was only possible with specialized systems and/or clusters, as discussed for example in Wright [Wri04]. Today, many researchers utilize the computational performance of GPUs[7] for virtually all kinds of simulations – often with interaction capabilities, as will be addressed in the following sections.

3.2.1 Controlling GPU-based Volume Rendering using Ray Textures

This contribution by Raspe and Müller [RM08] introduces a novel approach to control different rendering parameters of volume ray casting interactively. Since the introduction of ray casting implementations on programmable graphics hardware, both performance and

---

[7]Several groups even employ CPU–GPU clusters, which has become much more attractive due to dedicated programming APIs such as Nvidia CUDA or OpenCL.

flexibility have increased and are able to outperform texture-based techniques. In addition, by using rays for computing the volume integral instead of proxy geometry (see section 1.3.2), one has more control over local settings. Therefore, dependent texture lookups to user editable 2D textures are utilized, thus allowing for interactive parameter setting on a per-ray basis, at negligible performance overhead on modern graphics hardware. By those means, volume rendering can be controlled in a way impossible with proxy-based techniques and exemplary uses are demonstrated. Furthermore, data-driven initializations of the ray textures are going to be addressed as well.

Introduction

Direct volume rendering (DVR) plays an important role in visualizing three-dimensional data, with datasets from modern image acquisition systems in medicine being the most prominent. Several methods for solving this computationally demanding problem have been proposed in the past decades and form the foundations of many volume rendering systems in a variety of applications. Sections 1.3.2 and 2.3.3 discuss the techniques in general and in the medical context, respectively.

In this contribution, the control of rendering parameters at ray level by employing intermediate textures used as parameter lookup table is proposed. As a ray casting extension it is, of course, not limited to pure GPU implementations. However, to achieve reasonably interactive performance on commodity hardware the focus will be on a GPU-only implementation. In addition to the step size as the basic internal parameter for ray casting, these computations typically introduce different parameters. Controlling them individually across the volume domain (as proposed here) is usually not possible, but would offer numerous possibilities: starting the rays at different intervals for local cut-away views; decreasing the step size (i.e., better image quality) only in areas of interest or importance; weighting optical properties during integration, etc.

Related work

A clear advantage of ray casting is the easy integration with geometry, as is particularly interesting for clipping techniques or correct rendering. Kratz et al. [KSFB06] have established a flexible solution utilizing depth buffer information. Related to ray–geometry intersection is the correct rendering while moving the camera within the volume, which is can be regarded as interacting with the visualization as well. Therefore, the bounding geometry generating the rays must not be clipped by the view-frustum (i.e., near plane), but reset to resemble the "new" starting point of rays; details can be found in [SHN$^+$05], for example.

The concept of controlling the ray itself has been further extended by Rezk-Salama et al. [RSK06] to allow the flexible exploration of the volume. Especially in medical datasets, inner structures often cannot be revealed by editing the transfer function only, due to the viewpoint dependency of occlusion. Their approach aligns well with GPU-based ray casting and also exploits other hardware features for interactive performance, but does not work on individual rays or their properties. This idea has been proposed by Malik et al. [MMG07],

3.2. INTERACTION

whose method evaluates the profile of each ray through the volume, thus achieving a more flexible peeling technique.

Another category of research aims at controlling the rendering of the volume by defining clipping data, usually consisting of basic geometry like planes, spheres etc. This quite simple, yet effective technique is integrated in almost every commercial system and provides basic interaction functionality. In addition, this can also be extended to volume data (e.g., segmentation results) specifying the rendering/clipping of individual voxels. Although Weiskopf et al. [WEE03] have presented this approach originally for texture-based systems, their concepts can be easily extended to a ray casting environment.

Approach

Implementing the ray texture concept requires the discussion of several topics. Aside from technical issues for a flexible GPU implementation, different types of parameters and interaction modes are introduced and defined in the following sections.

As introduced before, the goal is to provide means for controlling volume rendering parameters down to the level of single rays. Of course, this implies that it should also be possible to build groups of rays for equal properties, thus simplifying user interaction. Thereby, the possible levels of control range from a single ray up to all rays at once, i.e., standard ray casting. Apart from the level of control, the parameters' type and semantics are of interest as well. One basic parameter in ray casting is the step size specifying the interval at which the volume is sampled along the ray: the larger the step size, the coarser the sampling, and vice versa. Another set of parameters closely related to the ray itself is the offset specifying the valid interval of sample positions along the ray. Figure 3.12 illustrates these *geometric parameters*, with the offset parameters defining only two intervals for clarity in the example.

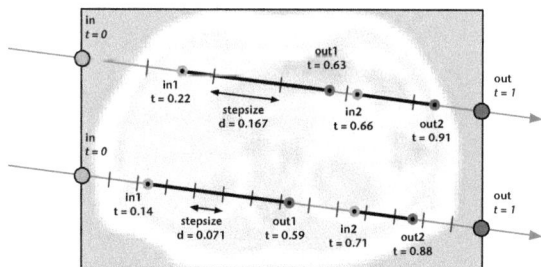

Figure 3.12: Controlling geometric parameters per ray: step size (blue dashes) and two intervals ("inN/outN") are set individually, thus sampling the volume along different intervals (thick black lines)

Classification of parameters In contrast to the ray geometry, another class of parameters can be defined as *value parameters* that control the computations during integration (i.e., within the ray casting loop for single-pass implementations). The following list names a few typical parameters:

- threshold for early-ray termination (ERT)
- weighting directional properties, e.g. gradients
- combining optical properties by blending different rendering modes (MIP, transfer functions, etc.)

In addition to the different applications, these parameters are of increasing complexity. That is, a simple threshold will be easier to implement and to control than the weighting of rendering modes or different transfer functions. As well as the geometric parameters described before, the uses are not limited to the examples listed here; they are rather to outline the idea. In addition, both sets of parameters can be combined in order to increase, for example, the quality of early terminated rays by reducing the step size for low ERT thresholds.

Controlling the texture To edit the ray texture during run time, two different approaches have been identified – no matter if the texture is set up automatically or via direct user input. As depicted in figure 3.13, the texture can be aligned with the screen or with the volume. For the former, the data in the texture is set in viewport coordinates, i.e., keeping the texels at fixed positions while changing the volume rendering in terms of rotation, position, etc. This method will be referred to as *view aligned*, also to emphasize the analogy to view aligned slices for proxy-based volume rendering. The second method maps the additional texture to the bounding geometry of the volume. This way the ray texture is transformed together with the volume and represents a *volume aligned* texture mode. Note the difference in the sampling of the volume with the ray texture specifying the step size, indicated by the different dashes in figure 3.13.

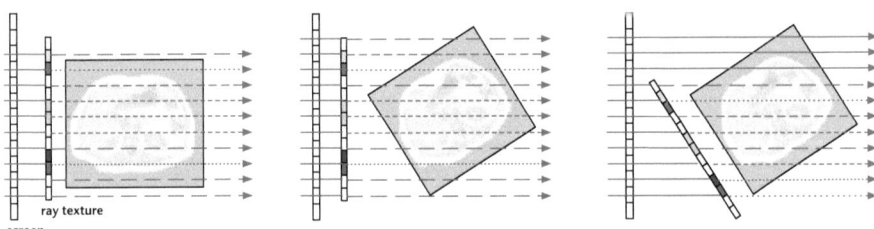

Figure 3.13: Different rendering modes: initial view (left), view aligned (middle) and volume aligned (right) application of ray textures to rotated volume.

Shader handling This approach focuses on a GPU-only implementation of ray casting which means that the computations are performed by shader programs. These programs are compiled once and loaded for drawing the geometry. Thus, the functionality of a shader

3.2. INTERACTION

cannot be changed without loading a recompiled program. To minimize the overhead of providing several complete shader program, two different strategies will be applied. Firstly, the framework developed in the course of this thesis (see chapter 6) supports the concatenation of shader code fragments. Using this approach, different modules integrating the parameter types introduced before into a default ray casting fragment program can be used. Depending on the user's selection the corresponding shader is then assembled and loaded. This approach is discussed extensively in chapter 5.

The second method does not employ the assembly of shader programs from small components, but uses one complete shader program. The different "semantics" (i.e., controlling the step size, ERT threshold, etc.) are used directly in the code by accessing different textures (or channels thereof) that have been initialized accordingly. Section 3.2.1 will show example code and the different approaches will be discussed.

Implementation

Setup   CASCADA already provides some basic tools for working with and rendering volume data. In addition to the data itself, which is represented as volume and array objects, respectively, the system also provides the corresponding texture objects for wrapping OpenGL states, handles, etc. Also mentioned before, "flat3D textures" are utilized that unfold volumetric data into a large two-dimensional texture.

The ray casting itself is implemented as a typical two-pass algorithm, as described in section 1.3. It should be noted that the approach proposed here is also applicable to optimized bounding geometry as presented by Scharsach [Sch05], because only the rays' parameters are controlled, independent of how the rays are computed. The shader program implementing the integration along the ray (i.e., the loop) is the main part of the ray casting algorithm and will be augmented with the additional texture for controlling the individual rays. In addition to extending the shader code as shown in listing 3.1, a two-dimensional texture is also initialized as needed for the further steps.

Application   As described in the section before, both controlling options have the advantage of providing a fast and simple setup and manipulation on the application side, and being easily accessed during the ray casting process in the shader program. The two approaches differ only slightly in terms of shader implementation, so that the whole procedure can be summarized as follows:

The first step should be clear and does not need further explanation. If the ray texture is initialized with pre-computed results, the second step is optional. In case the step is used, a circular neighborhood of the current pixel position, with varying size and fall-off has been implemented. Taking the basic idea of ray textures to controlling rays from a single ray to all rays at once one step further, a hierarchical approach has also been implemented. Therefore, editing the ray texture can be performed at different resolution levels: using a coarser level will result in many rays being changed at once, and vice versa. However, this permits only square areas to be edited due to the very nature of texture mip-mapping. A possible extension

---
Pseudocode 1 Ray Textures

  initialize 2D texture in viewport size
  manipulate the texels according to user input from window coordinates
  update the texture/coordinate information and load it to the GPU
  while (ray casting) **do**
    if (view aligned) **then**
      access the ray texture using the window relative coordinates
    else
      access the ray texture using the starting position of the ray
    end if
  end while
  control the ray parameters within the shader
---

to that will be reviewed at the end. In combination with the "manual" approach, this allows for further customization of the editing area, with results being presented and discussed later on. The subsequent step transfers the changes to the graphics hardware, so that this has to be done per frame. As this is the most expensive part, pure GPU implementations will be outlined at the end of this section to alleviate the communication burden. The following steps are performed within the shader and will be described in the next paragraph in detail.

Shader implementations As mentioned before, accessing the texture is done in the second pass of the ray casting algorithm for both methods. For the *view aligned* mode, the ray texture is simply indexed using the relative window coordinate of the current fragment via GLSL's `gl_FragCoord`. When using *volume aligned* access, the same texture coordinates as for the color-coded ray positions from the preceding pass (i.e., the fragments from rendering the bounding geometry) are used for fetching the corresponding texel from the ray texture. This is shown in the example code in listing 3.1, controlling the step size as an example. Note how the current ray texture's value can be used differently by using texture channels, sets of ray textures, etc.

Implementing the functionality itself is also straightforward, as will be shown with some examples that address both classes of parameters described before. For the first example, the effect of decreasing the step size in regions of interest to improve rendering with an initially low step size (1/10 instead of 1/256) is shown. Therefore, the user draws into the texture to lower the value stored in one of the channels. This value is then read within the shader to set the step size, which is then used as increment of the inner loop. Figure 3.14 shows a vessel data set ($384^2 \times 72$, 16 bit) with an accordingly edited ray texture to increase rendering accuracy in regions of interest.

The second example (figure 3.15) blends two shading modes by using a value parameter for linear interpolation. Thus, the user is enabled to control the exact application of transfer functions, simple shading, or other techniques on a per ray basis.

3.2. INTERACTION

```glsl
uniform sampler3D volTex;      // volume data
uniform sampler2D rayTex;      // control texture
uniform sampler2D startTex;    // ray start pos.
uniform vec2 rcpWinSize;       // reciprocal win size
uniform float stepsize;        // default: 1/256.0
uniform bool volAligned;       // mode (default: true)
varying vec3 texcoord;         // ray stop positions

void main()
{
  // compute ray
  vec2 tc = gl_FragCoord.xy * rcpWinSize;
  vec3 raystart = texture2D(startTex, tc).xyz;
  vec3 ray = raystart - texcoord;

  vec4 control;
  if ( volAligned )
    control = texture2D(rayTex, raystart.xy);
  else
    control = texture2D(rayTex, tc);

  // ...

  // set step size from first channel of rayTex
  stepsize = max( 0.00390625, control.x );  // limit: 1/256

  // integrate
  for ( float t = 0.0; t <= ray_len; t += stepsize )
  {
    vec3 pos = texcoord + t * ray;
    vec4 sample = texture3D(volTex, pos);
    // ...
  }

  // weight result from ray texture
  gl_FragColor = finalcolor * control.y;
}
```

Listing 3.1: GLSL shader code (simplified) showing the use of ray texture within a standard ray casting shader.

Results

In this section the results of the approach will be presented, both in terms of rendering performance and level of control. All implementations and tests have been done using the GPU-framework CASCADA 1, running on an Intel Core2 Duo (2.4 GHz) with 2 GB RAM and an Nvidia Geforce 8800 GTS under Windows XP. The viewport size for the ray casting has been 512^2 pixels, with a default setting of 256 loop iterations. Ray casting is performed as a two-pass approach as described before, without further optimizations. The data set used in the figures and the timings below is an MRI volume of 256^3 voxels, with 16 bit floating-point scalar values per voxel (represented as IEEE-754r compliant type "half"). The rendering performance is averaged over a full rotation of the volume to account for view dependency, with the volume covering at least 90% of the viewport.

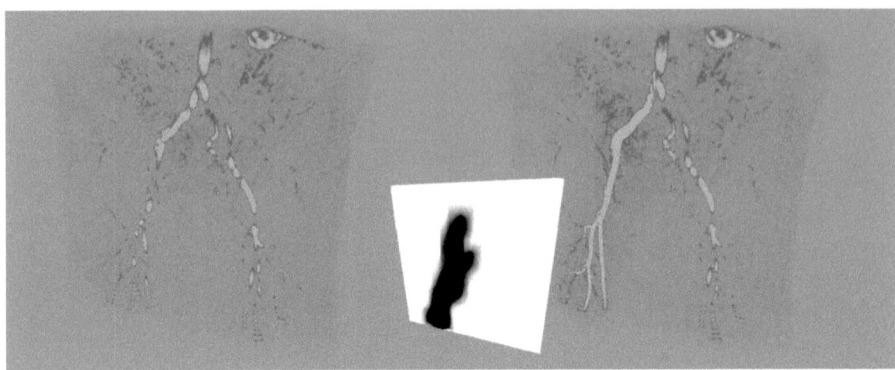

Figure 3.14: Decreasing the step size for a region of interest (right section vessel) in an example dataset. The inset depicts the corresponding ray texture.

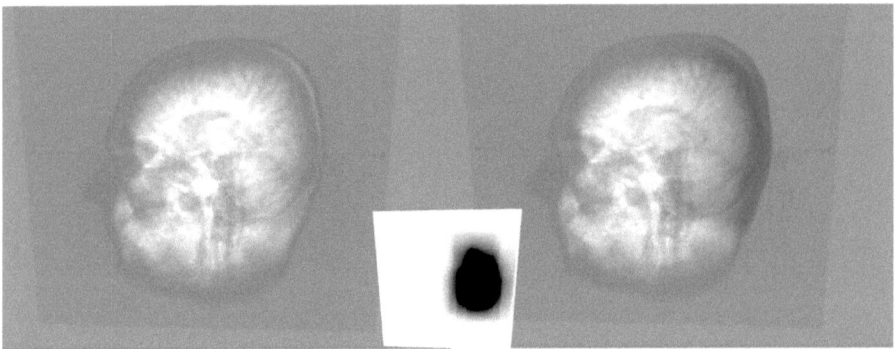

Figure 3.15: Blending a one-dimensional transfer function and simple accumulative shading by using value parameters, with the inset showing the interpolation weight.

Performance As stated before, the overhead for the additional texture lookup is negligible on current graphics hardware. Aside from the number of the pixels used for casting ray, the rendering performance is mainly influenced by the number of iterations due to the multiple texture fetches along the ray. Accessing the ray texture imposes only one additional texture fetch per fragment and does not contribute to the overall performance, as set out in the table below (static ray texturing).

While editing and reloading the texture as described in the preceding section, the performance is limited by the CPU–GPU communication bottleneck, of course. Note that this includes setting a whole neighborhood of values, not only the pixel currently "selected", so that there is some additional computation performed by the CPU. In order to reduce the performance hit by updating the texture per frame, the transfer should be limited to the actually edited region of the texture. In addition to the initial resolution of the ray texture,

3.2. INTERACTION

the hierarchical approach for updating an area of rays comparable to that of direct update has been used. This results in a clear performance gain compared to working with an equally large area at the full resolution. However, a detailed control of the neighborhood with arbitrary shapes is not directly possible when using the hierarchical approach.

Rendering Mode	Average FPS
Default ray casting (RC)	61
RC with static ray texturing	59
Direct update	9
Hierarchical update	33

Table 3.6: Average performance for standard ray casting, additional ray textures, and update strategies, respectively.

Although it is quite difficult to compare the two classes of parameters (geometric and value, respectively) due to their different usage, equally complex scenarios have been used to estimate the difference. Therefore, the intervals have been decreased in equal steps resulting in an increased number of loop iterations. For the value parameters the threshold for early ray termination has been increased likewise, which yields also more iterations (due to the delayed termination of the loop). As expected, the performance is not related to the direct type of parameter, but to its syntactic use within the shader.

Control The two methods of transforming the ray texture have led to different behaviour while editing the texture. For the *view aligned* approach, the functionality can be interpreted as looking through a "window of altered properties". This is similar to the idea of ray casting as image space method, where rays are cast through the viewing plane and sample the volume along the ray (usually within the volume's boundaries). As expected, this works only intuitively for fixed viewing positions due to the view dependency: for example, an increased level of detail applied to a specific region of interest will affect other regions once the camera is moved.

A more intuitive control is to transform the ray texture with the volume (i.e., *volume aligned*). This approach counteracts to some degree with the ray casting concept where the rays are all in viewing direction. Their properties, however, are changed only partially depending on the visibility and transformation of the edited ray texels.

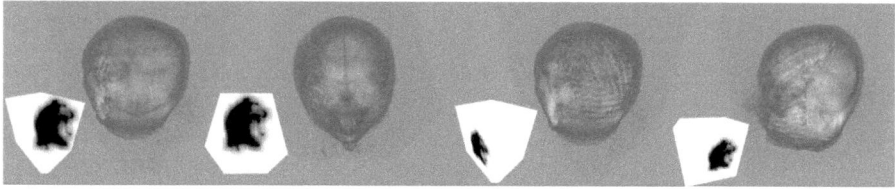

Figure 3.16: Comparison of the two editing modes: "view aligned" (left) and "volume aligned" (right). Note the inset illustrating the different effects

Thus, the former method can be used, for example, as a tool for inspecting parts of the volume, analog to a filter being applied to data. As both can be interchanged easily during rendering, manipulations of the texture can be made on-the-fly in one view or the other. Figure 3.16 shows the different results for the volume and view aligned mode, respectively.

Conclusion and Future Work

In summary, the concept of ray textures for controlling parameters of individual rays in volume rendering was presented as a tight coupling of visualization and interaction. Therefore, parameters were classified as *geometric* and *value* properties that can be edited and used separately, as well as in combination. Additionally, two modes of applying the ray texture were described: *view aligned* or *volume aligned*, which differ only slightly in terms of implementation and thus can be used interchangeably during run-time. In addition to a neighborhood of the current position for changing of a whole set of rays at once, a hierarchical approach has shown to be more efficient, if a simple quadratic neighborhood is sufficient.

As a direct improvement of the limitation imposed by the hierarchical approach would be a GPU-based solution. There, only the coordinates of the user's interaction would be transferred to the GPU, and preset textures of arbitrary size and shape would be applied. This would also enable procedural texturing or even an integration of feedback from the preceding rendering step. Initializing the ray textures is yet another direction of investigation. Therefore, the volume would be rendered first to an offscreen buffer to extract relevant information (e.g., gradients, silhouettes). Finally, the application of the ray texture concept to offscreen rendering would be of high interest for further parameter setting.

3.2.2 Controlling iterative algorithms

While the concept of ray textures provides interaction with the visualization, direct interaction is also interesting for the manipulation and control of computations. In general, two different classes of such techniques can be identified. At a very coarse level, the user interaction can represent parameter settings that control an algorithm. In the following, this concept is referred to as *global interaction*, to express the setting of properties for the whole process. In contrast, *local interaction* denotes the second level of interaction, where parameters are manipulated locally. As approaches for the former are rather obvious, the focus will be on concepts to implement local interaction.

Global interaction

In the context of iterative algorithms, one example for such a global interaction is the incremental region growing for vascular segmentation proposed by Selle et al. [SPSP02], and later by Boskamp et al. [BRL+04]. In their work, multiple thresholds are precomputed and the overall volume of the segmented region is evaluated. By plotting the data as graphs (see figure 3.17), the user or algorithm can select the optimal threshold with minimal error.

3.2. INTERACTION

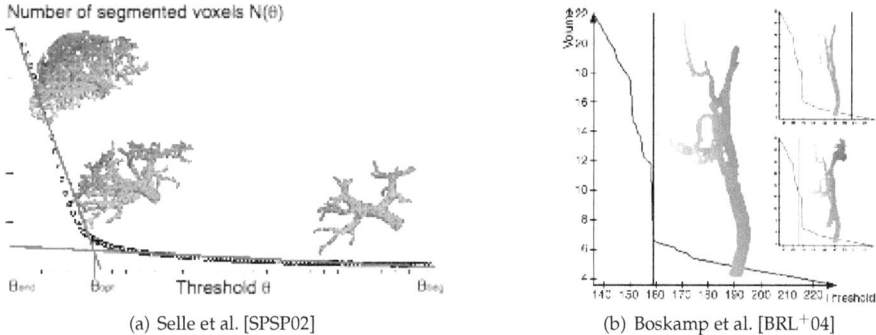

(a) Selle et al. [SPSP02]

(b) Boskamp et al. [BRL+04]

Figure 3.17: Interactive region growing to determine the optimal threshold in order to segment vascular structures from CT/MRI data sets. The graphs depict the total volume of the segmentation depending on the threshold. In (a) for liver vessel segmentation, in (b) for aortic vessels, with the insets illustrating the different results, respectively.

In Erdt et al. [ERS08] this concept has been adopted and extended to allow interactive settings based on transfer functions, to achieve real-time performance for whole volume segmentations on GPUs. Therefore, the segmentations results based on region growing are stored by augmenting the initial values with offsets from the different thresholds used. This results in high values where the voxel belongs to the region for a whole range of thresholds, in contrast to lower values for outliers; figure 3.18 illustrates the approach.

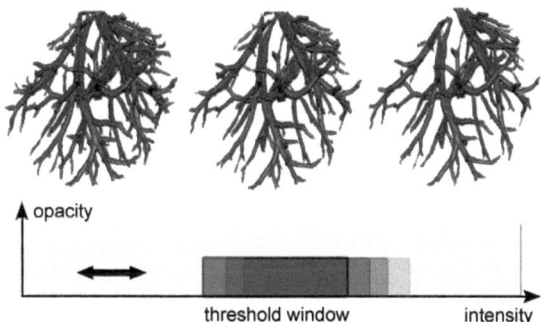

Figure 3.18: Real-time preview of region growing segmentation in [ERS08]. A dynamic transfer function is applied to a (precomputed) volume containing additional information from the iterative segmentation process of hepatic vessel structures.

Local interaction

Whereas the aforementioned examples provide only an indirect level of interaction, controlling computations locally is also desirable. There exist many applications for direct interaction with computations in the field of physical simulation, for example. Closer related to GPU-based computations are the fundamental contributions by Krüger and Westermann [KW03b] and Harris [Har04]. Based on the linear algebra operations and demo applications introduced by Krüger and Westermann, Harris implements Navier-Stokes fluid simulation on a two-dimensional grid. They have been able to run their simulations on reasonably sized grids in real-time on hardware available back then, mainly due to the high degree of parallelism of such applications. Nevertheless, this performance in combination with the direct mapping of the visual results to the underlying simulation (i.e., textures, see figure 3.19) allows the direct, local manipulation of the physical properties. As a result, the user can "draw" properties such as velocity, pressure, or temperature, or edit obstacles that interact with the simulated matter with immediate visual feedback.

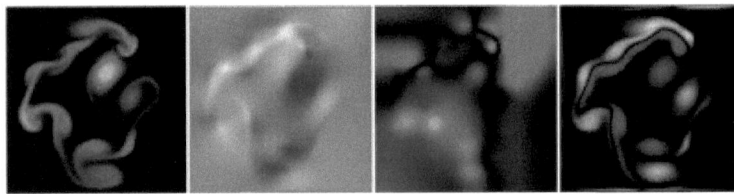

Figure 3.19: GPU-based fluid dynamics simulation by Harris [Har04] with direct interaction during rendering. The images depict from left to right: ink, velocity (scale-biased), pressure, and vorticity.

After many years of GPGPU research and the availability of increasingly programmable hardware, these applications have been extended to practically all kinds of physical simulations, three-dimensional grids, more complex solvers, etc. Due to the fact that the details of these implementations go beyond the scope of this thesis, the focus will be only on applications for (medical) image data, preferably of three-dimensional type.

During an early stage of this thesis, one project has been on interactively segmenting the liver from low-resolution MRI data of the human abdominal section utilizing graphics hardware (figure 3.20). While further details of the "LiverGPU" project will be presented in section 7.1, the following paragraphs discuss the concept of combining visualization, computation, and interaction.

Introduction The basic idea is the observation that region growing algorithms usually suffer from local artefacts. As a result, gaps in delineating structures (i.e., edges) give rise to leakage. That is, the segmentation process continues into regions that are not part of the desired object. Global parameter tuning can reduce this sensitivity to local irregularities, but is often too data dependent, time-consuming, and in the end the results are usually still not satisfying. Also, the approaches mentioned in the preceding section for detecting leakages as sudden increase in segmentation volume are only useful with well defined structures in terms of image contrast, modality, resolution, etc.

Relatively simple algorithms such as region growing usually do not have a high-level view of the structure to be segmented, whereas the human user generally does. While being good at detecting and recognizing known objects even in complicated settings, determining the exact contour of structures is often too tedious and error prone for the user. There are many

3.2. INTERACTION

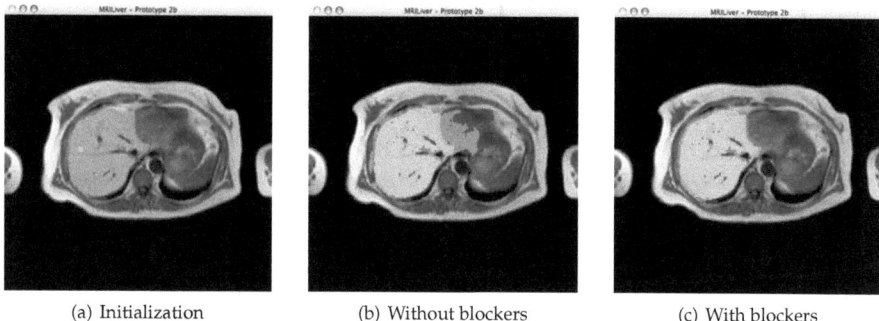

(a) Initialization (b) Without blockers (c) With blockers

Figure 3.20: Interactive region growing of low-resolution abdominal MRI in "LiverGPU". After initialization (a) the segmentation converges with severe leakage (b); blocking pixels are drawn to avoid such errors (c). (Green color depicts rough manual segmentation, red the automatically segmented region, and blue the manually drawn blockers. Iteration is performed in 3D, but for clarity only one slice is shown.)

approaches to combine the two advantages using semi-automatic segmentation tools, e.g., the LiveWire technique introduced by Mortensen et al. [MMBU92] and Udupa et al. [USB92], which is the basis for selection tools in many commercial products. The user draws a contour freely by dragging some pointer roughly along the desired border. The algorithm evaluates the neighborhood of the current position based on a cost function that has been derived from the image before. By choosing the path of minimal costs, the final outline of the object is created. In spite of several improvements of the technique, such as Falcão et al. [FUS+98], or Salah et al. [SOB05], this process can become quite tedious depending on the image's details to be segmented.

Quite recently, Chen et al. [CSS08] have presented a set of tools for interactive volume sculpting and segmentation. While the manipulation of the volume itself is beyond the scope of this chapter, interactively controlling the segmentation process is of high interest. In their work, the concept of splatting (i.e., combining a set of 2D point sprites into a volumetric structure) is implemented using geometry shaders and further advanced GPU techniques. Their segmentation framework allows the parallel execution of seeded region growing, where the seeds are defined by user-drawable primitives. In addition to the standard region growing, the shrinking of the segmented region is supported to provide further interaction. Their system achieves clear real-time performance for the parallel segmentation and visualization of typical volume data sets on commodity graphics hardware.

Blockers For iterative, non edge-based algorithms such as region growing, other methods are needed as the user should not guide the segmentation process completely. Therefore, the concept of *blockers* has been used in the project for interactive liver segmentation. These user-drawable structures define local boundaries or obstacles, which cause the segmentation process to stop at the "blocked" position.[8]

Although segmentation based on region growing cannot be directly compared with such, usually solver-based physical simulations, some of the concepts mentioned above can be adopted. In case of region growing the following computation steps describe the procedure discussed here.

Pseudocode 2 Region growing with local interaction

  preprocess image data, e.g., denoising filters, gradients
  seed definition for region growing by user input
  while (region growing is not converged) **do**
    add/remove blockers by drawing into offscreen image
    pause/re-run iteration
  end while
  postprocessing, e.g., morphological operations, volumetry

Adding or removing the blocking structures can be done on a per-pixel basis, with modifiable size, or predefined shapes, of course. For clarity, we limit the discussion and terms here to the two-dimensional case, where the mapping of the user's interaction is obvious. The extension of the approach to the final three-dimensional segmentation, as well as other features of the developed application, will be discussed in chapter 7.

By drawing such blockers, the growing process can be kept from leaking across weak or incomplete boundaries, as shown in figure 3.20. These small areas can cause the region to degenerate even if – depending on the algorithm's details – there are only few single pixels connected to the outer region[9]. As such critical spots are assumed to occur infrequently and only locally – otherwise the whole image data might not be suited for further segmentation – the workload for the user is rather low. The optimal case, however, would be to block just a single pixel.

Recorded iterations To further reduce the manual interaction needed by the user, the iterative nature of the region growing algorithm can also be exploited. This approach can be extended to other iterative algorithms as well, and is addressed in the discussion below. Reviewing the segmentation process from one time step to the next leads to the following observation. Given is a set R of pixels at time t. During the next iteration $t+1$ another set of pixels P from the region's neighborhood (depending on the algorithm) is determined to belong to the region, and thus should be added. This set then contains the "newest" elements, whereas the elements from set R become "older". This process is repeated until the segmentation converges. The pixels' age is stored as an integer value, so that the final region

---

[8]Note the resemblance to the local, user-definable modifications in the aforementioned fluid systems, where such obstacles influence or even steer the simulation.
[9]This becomes more obvious in the three-dimensional case, where such "bridges" cause the segmented region to expand across neighboring slices and then back to the area not to be segmented.

3.2. INTERACTION

consists of a set of pixels with increasing values towards the seed point/region. This concept is depicted in figure 3.21.

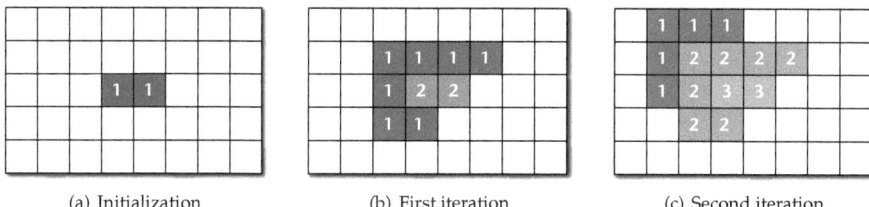

(a) Initialization (b) First iteration (c) Second iteration

Figure 3.21: Principle of recording the region growing process by using integer IDs. Starting from the seed region (a) each iteration increments the ID, thus providing means to separate the region later on (b,c).

In combination with flexible visualization techniques (e.g., via shaders), the approach using dynamic transfer functions mentioned in the beginning of this section can be used to interact with the "recorded" segmentation process. As shown in Erdt et al. [ERS08], the user selects the optimal threshold for the segmentation, and then further processing steps are performed. In contrast, the selection here is to determine the time in the segmentation where errors (i.e., leakage) occur. The user would then block the spots causing the leakage in the image data and restart the segmentation process, with the current segmentation as seed region to avoid redundant computations. As outlined before, the contribution by Chen et al. [CSS08] takes this concepts even further to realize a completely interactive segmentation based on seeded region growing.

Implementation issues

Until recently, graphics hardware has been limited to floating point data only. Although shading languages have provided integer formats, floats have been used internally and thus caused rounding errors in addition to extra computations for scaling/biasing; see also chapter 1. Due to the recently introduced integer formats, the aforementioned algorithm can be implemented without numerical issues, however.

Regardless of the data format, the upper limit of the ID values can be determined from the image data itself: in the limit case, the seed is placed at the very end of the image while the region expands to the other end. Thus, there are values in the range of $[1, ..., \lceil \sqrt{w^2 + h^2} \rceil]$, where w and h denote the image's width and height, respectively. For example, the values for recorded region growing of a 512×512 image would range at most from 1 to $\lceil (\sqrt{2} \cdot 512) \rceil = 725$. As a result, 16-bit unsigned integer values would support square images of more than 46k pixels per side, which seems to be sufficient for a wide range of data.

Extensions

The concept of controlling iterative algorithms is not limited to segmentation algorithms in general, or region growing methods in particular. Morphological operations such as dilation, erosion, or combinations thereof (i.e., closing and opening) can also be controlled by the technique described above. In spite of the fact that these operations resemble processing filters – in contrast to segmentation methods such as region growing – the concept of local "time-stamps" can be applied as well. The only difference to the recorded iterations as depicted in figure 3.21 is that the set of pixels does not represent regions; hence, the data elements can be processed independently.

Another category of algorithms are diffusion filters. These methods transfer the theory of diffusion processes to image data in order to reduce noise by equalizing "concentration" differences. Several types of diffusion algorithms exist and differ in the handling of edges, dimension, etc. In the following, anisotropic diffusion ([PM90, Jäh97]) as a commonly used diffusion filter should be discussed.[10] This anisotropic variant is an iterative edge-preserving smoothing process and has been widely adopted in image (pre-)processing. The basic idea is to use partial differential equations to describe the diffusion process over time, with intraregional smoothing being preferred over interregional diffusion. While the diffusion coefficient for inhomogeneous diffusion is directly dependent on the gradient strength, for anisotropic diffusion this process also varies in different directions. In discrete representations, this process is computed iteratively until convergence, while gradient information is usually approximated by differencing schemes (e.g., central differences).

Pseudocode 3 Recorded filtering (here: diffusion) with local interaction

Input image I_0
for ($i = 1$ to N) **do**
   if (Interaction performed) **then**
      Create interaction image I_i
      Store local change information in I_i
      Perform diffusion computation evaluating I_i
   else
      Perform diffusion computation
   end if
end for

In order to interact with the iterative process locally, an appropriate representation of every time-step has to be stored per data element. Whereas an integer counter has been sufficient for the aforementioned algorithms, diffusion processes require additional information: the change in image intensity from each iteration has to be recorded. There are different optimizations imaginable (e.g., only altered pixels are tracked, compression scheme to store differences only), but basically a sequence of (difference) images has to be kept for the whole procedure. This would be reasonable only for a moderate number of iterations, due to the additional dimension introduced by the difference images. As such, this strategy is somewhat related to the work presented in section 3.1.1 where sequential video frames

---

[10] Barash [Bar00] establishes a link between this iterative, computationally expensive diffusion process and bilateral filtering as non-iterative algorithm with similar results. However, here the focus will be explicitly on the iterative nature of the diffusion algorithm.

have been filtered volumetrically. As shown there, the computational complexity is feasible, especially when additional means such as compression would be used. In the preceding pseudo-code an approach for a diffusion filter with N iterations is summarized that does not store the change information of the filtering itself. Moreover, the local interaction is stored as image and is used to change the filter's parameter settings at the according iteration step.

This enables the compact representation of the user's input without the need to store any difference information of the iterative computations directly. While the roll-back of the filtering (e.g., to adjust some parameters locally for improved results) would still be possible by restarting the iteration from the very beginning, an intermediate "key frame" every k-th iteration would be a good trade-off between good performance and reasonable memory footprint.[11] As should become clear from this example, the concept of recorded local interaction can be extended to different kinds of operations that are of iterative nature and process image data locally.

3.3 Conclusion

Several approaches in the context of visual computing were presented and discussed in this chapter. In accordance with current developments of scientific computation and visualization, using the GPU was shown to be highly advantageous for computationally intensive tasks. Although individual processing steps can often be accelerated by hardware implementations, most applications benefit even more due to two aspects. Firstly, the utilization of the graphics hardware allows the direct visualization of (intermediate) results. If combined with advanced volume rendering techniques (see section 1.3) or concepts for directly interacting with the computations (as shown in the preceding section), there are even more possibilities. The second aspect is to execute as many sequential processing steps as possible on the graphics hardware, in order to minimize the bandwidth gap for data transfer. As will be discussed in detail in chapter 5, there are only few and very limited approaches available to date for implementing whole workflows on programmable graphics hardware. The framework CASCADA is an attempt to provide such functionality.

A final example for a well-suited integration of different disciplines in the medical context is the application presented by Dietz [Die05]. In this work, deformable registration methods are combined with direct visualization, while the acquisition of data points is updated interactively at the same time, based upon the visual feedback. The medical application is the registration of a generic bone model (here: femoral head) during navigated surgery for hip joint endoprosthesis preparation and placement. Therefore, the clinician uses a tracked

---

[11]Note that this bears resemblance to the concept of video compression, where intermediate frames are stored in total, and adjacent frames only as (encoded) difference information.

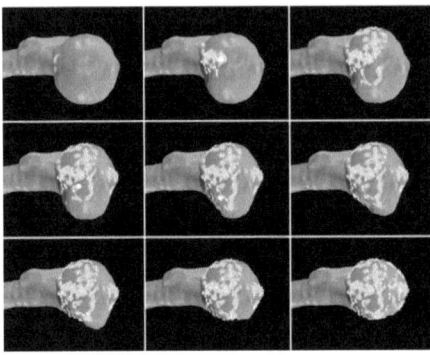 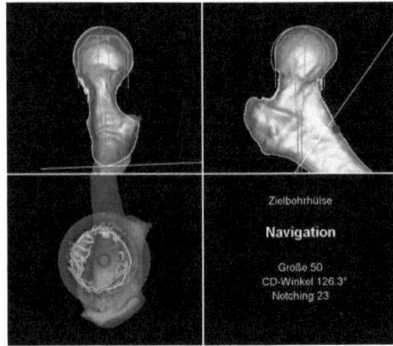

(a) Iterations of deformable registration (b) Final screen

Figure 3.22: Visualization of interactively acquired samples for deformable registration (a) of generic bone model to patient-specific anatomy in hip joint endoprosthesis surgery (b). (Image courtesy of [Die05])

input device to manually sample the bone's surface. In order to optimize the registration process, this procedure requires an equal distribution of the samples. As the positions already collected are not visible in reality, this information is only available through visual feedback (figure 3.22). Due to the fact that graphics hardware had not been widely available and flexible back then, all of the computation steps were implemented in software. The rendering was performed by the fixed-function graphics pipeline. In order to ensure an acceptable response time, the system is hence limited to a moderate number of samples, relatively coarse geometry representation and registration parameters, etc.

With respect to the methods introduced in this chapter, this scenario integrates many of these aspects and lends itself to be implemented completely in hardware. Firstly, the rendering of the bone geometry or sample points is obviously suited for graphics processors, with current generations being virtually unlimited in scene complexity and dynamic update/creation of geometry. Secondly, the transfer of tracking information from the navigation device also does not impose any restriction, as the bandwidth needed is clearly not performance critical. Finally, the deformable registration implementation based on radial basis functions (see Dietz [Die05] for details and discussion) is also well-suited for GPU implementation, as recent contributions in this field, such as Samant et al. [SXMOO08] account for.

CHAPTER 4

COMPRESSION COMPUTING

In the preceding chapter different approaches and concepts towards an integration of computation and visualization were presented and discussed. Following the term "visual computing" for such an integration, this chapter proposes the direct visualization and processing of *compressed* data. While the former has been subject of intensive research – especially in the context of GPU-based rendering – the direct processing has not been studied amply yet. The benefits for such algorithms, however, are obvious:

- the amount of data to be transferred is reduced due to the more compact representation, which enables
    - the processing and visualization of larger data sets (without additional techniques such as bricking etc.)
    - faster algorithms, if data transfers are required frequently
- processing operations can potentially be implemented more efficiently in a compressed representation
- depending on the compression method other techniques (e.g., multi-resolution approaches) are available

As mentioned in the introduction of this thesis, the increasing computational graphics performance provides means for more complex and interactive visualizations. On the other hand, the amount of image data acquired and generated today demands efficient solutions. Especially medical imaging technology has evolved rapidly and high-resolution three- and four-dimensional data sets are acquired on a regular basis today. With the latest dual-source CT scanners, for example, two data sets are created at the same time, each with different imaging properties. And as for the multi-slice scanning technology, the trend to even more sources is just a matter of time and market development. Although graphics hardware strives to keep up with such developments in terms of on-board video memory, the maximum size is limited by both technology and price. Advanced workstation graphics systems currently provide up to 1.5 GB of available memory per graphics board, where multi-GPU configurations usually share the memory and are thus limited to the amount of a single board.

In contrast, time-resolved tomographic scans of the beating heart easily exceed this limit, even at moderate resolutions.

Yet another example is virtual autopsy, where the amount of images is even higher due to the less relevant radiation exposure (see figure 4.1). However, the data set has to be analyzed as a whole for sophisticated diagnosis and visualization purposes, where bricking or other subdivision strategies are out of question, especially for time-resolved data. Therefore, there will always be a demand for handling data too large for the available (video) memory.

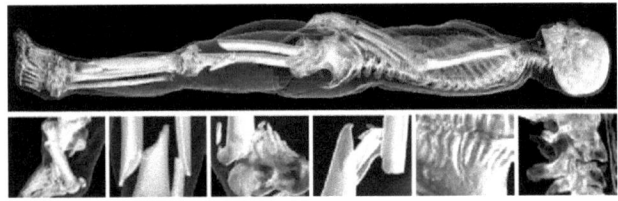
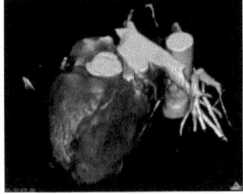

(a) CT scan used for virtual autopsy   (b) 4D cardiac CT scan

Figure 4.1: Full body CT scan from virtual autopsy (a) with approx. 3800 slices at 512×512 axial resolution. (Image courtesy Patric Ljung et al. [LWP+06]); 4D CT scan of beating heart (b) with approx. $400 \times 400 \times 300$ at 25 time steps. (Image courtesy OsiriX [Osi])

From a theoretical point of view, the basic idea is inspired by the relation between convolution in the spatial domain, and multiplication as its analogon in the frequency domain (see Jähne [Jäh97] for details). Whereas the Fourier transform does not provide any compression by itself, different compressed representations useful for image data will be discussed below. If it was possible to map different types of basic operations from the uncompressed, i.e., spatial domain into the "compression domain", image processing would be considerably faster in the ideal case. For reasons to be shown in the following sections, not all compression schemes are suited for such an approach, nor are all operations compatible with a compressed representation.

This chapter is structured as follows: In the first section, the notion of the compression domain and the resulting requirements are discussed, followed by a summary of mathematical and theoretical foundations of main compression methods. The different compression schemes are then compared and reviewed from a technical point of view. The second part of this chapter introduces the concepts for directly processing and visualizing the compressed data. Therefore, common operations are discussed in order to establish a mapping from an uncompressed representation into the compression domain. As some categories of algorithms are more compatible with the compressed representation than others, a classification leads to an evaluation and the proposal of alternative solutions where needed. While the implementation in general will be described in the third section, programming details in the context of CASCADA will be given in part three of the thesis. Sections two and three describe approaches for the direct rendering of compressed (volume) data, including a short review of relevant work in this field. The chapter finally concludes with an evaluation of the achieved results, as well as prospects for further research. Considerable work in this chapter has been contributed by Thomas Höllt during his diploma thesis [Höl08] and subsequent research.

4.1 Compression domain

The term "compression domain" has been first introduced by Westermann in 1995 [Wes95]. In this early work he proposed a multi-level approach to analyze and render time-resolved volumetric data. As this analysis requires the inspection of the whole data set, processing the uncompressed data is not feasible. Among several authors who have developed efficient techniques especially for rendering directly from compressed data, the contribution by Schneider and Westermann [SW03] makes explicit use of programmable graphics hardware. More recently, Fout and Ma [FM07] reconsider the transformation pipeline of data compression in favour of modern GPUs. They were able to improve the rendering performance considerably by reducing the decompression workload during the rendering process.

However, working in the compression domain has been limited to rendering directly from the compressed data as well as to GPU-based encoding (e.g., Wong et al. [WLHW07]), with few related applications so far. In the course of this chapter the concept of working directly in the compression domain is extended to reasonable (image) processing operations.

Compression generally yields a more compact representation of the same data by means of other bases, algorithms or storage methods. As an exhaustive discussion of this topic would be beyond the scope of this thesis, only compression methods and approaches related to graphics hardware will be reviewed. This is, however, not limited to rendering from compressed formats, which Fout et al. [FAM+05, FM07] and Kniss et al. [KLF05] provide thorough and up-to-date discussions for. Especially in Fout's second contribution [FM07], the *symmetry* of a coding scheme helps to assess the performance for rendering directly from compressed data sets. While the pipeline of compression and decompression is usually divided symmetrically between preprocessing and rendering (i.e., decompression together with visualization on the GPU), they propose a shift of computation steps towards the preprocess. While their improvement with respect to the rendering performance is only moderate, their approach achieves better compression rates and less intricate GPU programming for decompression and visualization.

Basically, there are two general classes of compression procedures: lossless and lossy algorithms. The former allows the reconstruction of the input signal without any change or error, while the latter introduces quantization. Lossy algorithms are (by their nature) able to achieve a higher compression rate on non-synthetic image data, depending on the specific algorithm and error tolerance. Such compression formats are typically used for audio, image and video material that should be consumed by humans and often exploit certain properties of the human visual/audio system to further improve the results.

In this section general information on lossless and lossy compression methods will be provided, with attention to medical image data. The theoretical and mathematical basics of selected methods, as well as details on relevant compression techniques will be given further in this chapter. A broader overview on data compression can be found in [Ble01], for example.

Lossless compression As the name implies, lossless compression allows the exact reconstruction of the original data from the compressed representation. While this is appealing for practically all applications, its use is limited due to the relatively low compression rate: only synthetic (image) data can be reduced reasonably, due to noise in all other images. There exists a wealth of such encoders which are usually categorized into dictionary-based and entropy methods.

In the context of medical volume compression, Komma et al. [KFDB07] provide a broad discussion of different techniques. As the different lossless methods only play a minor role in the remainder of this thesis, these methods will not be discussed in detail here; see the references in Komma's work. Quite interestingly, the authors also compare the results with the lossless variants of JPEG and Wavelet-based algorithms, which do not always provide the best compression rates. Komma et al. conclude that especially for sparse data sets with lower bit depth (in their case 8 bit) the lossless BZIP2 algorithm provides optimal performance, both in terms of encoding time and compression rate. Although the results are quite promising, the authors do not provide information about the details of the wavelet transform (esp. if multiple levels have been used).

Lossy compression Lossy algorithms are typically distinguished further into transform codecs[1] and predictive schemes. The former use another basis for representing (parts of) the signal, whereas the latter exploit coherence information to define errors and process these. Although transform codecs are more suited to the aforementioned mapping, and are in addition not restricted to sequential information (i.e., video or audio frames), practically all schemes include quantization steps where the transformed information is reduced. Consecutive entropy encoding reduces the resulting information further by applying lossless algorithms. These algorithms play an important role in the remainder of this chapter.

4.1.1 Requirements

As discussed in the preceding section, compression methods can be divided into lossless and lossy procedures. Whereas the former would be preferable – especially for medical data – they have two clear disadvantages. Firstly, lossy algorithms are much more suited to measured natural image data as they are not dependent on numerical sequences (e.g., for run-length encoding) or do not necessarily construct dictionaries that would become too complex for such image data. Secondly, the algorithms used for entropy coding, for example, provide no starting point for a mapping of common operations: a convolution filter has obviously no meaning on run-length or Huffman encoded data.

---

[1] Artificial term built from "*com*pression" and "*de*compression", describing both directions

4.1. COMPRESSION DOMAIN

Lossy procedures on the other hand provide more flexibility in terms of compression rate, underlying transform, and compatibility with further processes (e.g., direct rendering). Also, the internal representations, such as vector quantization or wavelet transform provide the possibility of mapping processing operations at all.

In order to establish the proposed mapping into the compression domain, the following requirements provide criteria for a discussion of the different compression methods:

1. All operations should be available in the compression domain, with an adequate fallback solution for operations that cannot be mapped.

2. The performance of operations in the compression domain should be superior, or at least equal to the standard approach.

3. The compression rate (alternatively, the signal-noise-ratio) should be controllable and reasonably high, including the possibility of no or lossless compression.

4. The additional memory consumption for compression and processing should be minimal.

5. The compressed representation should be compatible with direct visualization methods.

The first requirement is obviously the basic motivation for this chapter. Whenever the direct processing of compressed data is impossible and a fallback is needed (e.g., a block-wise decompression to apply standard operations), the computational overhead for (de-)compression is taken into account. In contrast, the second requirement does not include the (re-)compression of the whole data set, as the benefit of the operations themselves are of interest. Especially for medical image data, the third property is an important requirement as the error introduced by compression has to be known. The additional memory needed for the compression infrastructure should be kept as low as possible to maintain the overall memory requirements and exploit the savings from compressing the data. Finally, the key idea is not only to process the data efficiently, but to continue the approaches with the visual computing procedures that were discussed in the preceding chapter. Therefore, established volume rendering methods such as ray casting should not impose prohibitive computational overhead compared to displaying uncompressed data.

4.1.2 Methods

Based on the aforementioned requirements, several compression methods have been selected as potential candidates. As a basic understanding of their theoretical foundations is vital for the subsequent discussions, the mathematical basics will be presented in the following paragraphs. In addition, references to related work will be given where appropriate. As mentioned before, there is practically no way to realize computations directly on lossless (entropy) encoded data, so that these compression methods are not considered further here.

Wavelet Image Compression

Wavelet compression is a transform coding technique, which is used for example in the JPEG 2000 standard [JPGb] and consists of two passes: the first pass is the actual wavelet transform, and the second pass is the quantization or compression step. After the transform, the wavelet representation of the image consists of as many coefficients as there are pixels in the image. This first step is used because quantization in the original image domain (i.e., spatial domain and values) often results in poor quality. Applying the same quantization technique to a properly transformed image can yield remarkable results by exploiting certain features of the transformation domain. The following paragraphs only summarize the mathematical basics; for an in-depth discussion see Mallat's book [Mal99].

The basis functions for the wavelet transform are translations and dilations (scaling). These function are based on the function ψ, referred to as the mother wavelet. The one dimensional discrete wavelet transform of a function $f(x)$, with the discrete scale and translation step size a and b, and the discrete scale and translation variable m and n is defined by

$$W_\psi^{m,n}(f) = |a_0|^{-\frac{m}{2}} \int f(x)\psi(a_0^{-m}x - nb_0)dx. \tag{4.1.1}$$

Typical examples for mother wavelets are the basic Haar wavelet $\psi(x)$ with its scaling function $\phi(x)$:

$$\psi(x) = \begin{cases} 1 & \text{for } 0 \leq x < \frac{1}{2} \\ -1 & \text{for } \frac{1}{2} \leq x < 1 \\ 0 & \text{otherwise} \end{cases} \qquad \phi(x) = \begin{cases} 1 & \text{for } 0 \leq x < 1 \\ 0 & \text{otherwise} \end{cases} \tag{4.1.2}$$

or the Daubechies wavelet with the corresponding scaling function, respectively,

$$\psi(x) = \sum_{k=0}^{N-1} a_k \phi(2x - k), \qquad \phi(x) = \sum_{k=0}^{M-1} b_k \phi(2x - k) \tag{4.1.3}$$

where $(a_0, \ldots, a_{N-1})$ and $(b_0, \ldots, b_{M-1})$ are appropriate finite sequences of real numbers. Both mother wavelets are depicted in the plots in figure 4.2.

The wavelet transform can be regarded as a combination of low- and high-pass transformations. As such, the resulting coefficients can be represented as a low- and a high-band. The low-band coefficients usually consist of high energy and have no advantage over non-transformed values regarding compression. Thus in most cases the transform is applied recursively on the low-band. The number of recursions is called the level of transformation. For two-dimensional images the 1D wavelet transform is applied line-wise, followed by the same transformation applied row-wise to the intermediate result. This procedure yields four subbands at each level: one being low-pass filtered twice and three being high pass filtered at least once. The representations for one level are depicted in figure 4.3(a), and for three levels in figure 4.3(b), respectively. The low-band is on the top left, the high bands on the right and/or bottom, corresponding to the direction the high-pass filter has been applied. The two-dimensional transform can be applied in two ways, called the standard

4.1. COMPRESSION DOMAIN

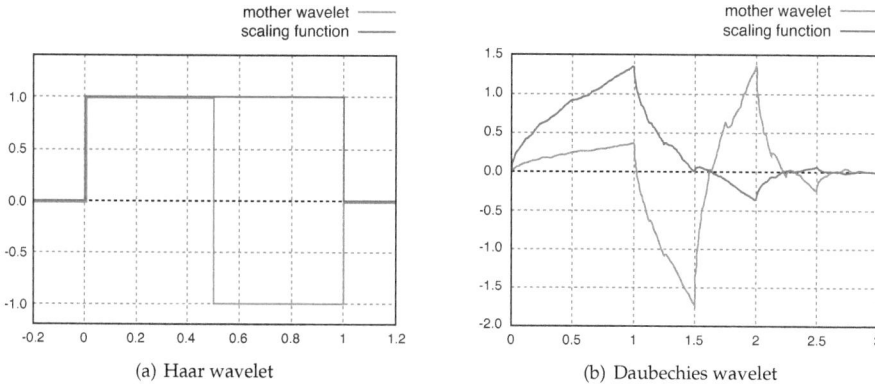

Figure 4.2: The Haar mother wavelet and the corresponding scaling function (a) and the Daubechies D4 mother wavelet with its scaling function (b)

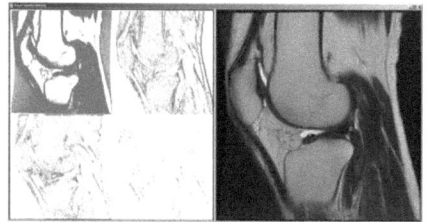 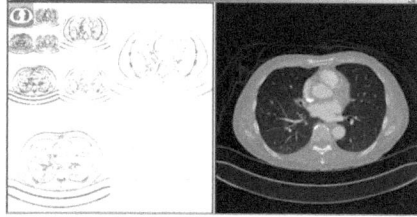

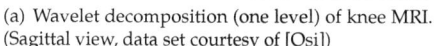

(a) Wavelet decomposition (one level) of knee MRI. (Sagittal view, data set courtesy of [Osi])   (b) Wavelet decomposition (three levels) of thoracic CT. (Axial view, data set courtesy of [Osi])

Figure 4.3: Slices from MRI- (a) and CT scan (b), respectively, each with Haar wavelet decompositions. For clarity, the coefficients are weighted and color-coded (red/blue depicts positive/negative values).

and non-standard transform. In the standard transform, the rows are transformed first until the desired level is reached, then the multi-level 1D transform is applied to the columns. In the non-standard transform the 1D transforms are applied alternatingly at each level. This representation is often advantageous with respect to the original image representation. Neighbouring pixels tend to have very similar or even the same values in natural images, meaning that the high-pass filtered coefficients are often (close to) zero. These characteristics of the coefficients can be used in the second pass to compress the image. Compression can then be done using different methods. Usually only the high-pass coefficients are compressed, while the low-pass values remain unchanged. Thus, in the following only the high-pass filter coefficients are considered.

The basic method is quantization, that is using fewer bits to store the coefficients than for the original image. As the coefficients are usually very small one can delimit the range to a smaller area around zero and use a smaller data type to represent the coefficients. As a naïve approach, cutting off the bits of higher values might be a reasonable solution as there are very few coefficients in the upper section of the interval. However, as these coefficients contain essential detail information, a more sophisticated approach is needed. Another possibility would be to divide the coefficients by a given value and store only the integer value of the results. In either case, quantization usually results in a loss of visual quality.

A second approach, the Wavelet Zerotree Encoding by Rogers and Cosman [RC98] is also a lossy compression scheme. The individual recursion steps in the wavelet transform can be interpreted as levels in a tree where the low-band coefficients after the last recursion step resemble the root node, and the coefficients after the first recursion step are the leafs.

Yet another approach stores only the non-zero entries. However, information of the position in the image is indirectly stored by the array position and would be lost if the zero-elements are discarded. Storing the array position with the value, however, is only reasonable if there are many zero-coefficients, because every coefficient that needs to be stored (i.e., all non-zero coefficients) needs additional memory to store the position.[2] A modification of this approach uses a binary importance map that has the same size as the original image. This technique will be discussed in more detail in section 4.3.

The last two methods are lossless by default, whereas the compression rate can be increased for all methods by specifying a certain threshold. All coefficients that are within this interval around zero are dropped as well. This is a lossy process, of course, and as such it affects the signal. On the other hand, lots of the coefficients are very close to zero anyway, so this often increases the compression rates considerably without introducing visible artefacts.

Decompression of wavelet transformed data is straightforward and only depends on the options discussed before. First, the coefficients belonging to the current section are indexed. Depending on the dimension of the data, such sections are often referred to as tiles (2D) or blocks (3D). The reconstruction can then be done according to the chosen mother wavelet. For higher levels these steps have to be done iteratively from the last to the first level.

Fractal Compression

Fractal image compression has been introduced by Barnsley and Hurd [BH93] as a vector based technique. It is a lossy compression that represents an image by using a set of transformations. Ideally an image can be stored as only one such transformation function. A unique fixpoint of this function has to be (a close approximation of) the image itself. In order to store such a function, only a fraction of the storage amount for representing the original image is needed. Decompression is then done by iteratively applying this function on an arbitrary starting image until the original image is reached. This concept can be illustrated with a simple fractal, the Sierpinski triangle (figure 4.4). The Sierpinski triangle is self-similar, i.e., one can copy scaled versions of the triangle into its corners, yielding the same image. In other words, if ω_1 is the transformation that maps the triangle in its upper corner, and ω_2 and ω_3

---

[2]This can take up considerable memory, as for example $2 \cdot 16$ bit for an image larger than 256×256 pixels are already needed.

4.1. COMPRESSION DOMAIN

map the triangle to the lower corners, respectively, the Sierpinski triangle can be described by the fixed point of the transformation

$$\omega = \omega_1 \cup \omega_2 \cup \omega_3 \quad (4.1.4)$$

as the transformation applied to the triangle leaves it unchanged.

The transformation ω is contractive, meaning the distance between two points p and q

$$d(p,q) = (p_x - q_x)^2 + (p_y - q_y)^2 \quad (4.1.5)$$

after a transformation is never larger than before, because all of the transformations ω_i are contractive. With the Sierpinski triangle as the fixpoint to the transformation ω, and as ω is contractive according to the "Banach Contractive Fixed-Point Theorem" (see [Val05] for details), the Sierpinski triangle is a limit of the sequence

$$X, \omega X, \omega^2 X, \ldots \quad (4.1.6)$$

with X representing an image and ω^i the composition of ω with itself i-times. That is, by iteratively applying ω on an arbitrary image the Sierpinski triangle with an arbitrary accuracy can be computed (see figure 4.4). In other words, the transformation ω alone can be used as a representation for the image of the Sierpinski triangle; a concept also known as Iterated Function System (IFS). Such a compact form as in equation 4.1.4, however, can only be found

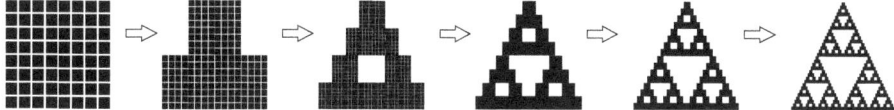

Figure 4.4: Multiple iterations from a random image to the Sierpinski Triangle

for fractals such as the Sierpinski triangle. On the other hand, also many natural images have areas of self-similarity. Therefore, so-called Partitioned Iterated Function System (PIFS) can be applied to real world images. The image is therefore partitioned into a grid commonly known as range blocks. These range blocks are all of the same size and non-overlapping. For each of these blocks a region in the image has to be found which can be transformed with a set of contractive functions to match the original range block as close as possible. In a typical application the range blocks are matched to a fixed set of domain blocks in the image. These blocks are usually twice the size of range blocks, and are not arranged in a fixed grid, i.e., they can overlap. The transformations applied to the domain blocks consist of scaling, translation, rotation and reflection, as well as adjustments in brightness and contrast. As only the transformations are stored and not the domain blocks, this codebook is called virtual.

In order to decompress the image, a new image with the size of the original image is created. The functions of the PIFS are then applied iteratively to the starting image until the changes in the image between two iterations are smaller than a defined threshold. Due to the nature of fixed points the starting image can be random. However, the time to compose the final image or the number of iterations may vary depending on the starting image, yet the image quality will be the same.

Discrete Cosine Transform

Just as the wavelet transform, the discrete cosine transform (DCT) is a transform coding technique, which is used for image compression. In fact, the DCT is a widely used image coding technique due to its use in the well-known JPEG compression [JPGa], which is the de-facto standard for compression of photographic images today.

A detailed description of the DCT used in the JPEG compression standard can be found in Wallace [Wal91], which will be only summarized here. The DCT-based encoder works in three steps. A forward discrete cosine transform (FDCT) is applied to the image first. Then the resulting cosine coefficients are quantized, and finally run through an entropy encoder. This process is not done on the complete image, but on 8×8 blocks. For color images, each channel is transformed separately. The image is usually transformed into the YCrCb (luminance-chrominance) color format in advance.

The decompression is simply the inverse of the aforementioned transform, that is, the inverse versions of all steps in reverse order. The compressed image data is entropy-decoded first, then dequantized, and finally the inverse discrete cosine transform (IDCT) is applied.

After the FDCT the quantization step is performed, where the resulting 8×8 coefficient matrix is divided component-wise using a quantization table. This table depends on the specified compression rate and takes the fact into account that the human eye is more sensitive to lower frequencies. Subsequently, the normalized quantized coefficients contain many zeroes which are usually separated from the non-zero coefficients by a diagonal line. This is used for the so called *zig-zagging*. Instead of coding the block line- or rowwise the coefficients are rearranged in a zig-zag line from the upper left to the lower right. The better coherence resulting from this pattern can then be exploited by a final entropy encoding step.

Vector Quantization

Just as fractal image compression, vector quantization described in Gersho and Gray [GG92] is a vector based image compression technique. By nature, vector quantization is a lossy compression scheme as its main concept is to approximate a range of values by a single value. A simple example for a one-dimensional vector quantization is rounding to the nearest integer: all values in the range $]x - 0.5 \ldots x + 0.5]$ are mapped to the single value x.

In image compression vector quantization is used in the following way. The input image is partitioned into a regular grid of non-overlapping blocks, just as for fractal compression, where these blocks build the set of input vectors. Then, the input vectors are matched with the codebook, which can be a set of vectors from the input image, similar to the virtual codebook in fractal compression, or a global set of vectors defined independently from the input image. Contrary to fractal compression, input vectors and codevectors need to be equally sized. When the closest match is found, a pointer to the vector in the codebook is stored (figure 4.5).

Also in contrast to fractal compression, the codebook needs to be stored to lookup the blocks in the decompression step in addition to a lookup map, which is the vector quantization equivalent to the PIFS. Thus, the compression rate mostly depends on the size of the

4.1. COMPRESSION DOMAIN

codebook[3]. The essential (and computationally expensive) part in this procedure is to find a codebook which is small enough to yield the desired compression ratio, yet large enough to map all input vectors with minimal error.

The decompression is a simple inversion of this process. For all entries in the lookup table the corresponding codebook vectors are fetched and placed in the appropriate position in the target image that is defined by the position of the pointer in the lookup table. Figure 4.5

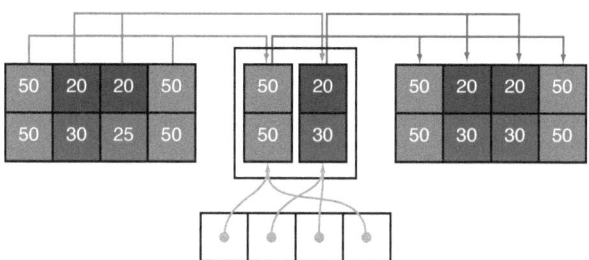

Figure 4.5: Vector quantization example

shows an example of a vector quantization. The input image on the left is partitioned in 1×2 blocks which are the input vectors. These are matched (red arrows) against the codebook (center) and instead of the input vectors the address in the codebook (green arrows) is stored in the lookup table (bottom), which has the extents of the input image scaled by the vector size. For decompression (blue arrows) codevectors are placed in the target image at the appropriate positions given by the lookup table.

Vector quantization can thus be regarded as an asymmetrical scheme, i.e., compression is computationally much more expensive than decompression. Therefore, this compression method is often used for applications that focus on direct rendering from compressed data.

4.1.3 Discussion

Based on the preceding introduction of common compression procedures, as well as the discussion of relevant criteria, the methods will be reviewed from a technical point of view. As not all of them can be implemented and evaluated in detail within the scope of this thesis, the following paragraphs discuss the methods to select the one most suited for further implementation of direct processing and visualization.

Fractal compression

With the utilization of graphics hardware for fractal compression algorithms, this time-consuming procedure can be accelerated several orders of magnitude, as shown by Erra [Err05]. This makes the extension to three-dimensional data feasible and is thus an adequate option for the target applications of this thesis. While the compression process is computationally

---

[3]The size of the lookup map is defined by the size of the input image, the size of the input partitioning and the size of the pointers to the codebook entries.

demanding because all possible transforms have to be determined, the decompression (e.g., for visualization) is markedly simple: the transformations only have to be applied to the seeds. In addition, fractal compression provides high compression rates, given optimal parameter settings.

On the other hand, however, there is no way to keep all information of the original image, as fractal compression does not provide a reasonable lossless representation. Depending on the implementation, notable artefacts can occur if some block-based processing is used. The most severe disadvantage of this method for direct processing is that there is no codebook or other intermediate representation to work with (see the preceding section for details). Therefore, it is practically impossible to apply any processing in the compression domain. In addition, if some block-wise standard processing was expedient, re-compression would require the whole original image as input – and thus would not be competitive anymore.

Wavelets

Compression methods based on wavelets have been thoroughly investigated for more than a decade. Aside from being the basis of the JPEG2000 image format, representative work has been done on volume data by Muraki [Mur93], multi-resolution volume rendering by Westermann [Wes94] and Guthe et al. [GWGS02], and general computer graphics applications in Schröder [Sch96]. Also, the utilization of graphics hardware for wavelet compression and direct volume rendering has been investigated by Hopf and Ertl [HE99], or more recently, by Kniss et al. [KLF05] and Fout et al. [FAM+05]. Wavelet compression offers relatively good control of the compression rate by means of different levels, with the multi-resolution property as an additional benefit for various applications. It should be noted that the wavelet transform itself does not introduce any loss of information and is thus also suited for applications requiring the exact reconstruction of the original data. However, the additional memory needed for the infrastructure might reverse the effect of data compression when storing/processing the data uncompressed.

The wavelet representation is also suited for direct image processing as shown by numerous contributions. Early work in this field has focused on image denoising due to the relatively simple relation between noise and image details in the coefficients.[4] Dorrell and Lowe [DL95] have proposed more general processing procedures on wavelet data. Although only basic operations such as scalar multiplication or image addition have been realized, several other operations can be built upon their concepts. Also, edge detection as fundamental procedure in image processing is inherently supported by the wavelet, because the detail coefficients resemble high frequency information (i.e., edges). For other types of processing methods, the usual wavelet compression cannot be used directly (or only with considerable overhead), as will be explicated later in section 4.2.3. Due to the compact block size, however,

---

[4]Noise appears in the wavelet representation as non-zero coefficients with small absolute values. Therefore, noise can be removed by thresholding approaches without sacrificing quality because important image details are usually represented by larger coefficients.

4.1. COMPRESSION DOMAIN

the fallback plan (i.e., to decompress locally and process the data using conventional methods) is still competitive.

DCT

Although the discrete cosine and Fourier transform are very closely related from a theoretical point of view, only the DCT is of practical use for data compression. As for the Fourier transform, there exist fast implementations based on the divide-and-conquer principle. In addition, the algorithmic complexity for three-dimensional data sets is usually reduced by applying a one-dimensional transform sequentially (see section 4.1.2 for background information). While the DCT-based approaches offer high, controllable compression rates, they suffer in some situations from the underlying block-size of 8×8 for two-dimensional (or $8 \times 8 \times 8$ for three-dimensional) data, respectively. First, the block artefacts can become visible with higher compression rates as the processing results per tile/block diverge too much. Also, the direct visualization of the compressed data is more expensive than for smaller block sizes, such as 2×2 for wavelet or vector quantization compression. This problem is even intensified by the additional dimension for volume data. Although there are some approaches based on the Fourier slice theorem for an efficient rendering of the volumetric data, these are by nature limited to simple projective visualizations.

In spite of these critical issues, several work has been done on the direct processing of DCT-compressed data, with fundamental contributions from Smith and Rowe [SR93, SR96] and Shen and Sethi [SS96] for algorithms such as edge detection based on convolution. While practically all types of operations are covered, the entropy coding step of the JPEG pipeline[5] requires the partial inversion of the process (i.e., decompression) to access the raw DCT data. Another disadvantage is the computational overhead of up to multiple orders of magnitude with their tensor-based representation. Furthermore, the aforementioned larger block size is a disadvantage for fallback solutions.

VQ

There has been a lot of research in vector quantization for data compression, going back to the fundamental work by Gray [Gra84] and, for volume rendering, by Ning and Hesselink [NH92]. The method has many applications and is usually implemented by determining vectors that approximate the input signal as close as possible, and store the set of vectors in a codebook. Therefore, the compression rate as well as the memory overhead depends on the size of the codebook. While the compression is computationally very expensive due to the exhaustive search for optimal codewords, decompression reduces to a simple lookup. This fact makes the method well suited for hardware implementations, and several direct rendering techniques have been proposed, e.g., by Schneider and Westermann [SW03].

The direct processing of vector quantization compression data has also been the focus of early research. In Cosman et al. [CORG93] different image processing methods are presented.

---

[5]This also extends to three-dimensional and time-varying data as well, but most work is based on the commonly used JPEG process for image data.

Simple point based filters can be realized by directly operating on the codebook. In order to maintain optimal compression, however, the codebook needs to be rebuilt afterwards. On the other hand, more complex operations involving a local neighborhood require additional information in the codebook, thus resulting in a significant increase in size and lower compression rates. Although the authors suggest another representation especially for edge detection, the results are not competitive with standard high pass filters, as illustrated in figure 4.6.

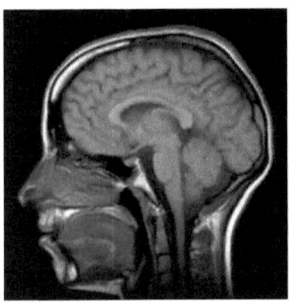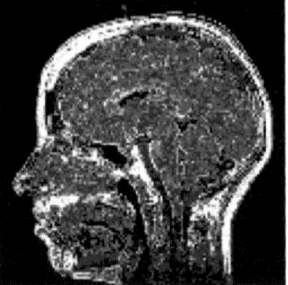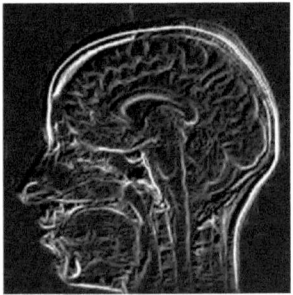

Figure 4.6: Edge detection using variable rate vector quantization (VRVQ) as proposed by Cosman et al. [CORG93], applied to an MRI scan (left). Their results (center) are hardly of use for further processing when compared to standard edge filters, such as Sobel filter (right).

Conclusion

After reviewing contemplable compression methods focusing on both the direct processing and visualization of the compressed data, one of the procedures has to be selected. At the beginning of this section, several criteria have been identified that are important for working in the compression domain. Also, the different techniques have been discussed against the background of these requirements. The following table and the subsequent facts summarize the properties of each method and lead to the final decision.

	Equal or better performance	Mapping/ fallback possible	Lossless mode available	Low memory overhead	Compatible with DVR techniques
FC	n.a.	no	no	yes	yes
DCT	no	yes	yes	no	no
VQ	partly	yes	yes	partly	yes
WVL	yes	yes	yes	partly	yes

Table 4.1: Table summarizing the criteria for comparing compression methods eligible for realizing the direct processing in the compression domain.

In spite of its hardware-friendly compression and rendering features, fractal compression is the least appropriate method due to the fact that the direct processing is virtually impossible. Also, a fallback implementation for operations not realizable would be far from competitive.

Finally, the application to medical images is problematic as there is no chance in maintaining the original data.

Although widely used in image compression, DCT-based approaches are not applicable because of mainly two facts. Firstly, the relatively large block size imposes a considerable performance penalty for operations requiring a block-based access and/or decompression. In case of a local decoding, the additional steps in the whole JPEG pipeline intensify the problem. Secondly, there exists no competitive approach to directly visualize the (volume) data by means of standard rendering techniques; only X-ray-like projection is possible.

Vector quantization is also discarded, although it seems to be a good alternative as the large number of contributions about compression and visualization indicate. However, due to the fact that local processing operations introduce a substantial loss of effective compression, this technique seems not well suited for the desired system.

Finally, wavelet based compression provides the most advantages. In spite of the relative memory overhead (especially for GPU-based implementations), the most important assets are the inherent multi-resolution property with many applications, the good compatibility with visualization techniques, and feasible fallback implementations for incompatible processing operations.

Therefore, the wavelet approach has been selected to be most advantageous with respect to the given criteria, and offers additional features that might be of interest for further extensions.

4.2 Wavelet compression

The general possibility and existing approaches for working in the compression domain have been discussed so far. Different criteria have finally led to wavelets as the underlying compression scheme for realizing the direct processing of compressed data, ideally in tight combination with visualization. This leads to the ultimate goal to utilize the graphics hardware for the whole pipeline, i.e., also for the encoding process. As this step is usually computationally very expensive – but also inherently parallel – it can benefit from hardware implementation, as shown by Wong et al. [WLHW07], for example.

However, the focus in this chapter is on designing a basis for the direct processing in the compression domain, as well as to propose an according implementation based on CASCADA. Therefore, approaches to GPU-based compression/decompression will not be addressed here. Once this foundation is established, further steps towards an integration of compression, computations, and visualization will be done.

4.2.1 Haar wavelet transform

The fundamentals of the wavelet compression have already been introduced before. In what follows, the Haar wavelet transform will be reviewed briefly and less general to discuss the processing of the compressed data. In addition to theoretical considerations on this direct processing, some alternatives will be described that are regarded as "fallback solution" for operations not compatible or efficiently feasible with the wavelet representation.

To simplify matters, only one-dimensional image data will be considered in the following examples. Also, the transformations will be limited to the first level of the wavelet transform. Although this limits the compression rate considerably in practice, it further simplifies the following theoretical explanations and notations; it will be considered in the implementation section below, however.[6] As explained in section 4.1.2, the wavelet transform using the Haar basis resembles an averaging and detailing process. For a one-dimensional image $i = [i_1, i_2, i_3, i_4]$ averaging of neighboring pixels leads to

$$\begin{aligned} a_{1,0} &= (i_1 + i_2)/2 \\ a_{1,1} &= (i_3 + i_4)/2 \end{aligned} \quad (4.2.1)$$

Note, that for averages the letter a, and for detail values the letter d is used, respectively. The first subscript denotes the level, whereas the second indicates the position in the sub-band. The result of this process is a coarser image consisting of only two pixels: $i_{\text{avg}} = [a_{1,0}, a_{1,1}]$. Information will be lost if i_1 and i_2, and i_3 and i_4, respectively, have different values: the original image can be reconstructed only to $[a_{1,0}, a_{1,0}, a_{1,1}, a_{1,1}]$. Therefore, the details (or coefficients) are computed

$$\begin{aligned} d_{1,0} &= (i_1 - i_2)/2 \\ d_{1,1} &= (i_3 - i_4)/2 \end{aligned} \quad (4.2.2)$$

and have to be added to the image representation for exact reconstruction, resulting in the wavelet form $\tilde{i}_{level1} = [a_{1,0}, a_{1,1}, d_{1,0}, d_{1,1}]$. The original image can then be reconstructed without introducing errors by:

$$\begin{aligned} i'_1 &= (a_{1,0} + d_{1,0}) \\ i'_2 &= (a_{1,0} - d_{1,0}) \\ i'_3 &= (a_{1,1} + d_{1,1}) \\ i'_4 &= (a_{1,1} - d_{1,1}) \end{aligned} \quad (4.2.3)$$

Although the discussion is currently limited to one-level decompositions only, the computation of higher levels is straightforward: the averaging and differencing process is performed recursively on the average image i_{avg}, where the image sizes have to be multiples of 2^{level} per dimension. Usually this recursion is done until the number of uncompressed averages is as small as specified by the user, or a certain threshold is reached. The transformed representation of the next level, for example, is then $\tilde{i}_{level2} = [a_{2,0}, d_{2,0}, d_{1,0}, d_{1,1}]$, where $a_{2,0}$ and $d_{2,0}$ are computed by:

$$\begin{aligned} a_{2,0} &= (a_{1,0} + a_{1,1})/2 \\ d_{2,0} &= (a_{1,0} - a_{1,1})/2 \end{aligned} \quad (4.2.4)$$

---

[6]Implementing multiple levels requires a considerable amount of additional computations for each pixel/voxel to be reconstructed (e.g., 8^{level} multiplications for three-dimensional data). However, the computational performance of modern hardware compensates for this, especially taking the clearly reduced amount of data into account.

4.2. Wavelet compression

The extension of this procedure to three-dimensional data is the same as for separable filters: the averaging and differencing process is performed consecutively in every dimension of the data. This process can be summarized in the following equation for first level decompositions of each $2 \times 2 \times 2$ block

$$f(u,v,w) = \frac{1}{8} \sum_{n=0}^{7} s \cdot c_n \quad , s \in \{-1,1\}. \tag{4.2.5}$$

where u, v, w denote the index in local block coordinates, and s the sign of the according coefficient c. The inverse process, i.e., image reconstruction can be formulated analogously by summing the eight signed coefficients.

Now that the averages and coefficients have been computed, the (lossy) compression process is finally realized by discarding coefficients whose absolute value is below a threshold (see sections 4.1.2 and 4.3.2 for more details). Performing this task and the layout of the remaining values is critical for efficiently reconstructing the image information. From a theoretical point of view, numerous operations are required for this "decompression" step, especially for multi-level representations. Thus, direct processing approaches should strive to avoid this reconstruction to gain performance over their uncompressed counterparts. As stated in the previous section, however, there should be an alternative available for operations that cannot be mapped into the compression domain. In addition, direct (volume) rendering also necessitates the unpacking of the compressed data, albeit the representation can be optimized for rendering-only approaches, as will be covered in the next section.

4.2.2 Rendering

After introducing the wavelet transform the focus will be now on the direct rendering of the compressed data. As this topic has been addressed thoroughly in multiple publications during the past years, only approaches utilizing graphics hardware with reference or applicability to wavelet based compression will be reviewed. For the implementation described in section 4.3, not all of the methods have been applied as the focus of this work is not on rendering only. However, the contributions provide good insights to the underlying concepts and foundations and inspire further development.

Hardware-Based Wavelet Transformations One of the first approaches for using the graphics hardware to render and transform volume data in the wavelet domain was proposed by Hopf and Ertl [HE99]. Although their performance results were comparable to software implementations, the lack of floating point data types back then degraded the accuracy visibly. However, as both the decomposition and reconstruction step were implemented completely in hardware, the expensive transfer of the data to be displayed could be avoided. They also commented on the fact that decomposition is approximately three times faster than reconstruction due to the much simpler implementation.

Interactive Rendering of Large Volume Data Sets The work by Guthe et al. [GWGS02] employed several techniques to increase the rendering performance. Their combination of a multi-resolution approach and wavelet based techniques allowed the decompression on-the-fly at optimal rendering quality. In a later work, Guthe and Strasser [GS04] extended the system by adjusting the resolution level using error estimations of the visual quality in screen-space. They used block-based wavelet compression with entropy encoding of the coefficients for further reducing the memory overhead. Also, their system employed higher-order wavelet basis functions that result in better visual quality than simpler approaches (e.g., Haar basis); at the expense of additional computations, however.

High-Quality Rendering of Compressed Volume Data Formats A completely different approach is described by Fout et al. [FAM⁺05], that was introduced in Kniss et al. [KLF05]. In their approach, the concept of *deferred filtering* is used to implement high quality rendering directly from compressed (or otherwise packed) volume data. By splitting the procedure into two rendering passes, redundant and potentially expensive work can be avoided. While the first pass reconstructs data in its original resolution and layout, the second pass renders the prepared data, thereby exploiting hardware features such as native texture filtering.[7]

Although the authors do not explicitly mention wavelet based compression techniques – vector quantization is described instead – the concepts can be applied for other schemes as well. In principle, the procedure uses offscreen textures to store adjacent, decompressed slices that will be processed and rendered onscreen in the second pass. This second step usually employs advanced techniques such as bi-/trilinear filtering, gradient computations, etc. The separation of the originally combined decompression and rendering procedure results in up to 20 times faster rendering performance on modern graphics hardware, despite the additional overhead from context and state changes.

4.2.3 Computations

After recalling the fundamentals of the wavelet transform, as well as related rendering approaches, the implementation of direct computations in the wavelet domain is the subject of this section. As discussed in section 4.1.3, there exist some approaches for working in the compression domain. Based on these experiences, a classification was established to evaluate different algorithms. In addition, an extended version of the wavelet basis will be utilized to account for incompatibilities with commonly used operations.

Classes of operations

In order to apply (image) processing operations on compressed data, a classification of operations seems reasonable. While the idea of an estimation of benefits from graphics

---

[7]Note that this technique has been originally introduced for graphics applications, where the *deferred shading* is used to speed up complex rendering computations, including multiple passes, lighting computations, etc. As a thorough discussion of such applications would be beyond the scope of this thesis, the focus is here on GPGPU implementations.

4.2. Wavelet compression

hardware implementations will be shortly outlined in section 8.2.1, Höllt defined different classes of operations on wavelet compressed data [Höl08]. Therefore, the mathematical definitions of various operations are reformulated, taking the properties of the wavelet transform into account (i.e., the separate data in the average values and coefficients). Details of these substitutions can be found in [Höl08], and eventually lead to the following four classes:

Class 1 Operations of this type (e.g., invert, histogram spread) are considered as point based and do not require any roll-back of the compression process. That is, these operations maintain zero coefficients and, if additional run-length encoding is used, the encoded sequences remain valid. These operations can be applied directly on the non-zero (i.e., compressed and sparse) coefficients and the average values.

Class 2 Operations such as image/volume sums or differences involve inhomogeneous additions and thus require the decompression of the zero coefficients, as well as changes on the run-length encoding sequences. The operation is then applied to all coefficients (and averages), but without complete re-compression.

Class 3 These operations are also point based, but cannot be performed in the compression domain. Therefore, the current voxel needs to be re-compressed after applying the procedure in the spatial domain. Examples are gamma correction, thresholding, and other operations that require comparisons, the absolute operator, or potentiation.

Class 4 This class subsumes all non-point based operations, i.e., where neighboring or other voxel data is required to be re-compressed (as in class 3). Both linear and non-linear local filter operations fall into this category and are applied in the spatial domain.

Especially the last two classes require additional discussion. Obviously, they resemble the "fallback solution" as the operator is applied in the spatial domain, and thus impose a considerable loss of performance due to the full re-compression. While the impact of class three operations is moderate (and of linear complexity with respect to the number of voxels to be reconstructed), the fourth class operation will be clearly outperformed by applying the spatial equivalent in the first place. Hence, the main reason for processing the compressed data is the more compact representation: larger data sets can be processed as they are unpacked only locally and thus still fit in the memory.

Convolution filters (as typical linear operations) can also be reformulated by shifting the image data spatially and using it multiple times in a weighted sum. The principle is shown in the figures below, with further details being discussed in [Höl08]. In figure 4.7, the traditional implementation of applying a convolution kernel with respect to its pivot (circle in center pixel) is depicted. While scalar multiplication and image addition can be transferred easily into the wavelet domain, the shift operation (for moving the filter kernel) is not directly possible, as the wavelet transform is shift-variant (see next section). Therefore, convolution is described by creating n copies of the original data, where n is the number of kernel elements. For every position in the kernel, the image has to be shifted in the opposite

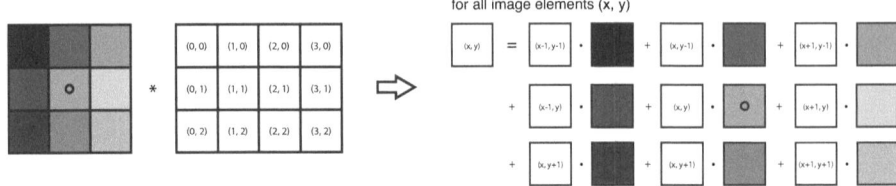

Figure 4.7: The principle of convolution in the spatial domain

direction relative to the kernel's pivot. The sum of these images weighted by the respective kernel value results in the desired convolution, as shown in figure 4.8. In the illustration pixels with dotted outlines are not part of the original image domain and require border handling (e.g., simple extrapolation).

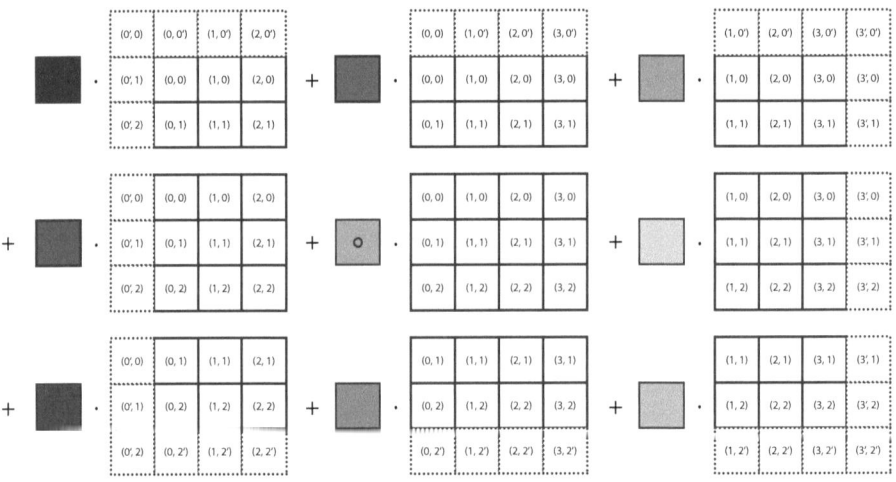

Figure 4.8: An alternative representation of convolution by applying the kernel to the input image at shifted positions.

Representing linear filters this way would alleviate the need for full re-compression, but also has considerable drawbacks. Copying the whole image or volume to realize the different filter window locations would lead to a prohibitively high memory consumption for reasonable kernel sizes: for $3 \times 3 \times 3$ kernels, 26 translations would have to be processed for one level, and $2^n - 1$ shifts per direction for n levels in general![8] On the other hand, using dedicated variants of the wavelet transform to avoid this complex workaround (i.e., shift invariant transforms) diminishes the effective compression rate and performance due to their additional requirements, as will be discussed in the next section.

---

[8] As will be shown later, this spiraling number of shifts can be reduced by discarding redundant combinations.

Over-complete wavelet representation

Many applications in signal and image processing, data compression, or multi-resolution analysis rely on the powerful basis provided by the wavelet transform, as is thoroughly described in the excellent book by Mallat [Mal99]. The benefits of this transform were also discussed in the first part of this chapter and ultimately led to using wavelets for the compression computing approach. However, the standard wavelet transform[9] (SWT) is based on a recursive down-sampling between the different levels (see sections 4.1.2 and 4.2 for details) that introduces a *shift invariance*: the coefficients are highly dependent on their location within the sampling grid. That is, minor translations in the input signal (e.g., frame-to-frame relations in image series, neighborhood information for filter kernels) result in severe changes of the wavelet coefficients that propagate and thus potentiate through the different levels. This process can also be regarded as aliasing, which – quite interestingly – disappears if (and only if) all of the coefficients are used for the inverse wavelet transform, i.e., the reconstruction of the original signal. However, as this is not practical for discrete, multi-level implementations due to quantization errors or partial (bricked) reconstruction, the shift variance still plays an important role for a wide range of applications in the wavelet domain; see Struzik [Str01] for details.

Therefore, several authors have proposed numerous representations and strategies that introduce redundant information for an (approximate) shift-invariance, as discussed in Bradley [Bra03]. While these extensions usually have specific names, they are usually based on the "algorithme à trous" or – the term that will be used in this chapter – over-complete wavelet transform (OCWT). The disadvantage of these approaches, however, is their inherent redundancy leading to an increase in required memory. Hence, Bradley proposes the combination of the standard method (i.e., the Mallat algorithm) for its computational efficiency and compact representation, and the à trous algorithm for the shift-invariance property. The two algorithms have been shown to be interchangeable by Shensa [She92]. In practice, the over-complete representation uses the Mallat algorithm for a given number of higher levels before switching to the full sampling of the second algorithm for the remaining (lower) levels, thus leading to an easily controllable trade-off between accuracy and memory footprint. As for the objective of this discussion – to increase the efficiency of class 4 operations – the conversion of linear filters as outlined in the preceding section can be directly implemented using the over-complete representation.

---

[9] As defined in Bradley [Bra03], the wavelet transform considered here is based on a discrete mother wavelet recursively applied at dyadic scales.

4.3 Implementation

The theoretical concepts described before and in [Höl08] have been implemented in the CASCADA framework[10], in the original version without multi-level support. However, information about the extension to multi-level decomposition and compression will be also given as it has been implemented in a second research phase. Due to the fact that the system works primarily on volume data, the wavelet specific computations are performed on three-dimensional data. While these concepts can be applied to data of other dimensions as well, most of the illustrations depict the two-dimensional case, mainly to clarify matters. In order to store the original data in the wavelet representation, some additional data structures are needed. This infrastructure will be described in the following paragraphs, with special attention to GPU compatibility. As already mentioned in the fundamentals section above, the non-standard wavelet transform is advantageous for image data, especially in the context of multi-level decompositions. Therefore, this type of transform is used throughout the implementation.

4.3.1 Data structures

Average values

Following the decomposition based on the Haar wavelet, the input data is separated into averages and detail coefficients. As the averages are not compressed, it is natural to store them in a dedicated structure. Therefore, an average volume is set up that contains all averages. Due to the fixed relationship between the averages and the input values – two data elements per dimension are averaged – the original position can always be reconstructed; this extends directly to multi-level decomposition via recursion. Hence, the data structure containing the averages is of size $n/2$ (for single levels), where n is the number of elements in each spatial dimension, as depicted in figure 4.9.[11]

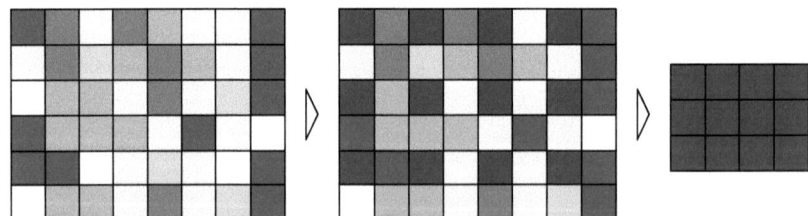

Figure 4.9: During decomposition, the pixels in every 2×2-block are averaged (blue) and compactly stored in a separate data structure.

---

[10]More precisely, all implementations presented here have been done in CASCADA 1 due to the fact that various underlying functions have been readily available by the time of the diploma thesis. Nevertheless, the second version of CASCADA will support compressed data and processing in a future release as well.

[11]Obviously, the size of the input data in each dimension has to be a multiple of two for single-level, and a power of two for multi-level decompositions, respectively.

4.3. IMPLEMENTATION

As all multi-dimensional data in CASCADA are represented internally as a linear vector, this extends naturally to the average data structure, including additional information for correctly indexing the original data. For a multi-level implementation, this would even simplify to a singe value for the highest level (i.e., a data structure with 1^n elements, for n-dimensional input data); the remaining averages are then reconstructed recursively.

Detail coefficients

In an uncompressed wavelet representation the input data structure for the detail information (i.e., coefficients) would have to be maintained. However, this case is just of theoretical interest, as there would be no benefit from the wavelet form at all: the additional infrastructure would even increase the total memory consumption. In the following it is therefore assumed that the coefficients are compressed by means of removing values below a certain threshold. As a result, all non-zero coefficients[12] resemble a sparse data structure and thus should be converted into a more compact representation. Storing the data linearly, however, would result in a loss of the original position that is in turn needed for reconstruction. This correlation can be implemented by storing the coefficients in a map with their spatial position as key. Querying a certain coefficient will then result in logarithmic complexity with respect to the number of elements in the map (for standard, tree-based internal representations), or even lower costs for specialized versions such as hash maps. However, the zero coefficients had to be included in both cases to ensure correct key-value mapping, thus leading again to a larger memory footprint. Therefore, a mixed strategy inspired by Grosso et al. [GEA96] is used, as indicated in figure 4.10.

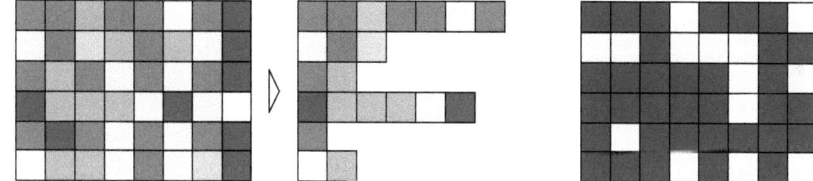

Figure 4.10: To maintain spatial information, the detail coefficients are stored in a mixed data structure (center image). For optimization only the non-zero coefficients (yellow) are marked in an importance map (right image).

For the two-dimensional case, the y-coordinates of the coefficients are maintained and used as index into a look-up table. For each entry, a list of the remaining coefficients of the same vertical position is created, resulting in vectors of different lengths. To further reduce the amount of memory needed, the data in each list is run-length encoded by actually maintaining two arrays: the first array contains the actual coefficient values, the second the number of repetitions of the according element. This extends analogously to other dimensions: e.g., for a three-dimensional setup two dimensions are used as index, while the third dimension is "substituted" by the run-length encoded list.

---

[12] This denotes coefficients that should be maintained, i.e., are above the given threshold.

Especially for higher compression rates, where more detail coefficients become zero, there are options for further optimizations. It is unnecessary for these coefficients to search the aforementioned data structure as zero values do not contribute to the result and are thus not stored in the list. Therefore, the first implementation introduced an additional data structure to decide whether the data to be reconstructed can be fetched from the coefficients list or not. In order to keep the memory footprint as small as possible, a binary "importance map" of the same dimension and size as the original data structure was used as lookup table (see figure 4.10). In order to achieve fast access to random coefficients for each two-dimensional coordinate of the current wavelet block volume, an offset for the two aforementioned coefficient arrays is also stored. This collection of offsets ("entry point map", EPM) is half the size of the original data in both x- and y-dimension as each block is comprised of two coefficients in each dimension.

While the first implementation required both data structures, i.e., importance map and EPM, the latter is sufficient for the second version. This helps reducing the memory footprint considerably, despite the higher bit depth that is needed to represent both coefficient values and run length coding in one data element. For a full n-level decomposition of a $2^n \times 2^n \times 2^n$ data set with 16 bit data elements the compression using the importance volume needs $\frac{1}{16} \cdot (1 + \frac{1}{8} + \frac{1}{8^2} + \ldots + \frac{1}{8^{(n-1)}}) + \frac{2}{z} \cdot (1 + \frac{1}{4} + \frac{1}{4^2} + \ldots + \frac{1}{4^{(n-1)}})$ of the data set's size for both the importance map and the EPM. The new representation, however, requires only $\frac{2}{z} \cdot (\frac{1}{4} + \frac{1}{4^2} + \ldots + \frac{1}{4^n})$. Using the example of a 256^3 volume with 16 bit per voxel (i.e., 32 MB of user data), this results in 12.95 MB of overhead for the first, and only 2.67 MB for the second implementation, respectively.

Discarding the importance volume does not only reduce the memory overhead. In the context of GPU implementations a reduced number of texture accesses can further improve the overall performance, especially for different data structures. Although the EPM has to be accessed more often than by querying the importance volume beforehand, the memory layout of graphics hardware is able to optimize sequential texture fetches.

4.3.2 Compression / Decompression

The theoretical concepts of wavelet compression were described in the introductory part of this chapter, as well as at the beginning of this section. Consequently, the implementation of this process is also comprised of two steps: the wavelet decomposition, and the actual compression.

The pseudo-code in listing 4.1 shows the block-wise, single-level wavelet decomposition for volume data. The decomposition function in line 8 is the implementation of equation 4.2.5 (page 109). Other basis functions than the Haar basis could be used here, of course. While the average coefficients can be directly written into the aforementioned data structure `averageVolume` (i.e., a volume with 1/8 the size of the input volume), the detail coefficients have to be processed further. Therefore, they are only separated from the values that should

4.3. IMPLEMENTATION

```
1   // single-level wavelet decomposition for volume data
2   for ( all even voxels )
3   {
4     // collect 2x2x2 block to be decomposed
5     waveletBlock[ 8 ] = getBlock( input( voxelPos ) );
6
7     // decompose
8     coefficients[ 8 ] = decomposeToWavelet( waveletBlock );
9
10    // extract the average coefficient
11    averageVolume[ voxelPos / 2 ] = coefficients[ 0 ];
12
13    // sort seven remaining coefficients temporarily
14    for ( remaining coefficients )
15    {
16      // coefficient not discarded?
17      if( abs( coefficient ) > compressionThreshold )
18      {
19        // volume position for current coefficient
20        position = volumePosition( coefficient );
21
22        // put coefficient into temporary volume
23        tempCoeffVolume[ position ] = coefficient;
24      }
25    }
26  }
```

Listing 4.1: Simplified code showing the wavelet decomposition of input volume.

be discarded by means of the user-specified threshold, and stored in a temporary volume at the original position.[13]

The entry point map and the coefficient vector are filled in the second step. This procedure is depicted in listing 4.2. For the current x, y-coordinate the `index` value is stored in the `entryPoints` map. Then all the non-zero coefficients in z-direction (that have been determined in the decomposition step) are put consecutively into the `coefficients` vector. Here a run-length encoding is applied, that is, sequences of equal values are reduced to a single value, and the number of occurrences is kept in a second list (`coeffSequence`). After the processing of one array in z-direction the next x, y-coordinate is processed. The updated *index* is recorded in the `entryPoints` map, and so on.

Decompression is the inversion of the preceding steps, which is accomplished blockwise by fetching the average value from the `averageVolume` first (listing 4.3, line 5). The corresponding coefficients are reconstructed from the encoded values afterwards. This process can be summarized as follows:

1. look up the offset at $(x/2, y/2)$ in the EPM
2. compute the sum of all repetition values, until the sum is equal or greater than the desired z-position

---

[13] As the importance map was discarded in the second version of the implementation, the according code section was also omitted in the example.

```
1   // initialize index, 0 for first level
2   index = coefficients.size();
3   // reorder and run-length encode detail coefficients
4   for ( all even voxels in slice )
5   {
6     // set entry point
7     entryPoints[ voxel.xy / 2 ] = index;
8
9     // sort coefficients in z-direction
10    for ( all even slices )
11    {
12      // get detail coefficients block from decomposition
13      tmpDCs[ 7 ] = getBlock( tempCoeffVolume( voxel ) );
14
15      // store coefficients run-length encoded
16      for ( all tmpDCs )
17      {
18        // if not the same
19        if ( current != predecessor )
20        {
21          // store and increment index
22          coefficients.push_back( current );
23          index++;
24
25          // store length (0 for separation)
26          coeffSequence.push_back( 0 );
27        }
28        // increase sequence length in any case
29        coeffSequence[ last ]++;
30      }
31    }
32  }
```

Listing 4.2: Simplified code showing the reordering and run-length encoding of the detail coefficients.

3. the coefficient can then be looked up by using the last value's index

The voxel values are then composed by applying the according equations (see [Höl08] for details), and stored in the uncompressed target volume.

Extending the (de-)compression to multiple levels is straightforward, especially given the aforementioned procedures for single level transforms. By looping over all levels (starting with the lowest), and using the resulting average volume from one iteration as input for the next one, an n-level transform was implemented. As the volumes' sizes must be multiples of 2^n for this operation, the volume might has to be resized to meet this constraint. The code listings have already indicated some data structures shared among the different levels (e.g., coefficients) to reduce the additional memory requirements during (de-)compression, and thus allow for more efficient computations.

Parallel implementations play an increasingly important role, especially with ubiquitous multi-core architectures nowadays. Although an excessive optimization in terms of parallel execution has not been the focus of this work, some of the preceding steps lend themselves

4.3. IMPLEMENTATION

```
// reconstructing values from RLE-based wavelet representation
for ( all even voxels )
{
    // get average coefficient
    average = averageVolume[ voxel.xy / 2 + zOffset ];

    // get entry point from x,y-position
    entryPoint = entryPoints[ voxel.xy / 2 ];

    // get remaining seven coefficients
    for ( remaining coefficients )
    {
        // seek coefficient position
        for ( half of output length )
        {
            // sum up sequence values
            seqLen = offset + coeffSequence[ entryPoint ];
            // break if exceeds desired z-position
            if ( seqLen > seqPos ) break;

            // update offset and increment
            offset = seqLen;
            entryPoint++;
        }
        // get value at computed position
        detailCoeffs = coefficients[ entryPoint ];
    }

    // recompose voxel data from current block
    composeVoxelValues( average, detailCoeffs );
}
```

Listing 4.3: Simplified code for decompressing the wavelet representation.

to be parallelized. Therefore, the decomposition and composition steps (listing 4.1 and partly 4.3) work on disjunct sub-regions of the input volume simultaneously. In contrast, the reordering steps used to construct the look-up tables etc. requires the coefficients to be set into the vector in the correct, deterministic order, so that (direct) parallelization has not been applicable here. All parallelization for CPU implementations has been realized by using the `omp parallel for` construct of the OpenMP library [OMP] with good results; for details see Höllt [Höl08].

4.3.3 Rendering

While the (de-)compression procedures were implemented in software only, the visualization is performed on the GPU. Therefore, the compressed data is reconstructed on-the-fly in the fragment shader. The main difference between compressed and uncompressed data is in accessing the current voxel: instead of a single texture look-up, the voxel has to be reconstructed from the compressed data. That is, the eight adjacent coefficients of the according 2^3 wavelet block have to be fetched, and the inverse wavelet transform has to be applied to this set of coefficients. As described before in section 4.2.2, native texture interpolation modes cannot be used directly on compressed data. Therefore, the interpolation has to be implemented manually or by means of deferred filtering. The latter would have required considerable changes to the underlying shader handling and management, and is left for future development; hence, linear interpolation has been implemented manually. Due to the clear impact on the rendering performance (see the results in section 4.4), interpolation is not activated by default. The required functionality (e.g., fetching single coefficients, accessing complete wavelet blocks) has been sourced out into a separate shader file.[14] This allows to reuse the code also in shaders that implement computations on wavelet data.

The transition from single- to multi-level transform required only simple adaptations to the rendering shaders, while most of the changes had to be done in the external shader file. As described before, additional data structures for the entry point map were implemented. While the latter is simply converted into a two-dimensional texture – just as the coefficient map – the entry point map utilizes mip-mapping for efficient access on the GPU. Due to the fact that the EPM's size always changes by a factor of two between adjacent levels, mip-maps are an ideal representation on the GPU. In addition, current shading languages provide dedicated functions for accessing mip-maps (`texture3DLod(...)` in GLSL, for example). Note that this mip-map is not used as traditional level-of-detail storage, however: the data in each mip-map level is completely independent from the content of the other levels. A disadvantage of using mip-maps for the EPM is the fact that mip-maps have to have complete levels in current implementations. That is, the additional memory consumption is independent from the number of levels actually used. Thus, in the worst case (i.e., single-level compression) 50% more texture memory is needed.

Reconstructing a single voxel from the (complete) multi-level representation requires the reconstruction of the average voxel from the average and detail coefficients of the next level. Unfortunately, (GP)GPU programming does not support recursion, so that all recursive algorithms have to be unrolled into iterative procedures. These functions are again implemented in a separate shader file to provide at least some modularity.

In addition to the support of multiple levels, the second version of the implementation allows enhanced rendering modes thanks to the increased decompression performance. Simple MPR-like rendering with enabled trilinear interpolation achieved only interactive framerates in the first version, compared to real-time performance with the revised one. This is mainly due to the more efficient coefficient access and thus enabled the implementation of direct volume rendering, including the use of one-dimensional transfer functions (see figure 4.11). Extending the functionality has been as simple as replacing "fixed" functions for voxel reconstruction with flexible versions that access neighboring values instead of a wavelet block.

---

[14] As will be described in chapter 6, CASCADA provides means to assemble valid GLSL shader programs from incomplete shader code fragments.

4.3. IMPLEMENTATION

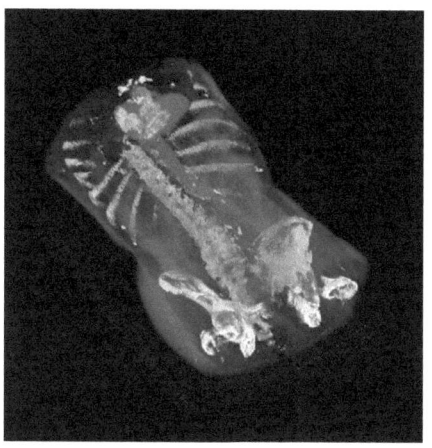
(a) Wavelet-based DVR

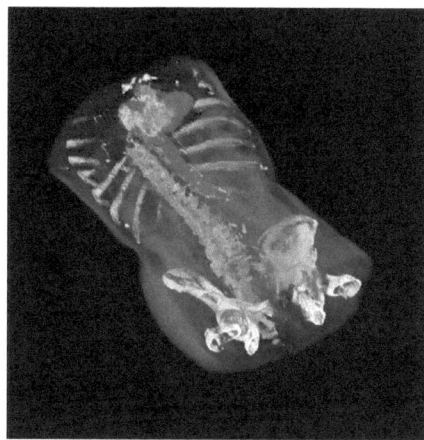
(b) Standard DVR

Figure 4.11: Wavelet-based DVR (a) of compressed CT data set ($512 \times 512 \times 256$, 16 bit, compression ratio $\approx 1 : 20$) at interactive frame rates, compared to standard DVR (b) in CASCADA. Both renderings use a one-dimensional transfer function and nearest neighbour interpolation.

4.3.4 Computations

While rendering can be regarded as a read-only process, computations performed on the compressed data require both read and write operations. As GPU-based implementations using textures cannot write into the same memory as is used for reading, an additional data structure has to be available. Some of the operations classified in section 4.2.3 do not require a complete copy of the input data, however. Homogeneous point-based operations, for example, do not require the reordering of the coefficients, so that only the average value and coefficient vector need to be copied. The result for all other operations has to be written into a temporary coefficient volume containing all coefficients, including even those below the threshold. The compressed coefficient map has to be rebuilt then in a postprocessing step.

For all of the classes introduced before, procedures have been implemented both on the GPU and in software. In particular for class 4 operations, a basic implementation of the over-complete wavelet transform has been evaluated as well. The following sections review the theoretical basis needed for implementing the algorithms and estimate the computational complexity. Experimental results with timings and further remarks are going to be summarized in the subsequent section.

Class 1: Inversion and histogram spreading

These two operations work directly on the compressed data and will be presented first. The main difference between the two operations is that the histogram spread operator incorporates a user-specified parameter; the invert operator is only dependent on the volume data. As a result, the input and output volume can be the same for the inversion.

As shown in detail in [Höl08], both operations can then be applied as gray value transformations on the wavelet coefficients. The software implementation can thus be realized by a loop over the average volume, where every value is transformed following $T_{\text{avg}} \cdot (-1) + g_{\text{max}}$ for the invert, and $T_{\text{avg}} \cdot \frac{(G-1)}{g_{\text{max}} - g_{\text{min}}} - \frac{g_{\text{min}}}{g_{\text{max}} - g_{\text{min}}}$ for the histogram spread operation, respectively; g_{max} denotes the maximum gray value of the volume data. The elements of the coefficient map are transformed in a second loop with $T_c \cdot (-1)$ for invert, and $T_c \cdot \frac{(G-1)}{g_{\text{max}} - g_{\text{min}}}$ for the histogram spread, respectively. Note that these loops can be implemented using multiple threads as there are no dependencies between elements in the data structures during the computations.

The implementation on the GPU is a bit more involved. In order to load the data on the GPU, both data structures are converted to two-dimensional RGBA textures. Using textures with four channels allows the parallel computation of four values in one step.[15] Each data structure has to be treated separately, because both the operations T_{avg} and T_c differ, as well as the two textures are usually of different sizes. The shader programs for the operations themselves are rather simple functions, as shown in listing 4.4, for the inversion operation, for example.

```
1 // invert averages
2 {
3    gl_FragColor = maxVal - texture2D( avgTex, gl_TexCoord[0].st );
4 }
5
6 // invert coefficients
7 {
8    gl_FragColor = - texture2D( coeffTex, gl_TexCoord[0].st );
9 }
```

Listing 4.4: Shader code detail for direct inversion.

Class 2: Image addition

Algorithms of this class can be performed directly in the wavelet domain in principle, but require both the decompression of all coefficients (i.e., also zero entries) and an update of the RLE sequences due to inhomogeneous operations. For the given implementation that uses additional run-length compression, this also entails the dissolving and reapplication of the encoding. Here, the addition of two volumes has been implemented, but extends trivially to subtraction as well.

Operations of class 2 require fundamentally different implementations on the CPU and on the GPU. The former consists of an iteration over the run-length encoded data and storing the coefficient at the respective position in the target array which resembles a scatter operation

---

[15]Of course, further parallelization techniques such as multiple render targets or data packing could be employed, but would require some more preparation and are out of scope here.

4.3. IMPLEMENTATION

(see section 1.2). For a GPU implementation based on standard shaders, this scattering is not available. Thus, every target coefficient has to be represented by a fragment and fetched independently from the run-length encoded data, i.e., converting the process to a gather operation. This is of course computationally much more expensive than the CPU algorithm.[16] Therefore, the estimated performance of class 2 operations depends on the platform used. While the results are going to be discussed in detail below, CPU implementations are expected to benefit to a much higher degree than their hardware counterpart, but are sensitive to the input due to the data dependency of run-length encoding.

Class 3: Binary thresholding

Binary thresholding has been implemented as example for operations that require block-wise decompression. As a point based operation, binary thresholding is ranked as a class three operation. Operations that require decompression are applied in two steps. First, the block that is to be processed is decompressed, followed by applying the operation in the spatial domain and transforming the result back into the wavelet domain. The second step is for reordering the resulting coefficient vector.

In order to reduce overhead for the decompression and recompression operations in the software version, the complete eight-voxel wavelet block is decompressed, processed and re-transformed. For binary thresholding this means that one indirect coefficient fetch is needed, instead of a simple array access per voxel. For computations on one level, seven additions are needed to transform each voxel (in the current block) from the wavelet into the spatial domain. After the threshold operator has been applied – as for non-compressed data – the re-transformation into the wavelet domain has to be performed and requires another seven additions.

Due to the fact that the wavelet data is encoded as colors in the GPU version, not all eight coefficients can be computed at once; RGBA textures offer at most four values. However, in order to compute the four voxels in the spatial domain, all eight coefficients of the corresponding block are needed, just as all eight voxels of the block are needed to compute the resulting coefficients of the re-transformation. Hence, the effective cost per voxel for decompression and re-transformation into the wavelet representation is twice the cost of the CPU version, i.e., two coefficient fetches and 28 additions per operation and voxel.

Class 4: Laplace filter (SWT)

Although Laplace filtering also requires block-wise decompression of the data, it is regarded as class four operation due to the fact that it accesses neighboring data. That is, applying the Laplace filter is very similar to the binary threshold operation described before, but additionally requires the neighborhood of the current block to be fetched. The Laplace filter

---

[16] As already mentioned in the first part of this thesis (and in chapter 5), dedicated APIs such as Nvidia CUDA provide scattering operations, shared memory, etc. Therefore, the "GPU" implementation will not require expensive workarounds and could thus exploit the performance potential of graphics hardware to a much higher degree.

is implemented as a $3 \times 3 \times 3$ mask, but can be extended to other sizes, of course.[17] In the special case of the Laplace operator, only the six direct neighbors of the pivot and the pivot itself are non-zero. Therefore, only the six directly adjacent voxels of each processed voxel contribute to the result, and thus have to be fetched. In terms of wavelet blocks this means additionally to the current block the six direct neighbors have to be fetched. However, for the $3 \times 3 \times 3$ filter mask only a $4 \times 4 \times 4$ voxel neighborhood has to be reconstructed for processing the current block, as a subset of the neighboring voxels is always within the current $2 \times 2 \times 2$ block.

This results in seven coefficient fetches and 21 more additions per voxel for the software implementation. On the GPU effectively 14 fetches and 42 additions are needed for reconstruction and recompression, that is again twice as much than the CPU version for the same reasons mentioned above. Although not implemented, the following statistics estimate the complexity for other kernels:

- For a $5 \times 5 \times 5$ Laplace filter kernel the 12 neighboring blocks sharing one edge with this block have to be fetched and reconstructed, increasing the number of fetches to 19 (GPU: 38), and the number of additions to 70 per voxel on the CPU (GPU: 140).

- A general $3 \times 3 \times 3$ filter mask would require 27 fetches and 28 additions on the CPU, and twice the amount on the GPU, respectively.

These indirect coefficient accesses are computationally very expensive, compared to simple array look-ups/texture fetches. Therefore, a significant performance decrease has to be expected for these neighborhood operations. After these computations the reordering of the coefficient map has to be performed (as for the wavelet compression), which is less expensive in total, however.

Class 4: Laplace filter (OCWT)

In section 4.2.3, the concept of the over-complete wavelet transform was introduced to provide a compression representation capable of handling shift operations that are needed for filter kernels. The implementation described here is regarded as proof of concept in that it does not exploit the full potential of the representation at the current stage of development. Hence, the focus was on the acceleration of class 4 operations by means of the over-complete transform, with less attention to memory efficiency and flexibility. As a matter of fact, the additional representation results in considerably larger data sets for the single-level decomposition implemented here. However, a similar benefit for a complete integration should be possible, just as indicated by the extension of the first version described in Höllt [Höl08] to the multi-level implementation.

As mentioned before, for an n-level decomposition based on Haar wavelets, in general $2^n - 1$ shifts in each direction are required. This results for single level decomposition and

---

[17]Note that this would result in much longer code (and thus might introduce problems due to instructions limits etc.), if larger masks were implemented straightforward. Basic approaches such as separable filter kernels should be applied then to limit the computational complexity and will be addressed in the context of compressed data in section 4.4.4.

three-dimensional data in 26 translated copies, plus the original volume. For the single-level Haar wavelet transform only two neighboring voxels per direction are dependent. That is, a translation by two voxels (or a multiple thereof) is equivalent to translating the wavelet transformed image by the desired number of voxels. As a result, all translations can be computed with inverted signs directly in the wavelet domain, i.e., a shift by $(-1,0,0)$ from the volume translated by $(1,0,0)$. Thus, only 7 instead of 26 shifted volumes are sufficient to represent the over-complete transform: $(1,0,0)$, $(0,1,0)$, $(0,0,1)$, $(1,1,0)$, $(1,0,1)$, $(0,1,1)$, $(1,1,1)$.

Based on these considerations – and recalling the fact that convolutions can be decomposed into translation, gray value scaling, and image addition – the over-complete wavelet transform supports all required operations. Thus, linear filters can be applied directly within the wavelet domain without any decomposition. In other words, procedures requiring class 4 computations can be mapped to class 2 operations which gives rise to a considerable speed-up. Just as for the standard implementation, a Laplace filter has been implemented both in software and hardware. This simplifies matters, as the Laplace kernel allows some optimizations due to several zero entries. Generalizing this to arbitrary masks is possible, of course, resulting in accordingly more texture accesses. Therefore, the performance gain with respect to the standard representation will increase for more non-zero entries, i.e., more fetches.

While the expensive workaround for shader-based implementations hampers the performance of the GPU version considerably[18], the software version can be expected to be orders of magnitude faster than the standard approach due to much fewer instructions.

4.4 Results

In the following sections, the results that were achieved by implementing the aforementioned concepts in CASCADA will be presented. As mentioned at the beginning of this chapter, the focus was on mapping computations into the compression domain, mainly as proof of concept. Therefore, the (de-)compression and rendering results will be outlined only shortly, as this has been already addressed in numerous other contributions in detail. Above that, both the memory efficiency and quality of the results will be assessed. The results will be discussed at the end, with references to particular implementation features, possible extensions, or open problems.

For most of the experiments, three different data sets were used that are depicted in figure 4.12. In addition to these rather moderately sized volume data, the data set shown in figure 4.11 on page 121 were used. The concepts can be translated to larger data sets as well, but would require the integration of further techniques such as bricking or more

---

[18]In addition, the performance varies significantly with different graphics cards (of the same GPU generation) and driver versions.

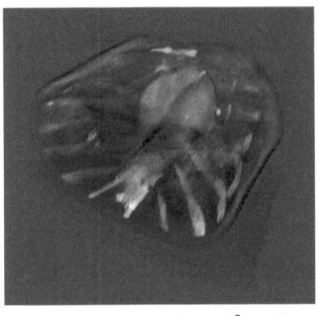 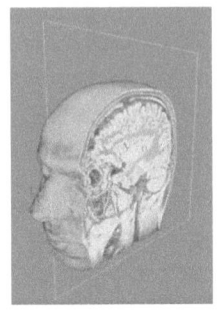 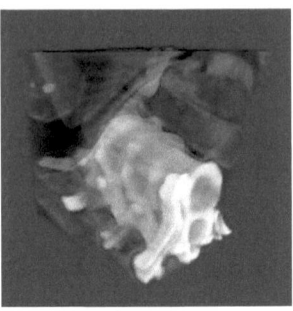

(a) Thorax (CT, 16bit, $512^2 \times 64$) (b) Head (MRI, 8bit, 256^3) (c) Spine (CT, 16bit, 64^3)

Figure 4.12: Data sets used for evaluating the compression computing approaches

general out-of-core approaches. All the experiments were performed on two systems running Windows XP:

- *System A*: Intel Core2Duo 2.4 GHz, 2 GB RAM, Nvidia Geforce 8800 GTS 640MB (G80)
- *System B*: Intel Dual Xeon Quad-Core 2.8 GHz, 6 GB RAM, Nvidia Geforce 8800 GT 512MB (G92)

4.4.1 Compression

The first version of the implementation, i.e., using only single-level decomposition and no run-length encoding, has been evaluated in detail in Höllt [Höl08]. As discussed in the theoretical part of this chapter, the wavelet basis allows lossless compression as well. For the single-level representation, this results in a compression rate of approximately 1 : 2 for the type of data sets considered here. However, for the multi-level approach, lossless compression leads to an increase in size of up to 50% due to the additional infrastructure. The over-complete wavelet transform applied here results – as expected – in excessive memory consumption of more than $10\times$ the original size for lossless, and between 400% and 150% overhead for lossy compression, respectively.

Lossy compression achieves much higher compression rates, of course, but at the cost of a worse signat-noise-ratio (SNR) due to information loss. This is illustrated in figure 4.14 on page 127, where the result for lossless compression (i.e., threshold of 0%) is infinity and therefore has been omitted. By introducing a parameter relative to the value range of the respective data set, the compression rate (or error) can be controlled. Here, this parameter denotes a percentage, i.e., a threshold of 2 results in discarding detail coefficients which are below 2% of the data set's maximum value.[19] The graphs in figure 4.13 summarize the achieved compression performance at different hierarchy levels for typical data sets.

---

[19]Other error measures, such as MSE, visual image metrics (SSIM), etc. are applicable for controlling the compression quality, as well. An integration and discussion would be beyond the scope here, however.

4.4. RESULTS

Depending on the bit depth, the compression results are considerably different, both in terms of total and relative compression rate.

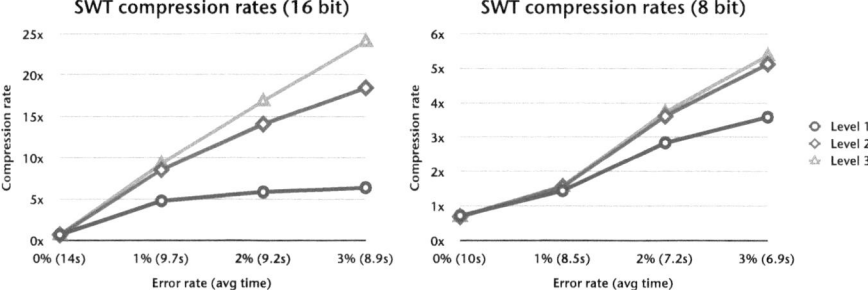

Figure 4.13: Compression results using the standard wavelet transform for the thorax (left) and head (right) data set. Both the compression rate at varying error thresholds and the timings are given for different hierarchy levels.

In terms of computational performance, the results mainly depend on the following three factors in descending importance: the size of the data set; the number of available processors; and the quality threshold. The first relation is rather obvious and scales linearly in practice, whereas the threshold parameter affects the performance almost constantly: except for lossless compression, virtually equal time is needed (see also figure 4.13). Finally, the compression is implemented only in software, but exploits multiple processors due to inherent parallelism, as described in section 4.3.2; this results in considerable speed-up for a multi-core system (esp. System A), as discussed in detail in [Höl08].

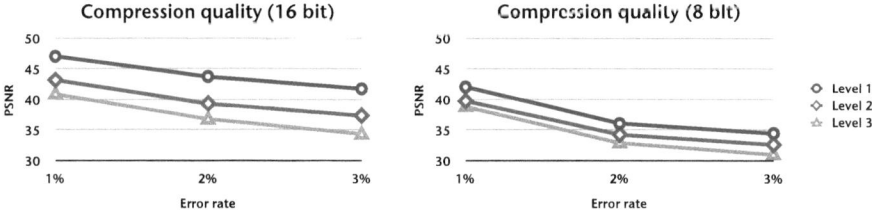

Figure 4.14: Compression quality measured by the peak signal-to-noise ratio (PSNR) using the standard wavelet transform for the thorax (left) and head (right) data set. The results are given at varying error thresholds for different hierarchy levels.

Decompression performance is approximately 25% higher than for the compression procedure. This is mainly due to the fact that compression requires the allocation of additional memory for the internal representation.

4.4.2 Rendering

As already mentioned in the preceding section, the rendering performance could be clearly improved by revising the first implementation and the extension to multi-level decomposition. Although rendering has not been the main focus of this research, some optimization strategies have been applied. This allows a comparable quality of direct volume rendering at interactive framerates, as depicted in figure 4.15. The differences originate from the block structure of the wavelet transform and lossy compression: coefficients below approximately 2% of the maximum value (i.e., 61 for the thorax data set) are discarded and cause high frequent noise. Obviously, the visual differences become less obvious for lower compression rates, whereas

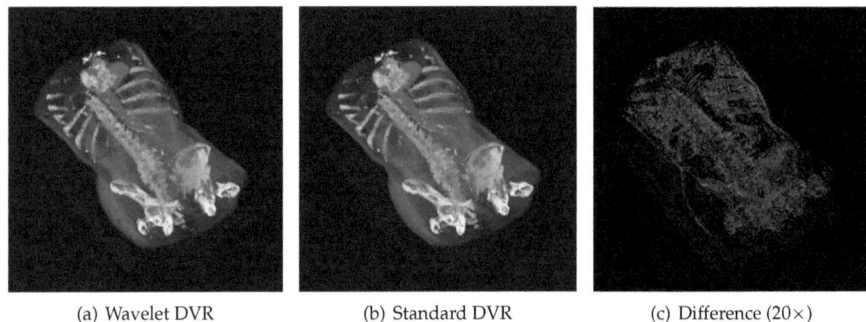

(a) Wavelet DVR   (b) Standard DVR   (c) Difference (20×)

Figure 4.15: Wavelet-based DVR (a) of Thorax/Abdomen CT data set ($512^2 \times 256$, 16 bit, compression $\approx 1:20$), compared to standard DVR (b) resulting in interactive performance. All renderings use a one-dimensional transfer function and nearest neighbor interpolation. Image (c) shows the amplified difference with negative values in blue, positive values in red.

the rendering performance remains practically unaffected, despite the larger amount of data.

In direct comparison to the first implementation, the MPR rendering performance could be increased by a factor of nearly 10 for nearest neigbour and trilinear interpolation, respectively. This is mainly due to more efficient texture fetches and the more compact multi-level representation, despite the considerably higher number of computations needed for reconstruction and run-length decoding. As addressed thoroughly in the preceding chapter, hardware implementations are much more suited for such computing intense tasks and unveil their full potential especially in combination with direct visualization methods.

4.4.3 Computations

After presenting the results for (de-)compression and rendering, major interest is in the performance of computations on compressed data. As motivated in the preceding sections, the Haar wavelet transform was chosen as compression method due to its flexibility and efficiency with respect to GPU implementations and visualization procedures. Therefore, evaluating the computational performance requires the consideration of the wavelet transform's properties and parameters, i.e., the compression level and threshold that were introduced in section 4.2.

4.4. RESULTS

All timings were performed using System A, with comments or additional information about the other system where appropriate. In addition, all measurements were performed on the Thorax data set (see figure 4.12 for details), except for the comparison of different data sets. Finally, for diagrams 4.16 and 4.18, two levels and a threshold of 1 are used as compression parameters, respectively.

Compressed / Uncompressed data

The first evaluation is the direct comparison of operations in the spatial and compression domain. As can be seen in figure 4.16, the performance of most operations on compressed data cannot compete with their standard equivalent. Especially for GPU implementations, all

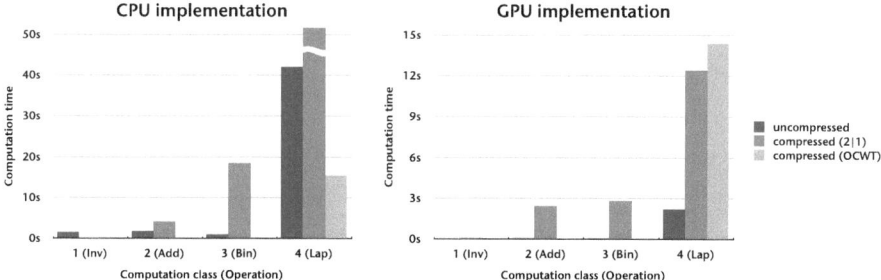

Figure 4.16: Comparison of different operations on uncompressed and compressed data, both for CPU (left) and GPU (right) implementations.

but the simplest computations (class 1) are considerably slower in the compression domain. However, the hardware implementation of the over-complete wavelet transform for class 4 operations is far from optimal due to programming limitations, as already discussed in section 4.3.4. The GPU version is even outperformed by the standard wavelet representation, and with a performance comparable to software implementations across different data sets. If the GPU code was able to use scattering, an acceleration comparable to the CPU would be possible and thus a clear benefit for complex image operations in the compression domain.

For CPU implementations, the situation is somewhat different. Class 1 operations are approximately one order of magnitude faster in the wavelet domain than in the spatial domain; again for different data sets. As these operations only have to process the average volume[20] and coefficient map, this depends strongly on the compression ratio; see the top-left diagram in figure 4.17. Operations of class 4 are practically unusable in the standard wavelet representation, as the computational overhead is prohibitively high. The performance results have been in the order of several minutes (e.g., more than 12 minutes for the Spine data set!), indicated by the discontinuous bar in diagram 4.16. On the other hand, the implementation

---

[20] Note that the size of the average volume depends on the hierarchy level and requires less time the more levels are used (i.e., down to a single computation for complete hierarchies).

of the Laplace filter using the over-complete representation clearly outperforms the same operation in the spatial domain.

Different classes

The diagrams in figure 4.17 show the influence of compression parameters on the computations' performance. With two sets of data points – for GPU and CPU implementations, respectively – in the diagrams, different aspects can be read from the results.

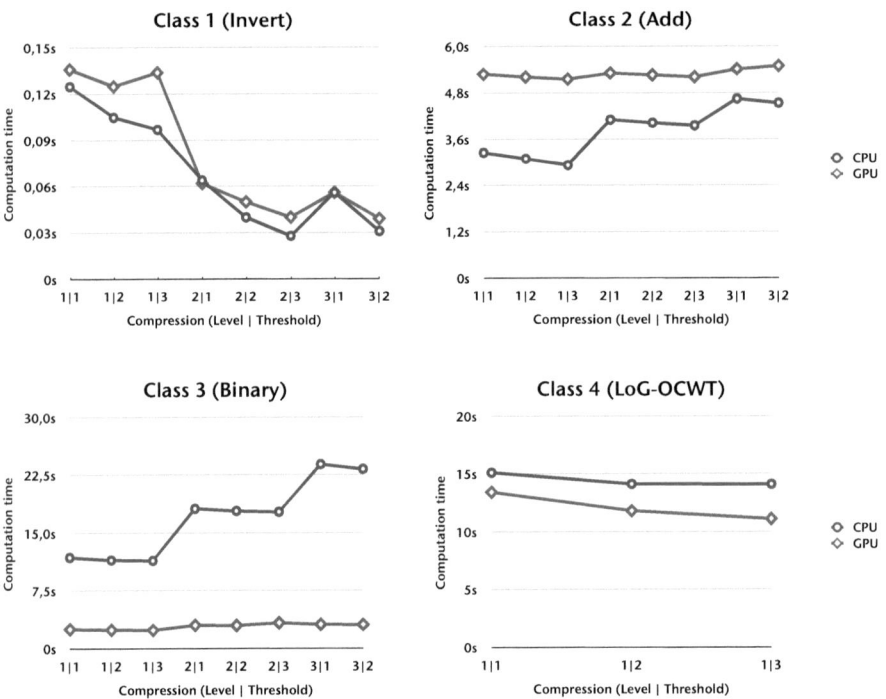

Figure 4.17: The computation performance of the different classes at varying compression parameters, for both CPU and GPU implementations. Note that class 4 operations have been realized using the OCWT implementation.

Firstly, the performance differs notedly between software and hardware versions for the different operations. While class 1 computations are practically comparable, the performance gap becomes more visible for class 2 operations. As noted before, however, the GPU version cannot exploit the full potential of modern graphics hardware due to the complicated workaround and is slower for all compression levels. In contrast, computations that require block-wise recompression, such as the binary threshold depicted at the lower left, benefit clearly from hardware implementations. Considering the results from the previous paragraph, the performance is obviously inferior for compressed computations with respect to

4.4. RESULTS

operations on uncompressed data. Although not directly comparable, the implementation of class 4 operations based on the over-complete wavelet transform indicates a trend similar to the one for class 2 computations. This becomes clear when reconsidering the fact that the additional information in the over-complete representation implies neighborhood accesses and therefore reduces the computational complexity to (approximately) class 2 operations.

Secondly, the results indicate varying dependencies on the compression parameters. In general, the GPU implementations are less sensitive to compression rates than their software counterparts. This is mainly due to the fact that accessing storage on graphics hardware (i.e., textures) is practically of constant complexity with respect to the texture's size. Software operations usually have linear complexity in this regard. However, the first diagram (top left) in figure 4.17 shows some variance, which is also due to the detailed scaling of the diagram's range. In this context, the performance for most computation classes varies at different hierarchy levels, especially for software implementations. As described in section 4.3, the extension to multi-level hierarchies introduced a computational overhead for traversing the levels in order to decompose or reconstruct the data. This becomes clearly visible for class 3 operations (bottom left of figure 4.17) where the performance drops significantly for each additional level: for the thorax data set of up to 50%, for example.

Data sets

The last criterion for assessing the performance of computations in the compression domain is for data sets of different sizes and bit depths. Therefore, the examples depicted in figure 4.12 are compared with respect to all operation classes. Again, the results are different for GPU and CPU implementations, as shown in the diagrams in figure 4.18.

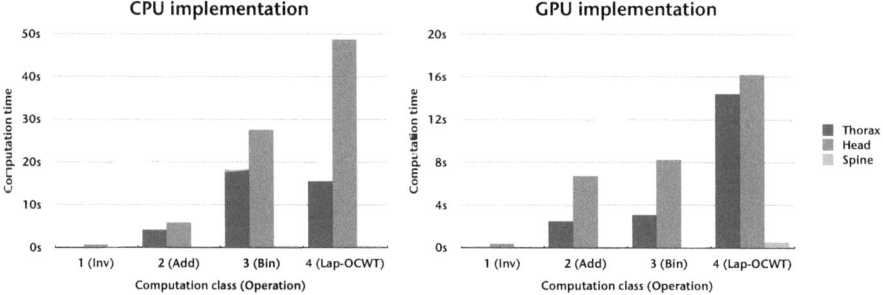

Figure 4.18: Computation performance for different data sets, using both CPU and GPU implementations. (See figure 4.12 for data set details)

Although the head and thorax are of same dimension, the former is half the bit depth (8 bit), resulting in half the size in memory – for the uncompressed data. After being converted into the wavelet domain using equal settings (i.e., level of 2 and threshold of 1), the compression ratio is significantly lower for the head data set (1 : 1.565 vs. 1 : 8.55); see also figure 4.13. This results in clear differences for the operations implemented in software.

The computations are in general slower than for the thorax data set, but can benefit from the over-complete representation to a higher degree.[21] In addition, for the data set of comparable compression ratio but different size, the findings are as expected in that the results scale with the according computational complexities of the operations.

For hardware implementations, the results align well with the aforementioned properties of the data sets (i.e., compression ratio, size). However, the internal data structures are more sensitive to hardware features, such as maximum texture sizes or data types, which results in several irregularities for differently sized data sets and are subject of further investigation.

4.4.4 Discussion

After presenting the results of compression computing described in the course of this chapter, some of the findings require further discussion. The concepts and results presented should prove the feasibility of the concept of performing computations directly on compressed data, as well as indicate trends and limitations. Especially these limitations have influenced the implementation on graphics hardware, as the (traditional GPGPU) programming model is not as flexible as for software implementations. Modern APIs such as Nvidia CUDA (see section 1.2 for details) provide several concepts such as shared memory or random write access, thus enabling more powerful and less cumbersome implementations.

Another example for optimization addresses operations that require neighborhood information (i.e., class 4 operations). A common approach to reduce the computational complexity in image processing is using *separable* filter kernels. This would be also possible in the wavelet domain, especially using the over-complete wavelet transform. Therefore, the application of the filter mask in one dimension would imply the parallel computations for multiple "filter rows" at once, as the representation already accounts for translation in different dimensions. However, as this separation pays off for larger kernels only, the over-complete representation has to be highly optimized to result in a performance gain in the end.

Yet another relevant factor of the methods presented here is the underlying representation. While advanced techniques such as the over-complete wavelet transform provides means for reducing the computational complexity of expensive operations, several simplifications are based on the Haar basis used throughout the implementations. Although this representation is in particular suited for discrete computations and hardware implementations, its quality is limited for reasonable compression parameters, i.e., hierarchy levels. As shown by several authors, other wavelets such as the Daubechies functions provide superior signal-noise ratios at equal settings – at the cost of more complex computations. But this computational intensity is exactly where GPU implementations can outperform software implementations. With more computations being performed "on-the-fly" the more compact representations would be possible at the same quality.

Finally, several classes have been defined to assess the different implementation approaches with respect to the computations. While simple operations are faster or at least of

---

[21] Although not directly comparable due to the missing multi-level support, the over-complete version has been included for reference.

comparable performance in the compression domain (as shown by several authors before), more complex operations usually cannot compete with operations on uncompressed data; this is especially the case for GPU implementations. On the other hand, graphics hardware provides only a limited amount of memory so that costly additional techniques such as bricking to process and visualize large amounts of data are needed. As mentioned in the beginning of this chapter, especially algorithms that require frequent transfer of data could benefit from performing computations directly on data stored in compressed form in the graphics memory – both to reduce the (initial) data transfer and the overall memory consumption.

4.5 Conclusion

The main objective of this chapter has been to evaluate the possibility and efficiency of mapping computations into the compression domain. In general, performing computations directly on compressed data has been shown to be feasible in the thesis by Höllt [Höl08] and by the extensions presented here. Although the performance is not as optimal as desired – especially for non-trivial operations – there is still considerable room for improvement regarding the implementation. This section is going to summarize the main findings before discussing further topics.

During the initial research phase, the wavelet transform was identified as the most advantageous one in different aspects. Firstly, practically all requirements that have been defined for realizing compression computing in section 4.1.2 are met by using the wavelet transform. Although the support of multiple levels requires additional memory, the compression results clearly outweigh this increase in terms of both storage and computational workload. Especially the possibility of lossless compression, the compatibility with GPU-based direct (volume) rendering, and the compact block size are key advantages for the target applications.

Secondly, the wavelet transform is flexible with respect to the underlying representation. On the one hand, there are several options for the wavelet basis, such as the Haar, Daubechies, or Meyer functions; see Mallat [Mal99] for further reference. On the other hand, the introduction of the over-complete wavelet transform to overcome the problem of shift variance would have not been possible for other comparable compression methods. With vector quantization, for example, neighborhood information can only be represented at prohibitively high memory consumption which cannot be reduced by algorithmic means (as for the over-complete wavelet transform). In addition, the flexible combination of both standard and over-complete representation allows for a convenient trade-off between memory consumption and computation performance.

Finally, the implementations have shown to cover different types of data. In the medical imaging context, different modalities produce data of varying bit depths and value ranges; see sections 2.1 and 3.1.2 for further information. First experiments have indicated that the implementations are applicable to higher bit depths as well, with clear performance advantages for operations performed on the GPU: modern graphics hardware is able to handle 32 bit floating point data at negligible performance penalties with respect to lower precision or integer types – in contrast to software implementations. Yet another aspect are multi-dimensional data types, such as fMRI imaging data. Although computations on compressed data are adaptive to these data types in theory, general problems as the independent processing of the individual channels also apply in the compression domain.

Aside from technical improvements (e.g., porting the (de-)compression to the GPU), an appealing extension is to exploit the multi-level support for hierarchical interaction and processing. Therefore, expensive computations can be performed and previewed interactively on a coarse level, and then applied to the full resolution after finishing parameter setting etc. This concept can also be extended to a combined GPU–CPU solution, where the GPU implementation is used for real-time preview by means of direct volume rendering on a smaller version of the data set due to the limited size of texture memory. Once the operation(s) are set up, the computations can be performed on the full data set on the CPU, or even by using out-of-core techniques for extremely large data sets.

In section 8.2.1, a classification of (GP)GPU procedures will be outlined in order to target at an (automatic) selection of the optimal implementation, i.e., hardware or software, for a given workflow. On the subject of integrating GPU and software implementations, this approach can be extended by the concepts presented in this chapter: depending on the data, given platform, and type/sequence of operation, a conversion to the compression domain might be beneficial. For example, if the data set to be processed exceeds the graphics memory, but should be frequently updated and rendered, transferring it only for display is likely to be slower than compressing it once and perform all further operations on the GPU. This requires all operations to be compatible with the compressed representation and the quality of the compression process being sufficient for the purpose at hand, of course. As evaluated in this chapter, some computations in the compression domain outperform their spatial equivalent while leaving considerable potential for further optimization, especially using dedicated computing devices and APIs.

CHAPTER 5

OBJECT-ORIENTED GPU PROGRAMMING

The exponential growth of computational performance for graphics hardware has led to an increasing interest in utilizing this additional resource, also for traditional graphics tasks. Until recently, however, programming GPUs has been complex, error-prone, and rather low-level – and required thorough knowledge of computer graphics concepts. Although graphics hardware has become more programmable and flexible, it can still be regarded as a special purpose device with its own distinct architecture. Hence, the creation of GPU-based applications is still not as established and proven as their software counterparts. McGuire et al. allude to this development in [MSPK06]: »Modern GPUs manifest another turn of Ivan Sutherland's "Wheel of Reincarnation", where general-purpose and specialized hardware alternate as the best implementation technology.« With respect to the development tools, for example, there are only few programs available for shader programming. Usually these are non-standard tools based on research projects which are often far from mature products. For other aspects of development, such as debugging, things are even worse: there is no support for maintenance or proper design at all.

Recently, some developments got the field of available programming interfaces for graphics hardware moving. During the last quarter of 2006, Nvidia introduced the dedicated API "CUDA" (Compute Unified Device Architecture) for using the graphics hardware as computational device. Along with their toolbox of special drivers and libraries, compilers, etc., the newly released generation of graphics hardware simplified or removed several programming limitations. Based on the stream processing concept (see chapter 1) that has been applied to graphics hardware mainly by Buck [Buc05], computer graphics concepts have been replaced by standard parallel-programming notions, such as threads, streams, barriers, etc. Also, the programming language is an extension of standard C, which both addresses the majority of programmers well and does not render existing code obsolete.

As such vendor-specific developments often turn out to become a problem for standardized and commonly used solutions, multiple vendors and research groups have joined the establishment of a standard in spirit of the widely accepted OpenGL. This so-called "Open Computing Language" (OpenCL), has been officially proposed at SIGGRAPH 2008 together with basic driver support [SIG], with the first version released in November 2008 [Khr].

Consequently, there are neither many experiences, nor mature applications available at the time of writing, but early details indicate some resemblance to CUDA.[1]

However, all of these developments have one thing in common: they use rather low-level, procedural programming concepts. While this aligns well with the underlying hardware and allows access to intricate, performance critical details, aspects from software engineering such as modular design or code maintenance are still not addressed. On the other hand, traditional software implementations benefit from an established knowledge and research in object-oriented programming, which is the de-facto standard for most applications. Hence, this chapter introduces higher-level programming concepts to GPU programming, based on the contribution by Raspe et al. [RLP08]. Existing work in the context of (GP)GPU programming is presented and discussed first, extending the investigations by Palmer [Pal08]. Different aspects of object-oriented programming are discussed in the subsequent section, with references to the framework CASCADA developed in the course of this thesis. In the third section, a hierarchical representation of functionality to provide different abstraction levels is proposed as a key feature of the system. The fourth section addresses several concepts from software engineering that are relevant for the implementation of the framework. The chapter finally concludes with a short comparison of the results, and leads to a technical description of the proposed concepts that will be introduced in the next chapter.

5.1 Related work

With the increasing programmability of graphics hardware, considerable research has been done on improving the creation of shader programs and abstracting from the intricate details of the underlying hardware. Quite naturally have most of the contributions focused on graphics applications, i.e., the utilization of the GPU in its original design. General purpose applications, however, often require other functionality or program logic. Therefore, this section will introduce representative and fundamental work in the field of shader programming, to lead to an object-oriented approach. Some of the languages and concepts have been already described in general in chapter 1, so the focus here is on discussing the programming features and possible limitations thereof.

5.1.1 Shader programming

As introduced in the first part of this thesis, shader programming has quite rapidly evolved from pure assembly programming into what is usually referred to as high level shading languages. The mainly used languages are Cg, GLSL, and HLSL, the latter being the DirectX variant of Cg. These C-like languages provide means for graphics-oriented programming, i.e., additional data types are available, textures are accessible, etc. Also, some higher level of

---

[1] For more details on CUDA see section 1.2 in the introduction, and chapter 6 for the CUDA interface within CASCADA 2.

5.1. RELATED WORK

description has been available for both Cg and HLSL, which are again practically identical: CgFX [FK03] defines self-contained shader units called *effects*. These text files bundle vertex and fragment shader code with render passes, states and parameters to describe a complete shading procedure that can be applied to any geometry. Many advanced modeling packages support this format to allow the creation of complex shaders without explicit programming, e.g., for artists in game development. This purely graphics-based approach has been extended by Eissele et al. [EWE04] for their system working with data in image-space. While providing support for multiple render passes and simple GPGPU-like operations, the effects cannot be used to model arbitrary computations, especially under dynamic, data-driven conditions.

The majority of authors have proposed strategies for combining shaders at the level of GLSL or Cg code, however. To this end, shader programs are usually split into smaller building blocks, and augmented with additional semantic information. Graph representations allow for a flexible logical representation and evaluation of common execution paths, shared variables, states, etc. This representation of shader functionality as directed graph, with nodes representing shader fragments connected by input and output parameters, has been proposed long before the advent of shader hardware by Cook [Coo84]. Abram and Whitted [AW90] have extended this seminal work by introducing additional dependencies between the nodes not realizable with the data flow paradigm only. In addition, they propose automatic type conversion for parameters where applicable.

Abstract Shade Trees McGuire et al. [MSPK06] have implemented automatic parameter matching, although their approach involves multiple steps including some intermediate representation and abstract connections between the parameters. Thus, they are able to represent complex functionality at a higher, more user-friendly level and deferring the specific type matching to internal processing. They were also the first to apply the concepts with programmable graphics hardware in mind. However, their effect-based abstraction does not map directly to non-graphical, offscreen computations and is thus not applicable to the context of this thesis.

Dynamic Shader Generation for Flexible Multi-Volume Visualization The work by Rößler et al. [RBE08] is also for visualization purposes only. However, their application to multi-volume rendering and interaction is of high interest. They separate graph nodes into structural and shader nodes: the former implement operations like splitting or transforms, the latter represent the visualization. The underlying graph is exposed to the user in order to provide an easy graphical interface for composing such functionality. Their approach achieves decent real-time performance on commodity graphics hardware, where some penalties from expensive structural nodes and the linear complexity in the number of volumes are the main limiting factors.

Automated Combination of Real-Time Shader Programs In contrast to the aforementioned approaches, Trapp and Döllner [TD07] make no explicit use of graphs. They propose a system for an automatic combination of high-level shader programs during run-time. Therefore, shader code is split into small fragments and augmented with predefined semantic information. A two-step approach converts these tagged fragments into executable code that is controlled by an additional shader[2]. The different execution paths are represented by a look-up table in combination with static branching, thus limiting the performance penalty on modern graphics hardware. Although the examples given are for building, combining, and reusing graphics shaders only, the extension to GPGPU shader programs seems possible.

Shader Algebra In 2004, McCool et al. [MTP+04] have proposed an approach that realizes the combination of shaders in an algebraic way. Therefore, their meta-programming system Sh (see next section) is extended to support two basic operations, connection and combination, that act upon shaders and kernels as objects. While the former operation concatenates shaders with matching interfaces, the second integrates multiple shaders with one unified interface. In addition, they provide further optimizations (e.g., dead code elimination) and manipulators. For more complex (GPGPU) applications they only suggest extensions such as striding, sort, or scatter/gather operations, however.

SuperShader Another approach has been proposed by McGuire et al. [McG05] with their "SuperShader". Here, the key idea is to utilize the preprocessor available in most programming languages (GLSL in their case) to "templatize" shader code. Preprocessor directives implement different feature sets for more general functionality, thus avoiding potentially expensive branches during run-time; all the program's logic is finalized at compile-time instead. In addition, a caching strategy within the application (i.e., the C++ code) optimizes the performance for (re-)loading the shaders. However, this approach can hardly be extended to GPGPU applications, as non-graphics computations such as offscreen passes cannot be directly regarded as "effects" built by their modular control shader.

Object-Oriented Shader Design Before current developments of the different APIs (i.e., CUDA, Direct3D 11) have started to provide object-oriented shader programming, Kuck has introduced object-oriented concepts to shader programming in [Kuc07]. His work is comprised of two main components that implement the proposed system: an object system for GLSL and corresponding proxy objects in C++. In order to achieve a lightweight system without any overhead, concepts such as compile-time polymorphism and template metaprogramming are heavily used and thus rely on compiler optimization. Although some examples are outlined and motivate the problem-oriented (rather than hardware-oriented programming), the problem of tight coupling is not addressed and might lead to less reusable code.

---

[2]These shaders are usually referred to as "uber-shader" (alluding to the German word for "over"), and are related to the SuperShader described below.

5.1.2 Programming systems

The approaches reviewed in the preceding section provide additional layers and/or concepts for existing shading languages. On the other hand, several authors have investigated systems that abstract the functionality even further from the underlying driver or hardware. Although the graphics hardware is, of course, also utilized in the end, these systems either extend the GPU programming tool chain with additional layers, or replace complete processing steps with custom tools.

Shader Metaprogramming In 2002, McCool and others [MQP02, MT04] have presented a completely different approach, which has become the basis for the commercial RapidMind[3] platform in 2006. Their meta-language concept integrates shader functionality directly into the application code, where special macros and an additional library provide information when and where the code should be executed. Different backends implement the functionality for the particular platforms, including standard software solution or support for other processor types. In addition, two modes are distinguished: the so-called immediate mode corresponds to using Sh as a standard matrix/vector library, with all commands being sequentially executed. The retained mode, in contrast, compiles the functionality into shader programs (or the equivalent for the specified target platform) and issues the execution later. As Sh is built within C++, no additional compiler or other tool is required. Also, by exploiting scope rules of C/C++, their approach can handle uniform parameters elegantly and is able to delegate the necessary API code completely to the according backend. However, the performance of the generated code is inferior to manually written GLSL code due to redundancies or suboptimal constructs, as shown in [Mar06]. Although this has improved with newer and more flexible hardware, complex GPGPU applications have been realized with the commercial RapidMind system only. In addition, the integration of the shader implementation into the application code impedes the modification of (shader) functionality during run-time.

Brook for GPUs Quite a different approach has been developed by Buck et al. [BFH+04, Buc05]. Their platform-independent system "BrookGPU", that is based on a more general streaming model, completely hides graphics concepts and can thus be regarded as a pure GPGPU system. In section 1.2.4 the further developed system "Brook+" was introduced, which is based on the BrookGPU system outlined here. BrookGPU requires an additional (pre-)compilation step with the source-to-source compiler "brcc". This separates the implemented functionality into legal C/C++ code[4] and shader code (Cg). The emitted code can then be compiled into a standard application that uses the additional library "BRT" to invoke the kernels.

While this is rather similar to Sh, the outstanding feature is the support of user-defined data types. In addition to the standard, graphics-oriented types (see chapter 1) arbitrary

---

[3]http://www.rapidmind.net/, last visit Feb 22 2009
[4]Brook programs are implemented using an extension of the C/C++ language that requires processing before handing it over to the standard compiler. This is a common approach for many programming systems.

representations are possible. However, as BrookGPU defers the specific functionality as well as Sh to backends (OpenGL, DirectX, and software), these data types have to be mapped to the underlying hardware. Yet another relevant contribution of Buck's work is the establishment of a performance model. Therefore, the notion of "arithmetic intensity" is extended to "computational intensity" to deduce influential performance factors during run-time. As these concepts are important for the overall performance of GPU-based implementations, this topic is reviewed in section 8.2.1.

Accelerator While for Brook programmers have to divide the computations into kernels manually, the system proposed by Tarditi et al. [TPO06] does this automatically. In addition, the system performs the compilation process at run-time and is thus more flexible to use, especially with older hardware. Accelerator is implemented in C# and is based on data parallel operations translated to pixel shaders on DirectX. Thus, parallel arrays, i.e., standard arrays without index operator, are the principal data type, both for application and GPU code. Several operations are defined for them: element wise operations are available, as well as reduction and transformation functions. The mapping to pixel shaders is performed by evaluating the computation in an internal graph representation, with additional operations on it. However, the performance that has been achieved is inferior to hand-written code, with some scenarios even reversing the gain: computing the sum or matrix-vector multiplication is multiple times slower than software implementations. In addition, the authors give no information on the capability of the system to integrate visualization shaders or the platform dependency of the system.

GPU++ Another integrated GPU programming system has been presented by Jansen [Jan07]. His system called "GPU++" is comparable to Sh in that it incorporates the shader functionality into the host application, but uses a more generic class interface that completely abstracts from graphics processing. It uses a unified kernel definition for hiding the individual shader types (i.e., vertex or fragment shader) depending on the computation frequency, thus providing better utilization of the different units.[5] Also, Jansen proposes a novel approach to ease the strict vector processing paradigm (i.e., SIMD data types) by vector component decomposition and an efficient vector fusion. In order to further improve the performance for processing the underlying expression graph, simplifications of otherwise expensive language features (e.g., run-time type identification) are applied within the limited conditions for shader graph traversal.

The concepts are evaluated by implementing various GPGPU applications that achieve a performance gain of (multiple) orders of magnitude compared to software implementations. Code complexity is reduced in almost all cases in addition to the less GPU-specific code and thus required knowledge. However, the author does not address the visualization of (intermediate) results or the performance of mainly graphical applications. In addition, the

---

[5]Current graphics hardware uses the unified shader model to address this load balancing (see section 1.1). However, this enhancement has not been available during Jansen's work.

influence of data transfer, especially for complex user-defined data types is discussed only briefly.

Bulk-Synchronous GPU Programming Recently, Hou et al. [HZG08] have transferred the paradigm of bulk-synchronous parallel (BSP) processing to the GPU. This model describes parallel computations by grouping code into sequential sections of parallel threads, communication between these entities, and barriers where all threads are synchronized. These groups – they are called "supersteps" in their approach – represent one unit of computation. This allows the utilization of implicit data dependencies, with shared and visible local variables within such a unit. A custom compiler transforms this code into valid GPU instructions, that are in their case implemented using CUDA. Special care has been taken to realize the barriers efficiently (i.e., without stalling the processing too much), as well as analyzing the data flow for rapid streaming code. Furthermore, they provide novel features like thread creation and deletion[6], efficient communication between threads (as is crucial for the BSP model), and typical GPGPU operations such as reduce, scan, sort (see section 1.2.2 for fundamentals).

When compared to the aforementioned approaches, BSGP is advantageous in several ways. Brook (and CUDA) implementations, as well as other GPGPU approaches require the explicit handling of data dependencies, so that larger applications can become too complex to realize. Sh allows for simpler kernel implementations, but is not aware of dependencies between the kernels. The authors also show the benefit of their approach both regarding runtime performance and code complexity. For different applications, the BSGP implementations is often clearly faster than hand-written CUDA code. In addition, the code is less complex and even allows for the realization of otherwise unfeasible applications, such as an X3D parser. Although not explicitly discussed, the examples suggest that the system addresses the visual computing concept well, i.e., a seamless and efficient integration of visualization modules is possible.

5.1.3 Summary

In most of the shader programming approaches reviewed before, little information is given about how parameters shared by the main program and the shader code – referred to as *uniform variables* in Cg and GLSL – can be handled efficiently with minimal programming effort. Modular approaches that concatenate shader fragments [RBE08, AW90, MSPK06, TD07] focus on input and output parameter handling between individual shading modules, but do not address the question of how to incorporate shader parameters into an application. Among the shader programming methods, the object-oriented framework proposed by Kuck [Kuc07] is the only one that addresses the topic appropriately. In his approach, parameters can be exchanged between main program and shader code as members of common objects. Kuck stresses the fact that his system is lightweight, which certainly applies to the fact that it has no additional run-time costs. Yet, implementing a class shared by C++ and GLSL using his

---

[6]This corresponds to the `fork` and `kill` commands for software processes.

framework seems to be less intuitive than proper object-oriented programming in standard C++, mainly due to the heavy use of templates and macros in his approach.

For the complete programming systems, most of them implicitly address parameter handling. The metaprogramming approach by McCool et al. [MQP02], as well as Jansen's work [Jan07] allow the simple exchange and update of parameters, since both the main program and the shader code are written in C++. Although not specifically designed for GPU applications, BrookGPU [BFH+04] also provides means for convenient handling and exchange of host and "device" data. While Accelerator [TPO06] is built upon a dedicated data representation and tailored operations with inherent updating facilities, its focus is too narrow and achieves only suboptimal performance. However, such an integration cannot be applied to the solution that is developed in this thesis, as the intention is to use manually written and optimized GLSL code instead of monolithic applications; the reasons are elaborated in the remainder of this chapter. As such, BSGP by Hou et al. [HZG08] pursues a similar strategy and integrates advanced parallel computation paradigms into an existing environment (CUDA implementations in their case), and is thus able to outperform preceding approaches.

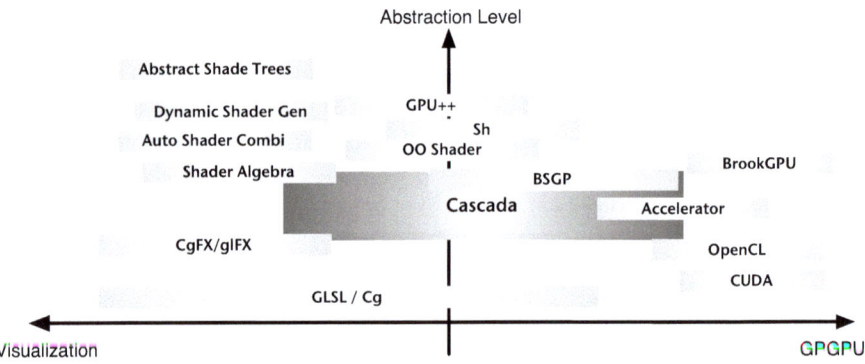

Figure 5.1: Classification of different GPU programming approaches with respect to general purpose or graphics applications. The illustration is based on [Pal08].

Although a direct comparison of the aforementioned approaches is not simple, an attempt to classify the systems is depicted in figure 5.1. Therefore, two dimensions have been identified: first, the focus of application, with pure graphics/visualization and pure GPGPU systems at both ends; the second axis is the level of abstraction from low-level programming to virtually no relation to the implementation details. Systems such as CUDA, for example, are mainly intended for GPGPU applications and thus ranked at the according position in the graph. While they are usually combined with visualization systems such as GLSL for display, their classification here is limited to their principal domain. Consequently, CASCADA covers a relatively wide range in both dimensions, as it integrates visualization and computation methods, and offers different levels of abstraction due to its basis on standard shading languages.

5.2 Object-orientation

Among the different programming paradigms, object-oriented programming has become very important, especially for large and complex software. Going back to the late 1960's (Simula) and later in the mid-1970's (Smalltalk), languages such as Java, C++, or C# have become mature and widely used systems. An extensive discussion of this topic would be way beyond the scope of this thesis, however. The focus in this section is moreover on introducing the elements that are relevant for "porting" object-oriented concepts to GPU programming.

Some of these ideas were already mentioned in the preceding section, where different existing approaches were reviewed. GPU programming based on high-level shading languages such as Cg or GLSL can be regarded as procedural programming, as these languages are usually both a subset and extension of the C language.[7] Therefore, the introduction of object-orientation to shader programming cannot be a full realization of all concepts of the object-oriented paradigm: the augmented functionality still has to be compatible with the underlying architecture, as GPUs are not general processing units as CPUs. In other words, as long as no object-oriented concepts are available for the graphics API[8], object-oriented programming is mainly limited to the application code, and shader code being extended only by few custom constructs.

In the following subsections, different aspects of object-orientation are discussed. After a short introduction of the main object-orientation concepts, entities that represent the building blocks for such an implementation on graphics hardware are outlined first. The communication of objects to realize data transfer, parameter control, etc., is the focus of the subsequent section. Although the concepts are not specific to one of the (currently) two versions of CASCADA, references to both version are given where appropriate.

5.2.1 Fundamentals

Following the object-oriented programming paradigm, the application to be implemented is comprised of objects that model the scenario. These objects usually encapsulate data and are so-called instances of classes. The classes serve as "templates"[9] for the objects' structure, where every single instance can have its own properties by setting the object's internal data accordingly. This control of the object's features is performed by methods with different access levels implemented by the object itself, thus defining a distinct interface to its environment (i.e., other objects). This principle is usually referred to as *encapsulation of data*.

Another key characteristic of object-orientation is *polymorphism*. Here, objects of different types can perform diverse operations (i.e., behave differently) through the same interface. This allows the system to implement dynamic behaviour that depends on the object and its internal functionality, and is thus not controlled in advance by the application logic. Therefore,

---

[7] A subset in the sense that not all constructs are available (e.g., pointers), and extension because additional means are provided (texture samplers, matrix types, etc.).
[8] Just recently, Shader Model 5.0 [Mic08] has been proposed and provides preliminary object-orientation within the shader/API, thus proving the concept of object-orientation for GPUs of being attractive.
[9] This is not related to the templates available in C++, or Java's generics, respectively.

entities can react at run-time by means of so-called late binding according to their current state, feature set, etc. Using this technique, the creation and/or replacement of objects that might be not known in advance is possible, for example.

Building upon the preceding concepts, and to enable the creation of complex applications, *inheritance* is another essential building block.[10] Accordingly, a subclass is a specialization of its base class and usually implements specialized features in addition to the ones inherited by the base class. This involves some issues regarding the implementation within the subclasses, that might be affected by different capabilities and specifics of the available programming languages. Where needed for the proposed C++ framework developed during this work, more details will be discussed; for information on other systems and languages, the reader is referred to the wealth of relevant literature on object-oriented programming.

5.2.2 Entities

The following paragraphs outline relevant parts of applying object-oriented concepts to GPU programming from the application's point of view. If there are noteworthy differences, both CASCADA versions will be described.

Wrapper classes Although there exist approaches to incorporate the shader code into the host application (see section 5.1.1), the underlying hardware is still controlled by API calls and programs executed in hardware. As mentioned before, applying object-oriented concepts to GPU programming is mainly restricted to the application. Wrapper classes provide therefore an additional layer of abstraction for this lower-level functionality. This allows on the one hand the utilization of object-oriented mechanisms of the respective language (i.e., C++ in this case), on the other hand concealing platform-dependent hardware details. Such a class that models a ShaderObject, for example, can provide a common interface to the user, while supporting implementations for different graphics APIs, generations, etc.; the term "back-end" describes this well.

Parameters Yet another fundamental entity in GPU programming are parameters, as they are used for the exchange of information. Although the details of this communication in the context of shader programs are subject of the next section, parameters are also interesting from an object-oriented point of view. Instances of classes such as ShaderObject, for example, represent specific functionality and are controlled by the application. Also, there are Parameter objects that contain (potentially complex) information to be passed between the application and the shader programs. When modeling reasonable scenarios, there will be several instances of ShaderObject that implement the workflow (usually on the graphics hardware), as well as a variety of Parameters. However, there would be some parameters that belong to one specific program only (e.g., a lookup texture), whereas others are the same

---

[10]For the sake of simplicity, inheritance will here be regarded as both inheriting the class's specification (i.e., interface) and implementation. Depending on the programming language used, multiple inheritance is used as well.

5.2. OBJECT-ORIENTATION

for several program objects (e.g., the current size of the rendering window). Obviously, some sharing mechanism is needed to prevent inconsistencies and, especially for large parameter objects, redundancies.

In CASCADA 1, parameters have been therefore separated into *local* and *global* entities, and require different handling. While local parameters can be implemented as instances created by the specific shader program, a superordinate mechanism is needed for controlling the global parameters' creation/deletion process, update of values, etc. Both are managed by a `ParameterSet` where one is part of the sequence or pass, while the other one is made globally available. Every set holds instances of the `Parameter` class template to support different types of parameters, such as single values, vectors, or textures.

Parameters play a different role in CASCADA 2. Here, each `Component` manages the input parameters that are needed for its computation, and provides the results as output parameters; both using the same interface via `ParameterSet`. Above that, there are local parameters available that represent properties (e.g., name) or states of the component. While `Modules` have "real" input and output parameters, hierarchical components such as `Sequences` and `Loops` merge the parameters of their child components by using different `join` operations. As will be shown below and in the third part of the thesis, the use of design patterns provides efficient and adequate solutions for handling the different, potentially shared parameters.

Containers Similar to the aforementioned wrapper classes, there are custom types and containers for representing data in the context of GPU programming. In addition to the standard low-level numerical types provided by the application programming language, elements of different complexity are needed for a convenient handling of data. At the first level, multi-component data types are provided that resemble the additional types in shading languages, such as `vec4` or `mat4x4` in GLSL. Since arrays of these basic elements are also directly supported in most shading languages, custom types can be created (e.g., for tensors). However, providing large amounts of data using such low-level `uniform` parameters is cumbersome, inefficient, and also severely limited by hardware resources. In order to overcome this situation, two more levels are used. Firstly, data can also be transferred per primitive, i.e., by assigning additional data to the elements the shader performs computations on: usually vertices for vertex shaders (as the first stage in the pipeline). These values are defined as specifically allocated memory and accessed in GLSL shaders using the `attribute` classifier. They are typically used to specify locally varying or sparse data.

The resources for such attribute data, however, are also limited per element. At the highest level in the hierarchy established here, texture objects are therefore the most commonly used representation for larger data, both for GPU and GPGPU applications. Consequently, there exist several graphics-oriented formats (e.g., `RGBA`), as well as "raw" formats that have become more flexible to use in recent years. These containers are also represented by wrapper classes in the framework to exploit object-oriented mechanisms, for example to hide the specific texture type. They use a single `uniform sampler` parameter of the particular type to be accessed from within the shader. Using textures for write-access is also a natural choice

– actually the only possibility in current APIs – to read data back from the GPU.[11] The details of this communication process, and the choice of the according hierarchy layer (i.e., default numerical types, custom uniform parameters, and texture objects) is the focus of the following section.

5.2.3 Communication

After considering different entities for an object-oriented GPU framework, the communication between these objects will now be discussed, again with a focus on GPU programming. Practically all the data that is transferred between the application and the shaders, and between the shaders themselves are referred to as parameters. However, there are certain limitations in the accessibility of these data elements (i.e., read-write modes), the size per parameter, or the overall number of parameters. Although depending on the specific graphics API that is used, most parameters can be separated by their classifiers:

uniform This type of parameter provides information for all shader programs during a single execution, i.e., one pass. These are read-only values for shaders.

attribute This parameter allows the transfer of data per primitive (usually per vertex). These parameters are also read-only for shader programs.

varying These values are transferred (and interpolated) between different shaders, but are not accessible from the application. They are writeable for the first stage (vertex program), and read-only for the subsequent stages (geometry/fragment program).

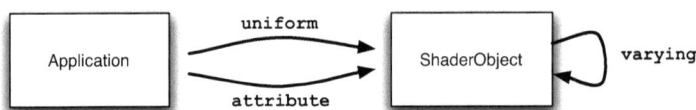

Figure 5.2: Communication between application and (GLSL) shader programs.

Figure 5.2 illustrates this relationship, where the unidirectional flow of information from the host application to the GPU dominates this communication. Actually, most of the data that is transferred in GPGPU applications is accessed via uniform parameters. Note that textures, for example, are also considered as uniform parameters. The application and/or framework employs optimization strategies to achieve reasonable performance. One of these strategies is the so-called "lazy evaluation", denoting the delay of data transfer until it is actually needed. This aligns well with the efforts to utilize the optimal device (i.e., CPU or GPU, depending on the algorithm, amount and type of data to be processed, etc.), which will be addressed in section 8.2.1.

---

[11]Especially for GPGPU applications the graphics-oriented notion of a texture is replaced by plain memory or buffer objects leading to a more flexible handling. Also, in dedicated systems such as CUDA, there exist other means for storing and exchanging data, but currently only under certain circumstances and performance considerations. See sections 1.1 and 6.3 for more information.

5.3. HIERARCHICAL REPRESENTATION

Setting up the connections between the host application and the parameters is only relevant for `uniform` and `attribute` data; `varying` values are set up within the shader code only. As stated before, the shader code is parsed before being handed over to the graphics API, so that for every `uniform` parameter an according `Parameter` object is created. For convenience, an initialization with default values directly from the shader code is also provided.[12]

The actual implementation of this communication process is realized by `Connection` objects in CASCADA 2. These objects resemble connections between output parameters of one component to the input parameter of another component. The input parameter is observing the output parameter in order to adapt its value. Such a connection instance is managed by dedicated `connect` and `disconnect` methods provided by each component. As already mentioned before, `Sequences` (as specialized components) can contain any other component, i.e., also sequences.

5.3 Hierarchical representation

After introducing object-oriented concepts for GPU programming in general, using a hierarchical representation for rendering and computation components offers additional benefits. Quite obviously, the abstraction from graphics programming details has many advantages, especially if performance-critical settings and functions are still accessible. While object-oriented programming already wraps low-level interfaces into classes, describing whole workflows would still be rather tedious in a one-level representation. Therefore, the developed framework represents its functionality using different hierarchy levels. The main benefits of this approach are:

1. Representing algorithms hierarchically emphasizes the desired workflow rather than the hardware-specific tasks (such as render texture setup, shader initialization, etc.)

2. The workflow's functionality and behaviour can be easily controlled at run-time in a graph-like structure.

3. Internal communication can be simplified at coarser hierarchy levels due to the higher-order semantics.

4. Different parts of the workflow can be easily re-used and interchanged, especially for both GPU and CPU implementations.

The first statement describes the overall motivation of the developed system, as a problem-oriented representation is more natural and powerful, while the lower levels allow a detailed and optimized implementation that takes the underlying hardware into account. As will be

---

[12]This feature can also be found in other systems such as CgFX [FK03]. The implementation details will be presented in chapter 6

discussed later, the workflow can be regarded as a graph[13] or, more specific, as a tree with additional constraints and conditions. Therefore, the behaviour at run-time can be easily controlled, e.g., activating a visualization sub-tree within an iterative computation only at certain intervals. The third aspect relates to the aforementioned communication between the different entities in such a system. While different kinds of parameters implement this communication at the shader code level, higher-order semantics can be defined for the exchange of (potentially data-driven) information for whole sequences, e.g., stopping criteria depending on preceding computations. Finally, re-using components is in general of high interest, whereas the approach proposed here also enables the interchangeability of different implementations (i.e., software, GPU code, or other bindings). These aspects are further introduced and discussed in the following paragraphs with respect to CASCADA 1. Where appropriate, additional information or references to related work is provided.

5.3.1 Hierarchical rendering components

The focus in this section is on the architectural and software engineering aspects in order emphasize the advantages over traditional approaches, i.e., using only high-level shading languages and standard APIs. The hierarchy of the framework is structured into three levels, as can be seen in the conceptual illustration on figure 5.3.

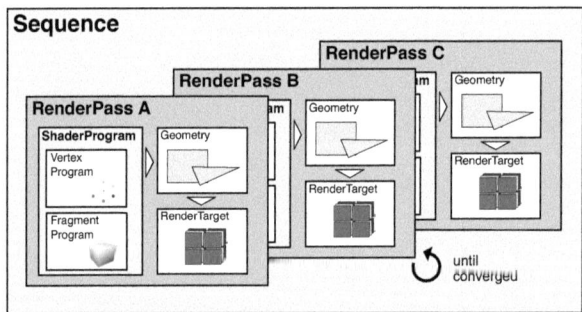

Figure 5.3: Conceptual illustration of the rendering hierarchy in CASCADA 1 with a focus on GPU functionality. `Sequences` are comprised of `Passes`, that in turn contain `ShaderPrograms`; note the additional semantics for data-driven control.

At the highest level there are *sequences* that encapsulate procedures ranging from simple thresholding to more complex operations such as region growing, for example. Although one sequence can contain all stages of a workflow, it is advantageous to keep sequences smaller to enable the reuse of their functionality in different contexts, as will be described later on. By utilizing the composite pattern (see 5.4.1), sequences are implemented as subclasses of `RenderComponent` and thus can contain sequences themselves, which allows for even more

---

[13]Actually, the graph representation has many features in common with scene graphs that are widely used in real-time computer graphics. For more information on scene graphs, see Akenine-Möller et al. [AMHH08], for example.

5.3. HIERARCHICAL REPRESENTATION

flexible and complex designs. Additional control is given by (de-)activating each component separately by setting according flags during run-time.

At the next level are *passes* that draw geometry with assigned shader programs to a defined target. For convenience, subclasses that already allow for offscreen rendering (i.e., screen-filling quadrilaterals to offscreen buffers), onscreen rendering of arbitrary geometry, volume raycasting, etc., are provided. These passes can resemble single operations or repeatedly run passes, controlled by a fixed number of iterations, or until some condition is met (e.g., region growing has converged). Especially for iterative algorithms, RenderLoops that wrap a render sequence being executed multiple times are additionally provided; this loop is then controlled by some RenderLoopCondition, which serves as an example for the higher order semantics mentioned above. The output of one pass is then used as input to the subsequent pass by setting the texture parameters accordingly.

Finally, *shader programs* resemble objects that contain GLSL programs. Figure 5.4 summarizes the relations of the hierarchical layout in a simplified class diagram:

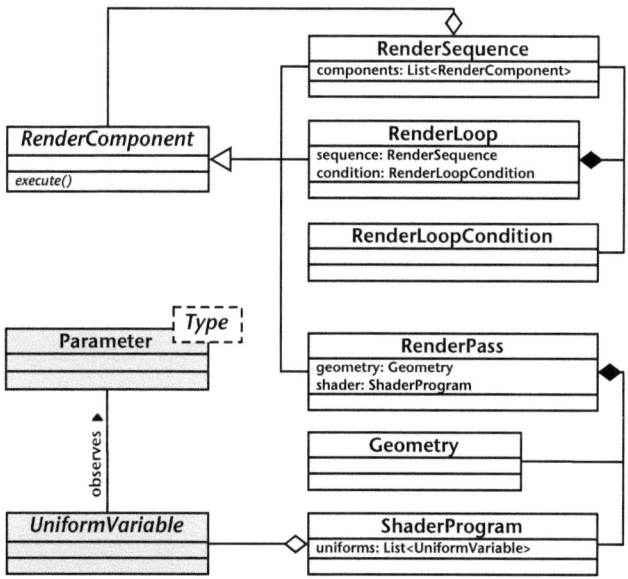

Figure 5.4: Simplified class diagram illustrating the main rendering components (yellow) and uniform variables (blue) in CASCADA 1.

5.3.2 Case Study

After describing the approach from a conceptual point of view, a reasonable scenario will be described. In this example, a segmentation sequence based on region growing is implemented. Input data in this case is volume data, but translates also to other data, of course. As can be seen from the legend in figure 5.5, most components of the sequence are implemented on the GPU, as the system focuses on GPU implementations. In addition to the superior performance – especially for volume algorithms – the data can be visualized during run time with a negligible overhead, as the data being processed is already in video memory. See chapter 3 for an extensive discussion of the benefits for such applications.

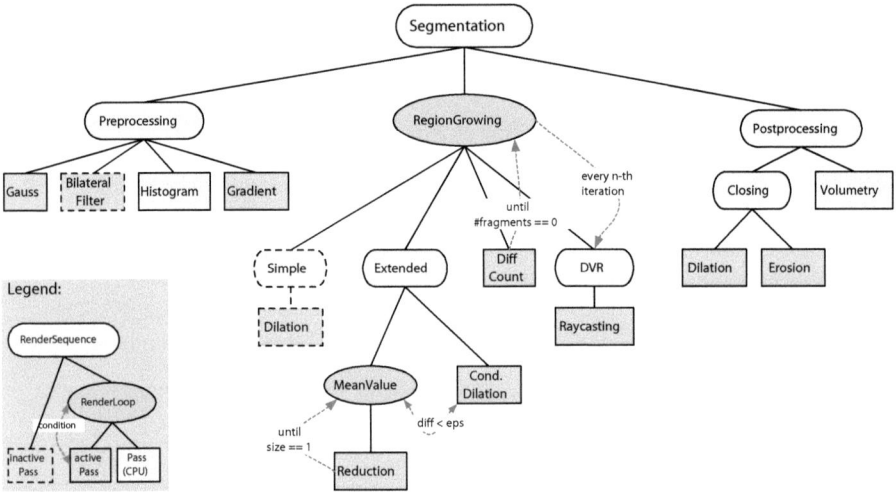

Figure 5.5: Example workflow for a volume segmentation procedure using the hierarchical approach and illustrated as graph. Note the annotations and the different components (specified in the inset legend).

The whole workflow of the segmentation example depicted in figure 5.5 is represented as a (simplified) tree that is traversed in depth-first order. The preprocessing sub-sequence is executed first by traversing all active components. In the example the bilateral filter has been deactivated, for instance, and is thus omitted. Additional information such as the histogram or gradients is computed on the following steps. CPU and GPU algorithms can be used interchangeably, for example based on a strategy taking the underlying hardware and the respective funtionality into account, as will be outlined in section 8.2.1.

The region growing (as example for iterative algorithms) is implemented as a `RenderLoop` that is executed until convergence. In the example, a simple implementation is skipped leading directly to the computation of the input data's mean value. A reduction shader iterates until the texture is at minimum size to compute the mean value (see section 1.2.2 for details). Afterwards, a conditional dilation is performed that uses the mean value for determining neighboring voxels. Then the difference between the current output and the output of the step before is computed, resulting in the number of fragments determined via occlusion queries (as optional property of `GLRenderPass`). If this number is zero, the region growing has converged (i.e., iteration n and $n-1$ do not differ) and the `RenderLoopCondition` can be set accordingly. Also, a visualization sequence is executed every n-th iteration, which comes at almost no performance overhead for GPU computations because no image/volume data has to be transferred. Finally, postprocessing is applied to the segmentation data: a typical morphological operation, followed by counting the number of voxels segmented in the given example. As mentioned before, different parts of the tree can also be reused, either separately (e.g., the DVR sequence) or in other sequences such as preprocessing.

This approach makes explicit use of the parameters involved in such a sequence to implement the communication between the components, as described in the preceding section. Examples for global parameters are in this case study the texture size (for neighbor access) or statistical values of the data itself. Local parameters, however, are specific to the individual sequences and/or passes: a threshold for the region growing, a structuring element for the morphological operations, etc. Most of the parameters are provided during run-time, that is when data-specific properties are available with each data set loaded. This results in an immediate update of all dependent parameters such as the number of iterations for the reduction shader, for example. The remaining values such as thresholds or quality settings for the raycasting sequence can be specified by the user, usually with a default initialization.

Although the proposed hierarchical representation offers a convenient model both for the internal implementation and the external description, the additional infrastructure and layers might impose a loss of performance with respect to plain GPU programming. In addition, the approach presented here does not built upon run-time neutral techniques such as macros or template meta-programming, as used extensively by Kuck [Kuc07], for example. Quite contrary to such thin layers, CASCADA actually utilizes multiple concepts from object-oriented programming including design patterns, in favour of clarity, extensibility and maintainability. Hence, this approach has to be evaluated in terms of run-time performance in order to justify the use of these potentially expensive concepts. Before assessing the system in section 5.5, however, some aspects of software engineering and related topics will be introduced first to complete the discussion of employed concepts.

5.4 Software engineering aspects

As discussed throughout this chapter, introducing object-oriented concepts to GPU programming is beneficial in different aspects. In addition to clearly definable interfaces, exchangeable and modular components, and hierarchical concepts, the maintenance and scalability of such software can be improved considerably. Without covering the full range of methods and strategies from software engineering, some aspects will be introduced and outlined here. More details with respect to the implementation in CASCADA will be provided in the next chapter.

5.4.1 Design patterns

In general software design, reusable approaches for common problems are usually referred to as design patterns. There exist different categories of these patterns, with more than 20 patterns being defined and extensively described in the seminal reference by Gamma et al. [GHJV95]. During the discussion of applying object-orientation to shader programming, some problems suggest the use of patterns. Actually, the evolution of CASCADA has led to the dedicated integration of commonly used patterns, either directly implemented within the system or indirectly through the use of libraries, such as Boost [Boo08]. While further technical details are going to be provided in chapter 6, the application of important patterns in the second version of the framework is outlined in the following list:

Observer In order to propagate change information, the observer pattern is a useful approach. Therefore, a subject notifies registered observers by calling their update function. The current implementation uses Boost's `signals` concept.

Composite This pattern is used for uniformly representing objects and compositions of these objects by means of an abstract class `Component`. While standard computations are referred to as `Module`, dedicated classes such as `Loop` or `Sequence` are further specializations.

Singleton Global data, such as preferences or universal states are implemented by means of the singleton pattern. The implementation often uses templates to allow a lightweight infrastructure.

Visitor Separating object structures and algorithms performing computations (or other operations) on these structures is the idea of the visitor pattern. Boost's `Variant` package provides means for using different objects uniformly and implements different versions of visitors.

Factory As another creational pattern, the factory method pattern is implemented to provide deserializations, i.e., to load and recreate objects persistently stored in files.

Proxy As a structural pattern, a proxy implements a substitute for other objects and controls the access to the real subject. This concept is used for referring to components being loaded at run-time by the `PluginLoader`.

Usually, the final implementation differs slightly from the general pattern, as is typical for applying design patterns to individual programming problems. In addition, some programming concepts are not directly implemented as patterns but realize related functionality; examples can be found especially in CASCADA 1. Finally, external libraries such as Boost or toolkits such as Qt [14] provide powerful and proven implementations of patterns, e.g., the signals-and-slots concept as realization of the aforementioned observer pattern. Where appropriate, existing implementations are thus preferred over self-written code.

5.4.2 Plugins

Plugins are widely used in software engineering and provide several advantages in contrast to static implementations. Due to the fact that these modules are external components, the

---

[14]`http://qtsoftware.com/products` (last visited: Jan 12th 2009)

5.4. SOFTWARE ENGINEERING ASPECTS

main library or application can be very lightweight and compact; only the interface has to be disclosed. In addition, plug-ins are usually connected to the host application during run-time as shared library, i.e., they do not require any changes or recompilation of the whole application. Hence, the host program can be extended dynamically with additional functionality. Plugins are above that often provided by a third party.

Although the exact definitions vary, there are some concepts related to plugins. *Extensions* actually modify or augment features already provided by the host. *Services*, on the other hand, resemble an addressable set of operations that implement further functionality. The boundary to the functions provided by the host application is in contrast well-defined for plugins, due to the clearly specified interface.

Implementing plugins in a cross-platform[15] environment is, however, rather challenging: for every operating system there are different concepts and techniques to implement the dynamic loading of external functionality. Although there exist implementations for handling plugins across all major platforms (e.g., the plug-in system of Qt) CASCADA's implementation is custom-built. On the one hand, this keeps the infrastructure as lightweight as possible, especially as no external library is involved. On the other hand, different wrapper classes hide the platform-specific details from the user, but can be adapted or extended, if needed. The `PluginLoader` uses the aforementioned instances of `Component` implementations as template parameter. Its use is related with the proxy pattern, in that a `ProxyComponent` can be used as base class for components that wrap other components. For example, the `PluggedComponent` encapsulates a `Component` dynamically loaded from a plugin.

5.4.3 Further concepts

Introducing object-orientation to GPU programming is usually limited to the application code, or at least the API binding. As mentioned in section 5.2, the lately presented Shader Model 5.0 [Mic08] transfers classes, interfaces, and other object-oriented concepts into the HLSL shading language. Although this enables shader programming at a higher level, it is currently restricted to the DirectX API. The OpenGL standard faced severe problems with its latest version in that it lags behind the developers' needs and recent hardware advances: no information about the implementation of an object model has been available yet. Therefore, the discussion here is mainly limited to application code, where relevant previous work was already presented in section 5.1. The evaluation in the subsequent section provides more detail on shader code.

Unit tests have been introduced as another software engineering method for CASCADA 2. It is used for verifying the proper functionality of small, testable source code units. In object-oriented programming these units are usually methods that belong to classes within a limited scope of the class hierarchy. In order to benefit from the advantages of unit testing (faster identification of errors, integration support, additional documentation, etc.) and keep

---

[15] As will be described in chapter 6, CASCADA supports the major operating systems Windows, Mac OS X, and Linux. For graphics hardware, there is no such separation needed, whereas Nvidia systems are preferred due to their wider and more flexible driver support.

the additional workload to a minimum, the external framework "UnitTest++"[16] is used throughout the development and testing of CASCADA 2.

Finally, the concept of persistence has become an integral part of practically all components within the framework. Persistence refers to the possibility of storing information about the program beyond its execution, e.g., after restarting the application. Therefore, all relevant data has to be collected and written into one or multiple files. The files' format should allow the reloading of this information to restore all components, data, etc. In CASCADA 2, persistence is implemented using XML, where all relevant classes provide writing functionality. Reading is realized by applying the factory method pattern mentioned before.

5.5 Evaluation

After discussing related work and several concepts for hierarchical, object-oriented GPU programming, these concepts should be evaluated with respect to code reusability and flexibility, as well as overall performance. While the former aspects are discussed based on examples and representative scenarios, the rendering performance is compared to plain OpenGL code, as far as possible in practice. Hence, the main questions are:

- How well can the (shader) components be re-used in practice, also with respect to the different versions of the framework?
- What is the impact on the computation/rendering performance introduced by object-oriented methods?

In order to answer the questions, the different approaches will be outlined from a technical point of view first, with reference to related systems or current (GP)GPU developments. Although CASCADA is presented in-depth in the following chapter, the required details are introduced here. Subsequently, the results are presented and discussed, and the chapter is finally concluded by a short summary. Other criteria such as code maintenance, debugging, or the level of difficulty (i.e., the training curve) do not differ from standard applications programming and are thus addressed only briefly.

5.5.1 Reusability

In section 5.1 several approaches in different fields of application were discussed. While most of them differ substantially from a technical point of view, the common purpose is the simplification of shader programming by means of abstraction, modularization, etc. – either on the application side or directly in the shader programs. Some systems (e.g., Sh/RapidMind) integrate both aspects, but virtually no information is provided about factors such as code reuse or flexibility in real life examples.

---

[16] http://unittest-cpp.sourceforge.net/ (last visited Jan 12th 2009)

5.5. EVALUATION

CASCADA has evolved from a specific project in the medical context (see section 7.1 for background information) in two diverse directions, that will be described in detail in chapter 6. Although at different stages of development, the concepts and techniques for handling shader code are practically equal for both versions.[17] On the other hand, the non-rendering, i.e., application-side components are much more coupled and interrelated in CASCADA 1 than in the second version. Thus, the two frameworks are treated alike for shader code reuse, whereas in the discussion of application code the systems are differentiated.

Shader code

Reusing shader code is a highly relevant topic for practically all rendering systems which is mainly due to two facts. Firstly, the utilization of custom shaders has superseded the use of the fixed function pipeline almost completely today. This results in a large number of shaders that are created for advanced effects and computations. Secondly, using the different shaders in various contexts leads to what is usually referred to as "combinatorial explosion": for every new effect to collaborate with all other shaders another dimension is added, thus entailing a factorial number of combinations. For example, if there are three different materials that should be lit by six types of lights, this already totals to 18 shaders. Adding four different environmental effects (e.g., fog) leads to no fewer than 72 combinations, and so on.

Although the situation for GPGPU shaders is less dramatic – there are fewer "dimensions" with less variations – reusing as much shader code as possible will be of great benefit. As complete object-oriented concepts are not fully available in shader programming today[18], different authors have proposed to assemble fully functional shaders from small code fragments; see Trapp and Döllner [TD07] or McCool et al. [MTP+04], for example. This concept is also available in CASCADA by means of either application-controlled concatenation of different shader programs, or the direct inclusion within the shader code; a feature that has not been available in GLSL until recently. While the latter approach is limited to shader fragments of one shader type (i.e., vertex or fragment programs), the concatenation of various types into the shader object provides even more flexibility. This has been shown in the preceding chapter where convenient access to compressed data is provided, for instance: the external shader fragment waveletFunctions.frag.glsl is integrated by several shaders working with wavelet data. Technical details of this feature are provided in section 6.3.4.

Yet another example for reusing shader code is in the context of computations, that is explicitly for GPGPU applications. The case study described in section 5.3.2, for example, contains several computations that are relatively similar and therefore potential candidates for reuse. As depicted in figure 5.5 on page 150, the preprocessing stage provides a Gaussian filter, a (deactivated) bilateral filter, and the computation of gradients. All of them can be described by a standard convolution filter, each with different coefficients and potentially varying mask

---

[17]CASCADA 2 also supports Nvidia's CUDA, which requires rather different handling and cannot be directly compared here. However, the CUDA module is designed to directly interface the GLSL components, so that the discussion is relevant for the CUDA module as well.

[18]Recently, DirectX 11 [Mic08] has been released with respective advancements, esp. dynamic linkage for reducing the number of shaders.

size, respectively. Different kernel sizes were successfully used in the collaborative work by Langs and Biedermann [LB07] and Erdt et al. [ERS08], both outlined in chapter 3. The following example shows a general convolution filter of fixed size:

```
uniform sampler2D inTex;     // input data (flat3D RGBA)
uniform float kernel[27];    // weights (3x3x3 mask)
uniform vec3 offsets[27];    // neighborhood info

void main()
{
  vec4 sum = vec4(0.0);

  // convolution
  for ( int i = 0; i < 27; i++ )
  {
    // get current neighbor and sum up with corresponding weight
    sum += getNeighbor( offsets[ i ], inTex ) * kernel[ i ];
  }
  // output
  gl_FragColor = sum;
}
```

Listing 5.1: General convolution shader for $3 \times 3 \times 3$ kernels.

As CASCADA has been designed to perform complete workflows that are comprised of single computation steps, the implementation of a filter sequence is straightforward. The different shaders are usually parameterized, that is, the individual functionality is controlled either by internal computations (e.g., iteration count) or upon user input (e.g., thresholds).

In addition to arbitrary combinations, dedicated filters such as the Laplacian of Gaussian or morphological closing (see the postprocessing stage in figure 5.5) are also possible. Nevertheless, their performance can be expected to be inferior to combined kernels due to additional overhead introduced from multiple shader executions, as will be discussed below. Also, separating filter kernels into one-dimensional vectors that are applied n-times for n-dimensional kernels would also result in a reduced number of operations. In contrast to CPU implementations, however, the kernels have to be extremely large for the optimization to pay off; again due to the organizational overhead.

Application code

On the application side, most of the general concepts were already addressed in section 5.4. As mentioned above, the two versions of the framework vary considerably. Whereas the second version is in essence designed as a library consisting of different packages (e.g., `CascadaCore` or `CascadaGL`), the first variant does not provide such a clear separation.

In addition, CASCADA 2 implements several software engineering concepts, where especially the plugin architecture helps to reuse code. It allows the flexible handling of modules which can be loaded and combined in different contexts during run-time. Another, rather obvious feature of object-oriented programming is the concept of having instances of a class with individual properties. Translating this to the aforementioned example of the convolution filter, a (notional) class Convolution would contain the particular settings and coefficients to represent different kernels for CPU implementations.

5.5.2 Performance

Performance issues are often mentioned as a disadvantage of design patterns and other object-oriented programming techniques that involve indirections, virtual methods, etc. Unfortunately, evaluating the performance of such approaches is rather complicated in comparison to traditional, procedural shader programming, and can be found only rarely in literature. Most of the publications discussed in section 5.1 describe their approaches in principle and use some representative examples to prove the concepts. An extensive evaluation and comparison for the meta-programming language Sh can be found in the thesis by Michelle Martin [Mar06]. However, due to the cessation of the open source development of Sh and the rapid advances of graphics hardware since then, the results can be transferred to today's systems only to a limited degree. Another, more recent example of thorough assessment can be found in [HZG08] by Hou et al. In their work, code complexity and style, as well as the resulting performance and memory consumption are compared to a CUDA-based system by implementing different scenarios from various fields of applications. In addition to criteria such as developer time and code complexity, objective metrics such as rendering/computation performance and memory consumption are clearly in favour of their approach.

To assess the performance of the framework developed in the course of this thesis, an evaluation as complete as Hou's would be beyond the scope of the chapter. In addition, CASCADA is currently based on standard GLSL shaders implementing (mainly) image processing and segmentation functionality, thus leading to a much narrower focus of applications. A rather coarse estimation of the system's performance with respect to software implementations was already described in section 3.1.3, with a clear advantage for the GPU, especially when whole sequences are executed on the graphics hardware. In what follows, the performance achieved by using object-oriented programming is going to be compared to an "unrolled" version of the (on- and offscreen) rendering steps[19], i.e., sequential OpenGL calls. Two different approaches have been developed and are described in detail below. Firstly, all OpenGL calls are logged within CASCADA and replace the original high-level code. Secondly, an additional tool is used for recording OpenGL calls independent from the underlying implementation and transforming the information into a code module. While the first method has been implemented using CASCADA 1 and was used for the measurements below, the second approach is still under development and outlined only briefly.

The measurements were performed on a commodity PC (Intel Core2Duo 2.4 GHz, 2 GB RAM, Nvidia Geforce 8800 GTS 640MB (G80)) and an MRI data set ($256 \times 256 \times 16$, 16 bit). The assessed operations are binary thresholding, Laplacian of Gaussian ($3 \times 3 \times 3$ mask

---

[19]Note the resemblance to "loop unwinding" that is used for optimizing the run-time performance of code by transforming loops into sequential code, resulting in a trade-off between code size and efficiency. This technique was the only method of realizing loops in shaders for early shader generations.

size, two separate passes), and a region growing sequence similar to the one discussed in section 5.3.2; measurements for the first two operations were averaged over 100 runs.

Embedded logging

In order to convert object-oriented GPU computations into linear OpenGL code, a Python script adds code fragments for extracting relevant OpenGL calls from an executed sequence. This results in a modified version of CASCADA, where for every OpenGL call an additional message is assembled from the current function name, its parameters (e.g., texture units, memory addresses) and other relevant information as conditional macro. This logging mechanism records all the executed commands into a file, which is afterwards included and compiled instead of the high-level method call. By embedding this logged sequential code into the application, the memory addresses, textures, input parameters etc. are ensured to be initialized and valid.

Operation	OOGPU	OpenGL	Difference
Binary	6.25 ms	6.87 ms	+9.9%
LoG	11.56 ms	12.19 ms	+4.6%
RegionGrowing	6.97 s	6.38 s	−8.46%

Table 5.1: Performance comparison for different GPGPU operations.

As can be seen in table 5.1, the run-time performance of the smaller sequences is even slightly better than the plain OpenGL version, whereas the rather complex region growing implementation does not benefit from object-oriented GPU programming. This seems to be related to the fact that especially the region growing sequence consists of multiple shader programs and requires more than 200 iterations to converge for the given data set. Another factor is the compiler's output, as the object-oriented code can be processed differently than the linear equivalent.

Wrapper library

While the first approach has been customized for CASCADA 1 and requires the manual modification for every feature addition or code change, the second method employs the external tool GLIntercept[20] to record the OpenGL calls. As before, this intermediate layer between the framework and the graphics API creates different types of logs and saves them to files, with XML as the preferred format due to its inherent structure. Finally, these log files can be transformed into source code by using XSLT scripts.

The main advantage of this approach is the improved flexibility to changes in the application, to support new OpenGL extensions, and a much cleaner integration into the test system. As CASCADA 2 utilizes the concept of plugins, the complete sequence that should be assessed will be logged into the file and then compiled into one plugin replacing the

---

[20] http://glintercept.nutty.org, last visited Feb 10th 2009

whole sequence. Just as for the first approach, the "environment" for correct execution of the recorded functionality has to be ensured by loading the according input data, parameters, etc. This can be done by specifying all data as input parameters of the plugin.

5.6 Conclusion

In the course of this chapter, several approaches for adding object-oriented and hierarchical approaches to traditional GPU programming were proposed. After reviewing various contributions of different development stages and generations of graphics hardware, object-orientation was introduced first. Although this has been mainly limited to the host application due to current restrictions of shader programming, some useful extensions and simplifications have been applicable to shaders as well. The introduction of hierarchical concepts allowed a further abstraction from low-level details in order to provide a more workflow-oriented view. Therefore, existing entities are represented at different levels of granularity by exploiting object-orientation mechanisms such as inheritance or design patterns. This enables the flexible control of detailed features and parameters on the one hand, and the efficient and integrated specification of GPU functionality on the other hand. After outlining further concepts from software engineering that have been used especially in the second version of CASCADA, the results were evaluated in terms of code reuse and performance.

The methods introduced in this chapter had a positive effect in regard to both aspects. Firstly, the flexibility and reusability of code has been increased, especially for shader programs. Modern applications in the field of visual computing already make use of object-orientation, so the benefits are more of structural nature. However, several improvements for shader programming led to a considerable reduction of code complexity and thus enabled reuse and flexible parameterization. While such techniques usually have a negative influence on the rendering and/or computational performance, only moderate additional run-time costs – depending on the operation performed – were measureable. Given that the implementation of complex workflows is greatly simplified by using the aforementioned approaches, in practice the performance penalty is clearly outweighed. In addition, both the application and the shader implementations have not been fully optimized yet, so the performance gap can be expected to become even smaller.

Recent advancements of graphics hardware and programming platforms indicate that some of the concepts are going to be provided directly by the drivers or run-time environments of the according graphics APIs. For example, the latest release of DirectX introduced further techniques from object-oriented programming right into their shading language HLSL. Also, the once fixed-function pipeline continues to become a fully flexible and highly parallel infrastructure, with larger local memories, additional types of processing units (e.g., compute shader, hull shader), etc. Finally, dedicated computing systems such as Nvidia's CUDA or OpenCL provide a more general, yet still rather low-level view to the hardware. Approaches towards a higher level of abstraction are still going to be relevant for these non-graphics systems as well.

Part III

Applications

CHAPTER 6

THE FRAMEWORK "CASCADA"

This chapter describes the programming framework that was developed for GPU-based processing and visualization, as well as the projects and applications based on it. During its evolution, the system has been named CASCADA because of the suitability and descriptiveness of the word. With the meaning "waterfall" in several languages, it describes the framework's intention very well: (volumetric) data is flowing through different stages or levels. In addition, the word contains the acronym "CAD" for computer assisted diagnosis/detection as introduced in section 2.1.3, and as was the main focus of several applications for this work.

After outlining the motivation for implementing such a framework, the subsequent section will provide an overview of the system. Here, the focus is on discussing design choices, outlining system requirements and external libraries, as well as selected extensions. The third section will provide a closer look on implementation details, also based on the discussion from the preceding chapters about compression computing and object-oriented concepts. As there are several differences between the two versions of CASCADA regarding key concepts such as volume representation or the rendering system, they will be described separately. Also, the generalization of GPU programming by means of the CUDA API will be covered as well. The chapter will conclude with final remarks and prospects to further developments after a short presentation of approaches for application development.

6.1 Motivation

There exist several ways of programming the graphics hardware, as already mentioned in the preceding chapters. While in section 1.1 the focus was primarily on shading languages, these can serve only as the basic layer of a system for processing and analyzing data: neither the programmer who, for example, implements a segmentation method, nor the user who is supposed to control parameters while interacting with the data should care about intricate details like texture coordinates, the layout of the render target, and so on.

Therefore, the system should provide an *abstraction* from its low-level components, but at the same time maintain means for programming specific functionality if needed. Hence, the introduction of object-oriented programming concepts and hierarchical approaches in chapter 5. However, the benefits of an improved programmability, maintenance, and structure should not be alleviated by comparatively high performance penalties on the application and/or algorithm due to the abstraction. This led to considerations towards a *classification* of computations: for the current situation (e.g., hardware configuration, size/type of data, algorithm), the most efficient implementation method should be (ideally) automatically estimated; see section 8.2.1 for further considerations.

Providing a basis for different projects and theses in the *educational context* was yet another objective for the framework. The building blocks in shader programming play an important role in learning modern computer graphics. However, at a certain level programming everything from scratch hampers advanced development, becomes error-prone, and might have a negative effect on the overall motivation. Becoming acquainted with considerable amounts of external code is also of great importance during student projects. These considerations finally gave rise to the development of a more modular architecture with clearly defined interfaces in CASCADA 2. Although this version is still work in progress, several features were addressed in sections 5.2 and 5.4 already. In the next section, key concepts and related topics are going to be described from an implementational point of view.

Finally, CASCADA was used for several example applications and *projects* during the course of this thesis. The project "LiverGPU" that will be presented in the next chapter has been the origin of the framework, and was extended by many subsequent developments. As this first version has become a rather unwieldy mixture of both library functionality and application, the second development started from scratch, with special attention to modular design and utilization of software engineering concepts and tools. Thus, both versions of CASCADA will be described in the subsequent paragraphs from different points of view in most cases: the first version for describing several GPGPU programming concepts, fundamental representations of data, rendering infrastructure, etc.; the second because of its advanced object-oriented design and overall flexibility.

6.2 Overview

6.2.1 Structure

Due to the fact that the implementation of CASCADA 1 originally started to develop a GPU-based segmentation system, its architecture depicted in figure 6.1(a) consists of both library and application components. Based on different types for software and hardware implementations alike, denoted as `BaseTypes` and `GLTypes`, respectively, data and rendering infrastructure provides a toolset for implementing visual computing algorithms. Supplemented by means for reading/writing data (`I/O` component) and further tools for type conversion, logging, etc., as well as a graphical user interface, several entities make up the application; details about these "managers" are provided in section 6.3.5.

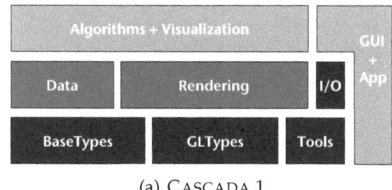
(a) CASCADA 1

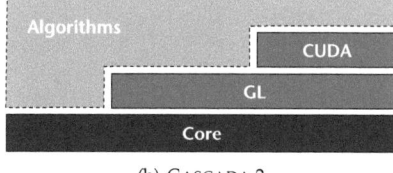
(b) CASCADA 2

Figure 6.1: Comparison of both CASCADA versions as broad overview. While CASCADA 1 (a) is a conglomerate of library and application, CASCADA 2 is realized as library (b) for implementing algorithms.

The building blocks of the framework's second version are shown in figure 6.1(b). As can be easily seen, CASCADA 2 consists of a basic core library that is supplemented by two additional libraries providing support for OpenGL and CUDA, respectively. Algorithms can either use `CascadaCore` for basic software implementations of volume processing, but usually displaying the data is also desired: therefore, `CascadaGL` is available, or additionally `CascadaCUDA`. While the latter provides a more general programming interface, visualization resorts to the graphics API. The creation of applications and algorithms can be done as for CASCADA 1 via direct programming, or using an external editor, that will be shortly outlined in section 6.3.5 as well.

6.2.2 System requirements

Since the first prototypes and implementations starting in September 2006, CASCADA has been developed with platform independence in mind. This includes both the support of all major operating systems (Windows, Mac OS X, and Linux), and the cross-vendor (Nvidia and AMD/ATI) implementation for graphics functionality – as far as was practical. Therefore, only few external libraries have been employed: firstly, GLEW [IM08] to allow the convenient use of OpenGL extensions; secondly, OpenEXR [KBH04] for the `half` data type, in combination with the OpenGL extension `GL_HALF_FLOAT_NV` for the hardware equivalent; finally, the

`FramebufferObject` (FBO) class provided by the GPGPU community[1] has been integrated into the framework.

In addition to utilizing unit tests during development (see section 5.4.3), CASCADA 2 employs the cross-platform build system "CMake" [CMa08]. This tool is used by numerous other platforms, and supports practically all programming environments and external systems such as CUDA.

As mentioned in the introduction, the framework uses the OpenGL Shading Language (GLSL) for all graphics hardware implementations. This is mainly due to the fact that GLSL was less vendor-dependent than other languages (e.g., Cg), despite the somewhat limited flexibility. Additionally, GLSL's architecture does not require external tools: the hardware driver contains compiler, linker, etc., as outlined in section 1.1.2. Although there exist fallback implementations for systems that support only OpenGL 1.5, the de-facto standard OpenGL 2.x is recommended, especially for advanced shader functionality. This corresponds to the actual hardware supported by the framework: Shader Model 3.0 compliant systems (i.e., NV4x and above) are needed for most implementations. However, if advanced techniques such as geometry shaders or integer textures are used, recent hardware (Shader Model 4.0) is required.

CASCADA 2 uses GLSL for shader implementations as well, but additionally features the support of Nvidia CUDA. While this would have been possible for the first version, too, the much clearer interfaces and separate modules were better suited for targeting at the second version. In order to use the CUDA module, hardware supporting the API as well as corresponding drivers are obviously needed. In practice, all Nvidia graphics cards of the Geforce Series 8 or above are required.[2]

6.2.3 Extensions

During the development of CASCADA 1 several student projects extended the framework's functions with respect to user interaction. Firstly, standard mouse functionality can be augmented with 3D input using the SpaceNavigator [3Dc08]. This is useful for coarse navigation or manipulation of the volume visualization, especially in combination with the mouse for fine-grained control. Secondly, the Phantom Omni [Sen07] has been integrated to support three-dimensional interaction at different scales, that is, for coarse navigation as well as for picking, drawing, etc. As the device also features force feedback, example implementations demonstrate haptic volume rendering. Combining this with the concept of RayTextures (section 3.2.1) would be an interesting extension, because of both the straightforward 3D-to-3D mapping of user input, and the tangible interaction with parameters.

In addition to the different visualization options for volume rendering introduced in section 1.3, the utilization of three-dimensional displays is another extension. Based on

---

[1] http://www.gpgpu.org/developer/ (last visit Mar 9 2009)
[2] CUDA is also supported on dedicated GPGPU hardware such as Nvidia Tesla systems. Although these have not been available for development during the course of the thesis, "porting" `CascadaCUDA` should be straightforward, if required at all.

a student's project, any OpenGL rendering can be enhanced for being displayed on a 3D screen by means of shaders. Although the original implementation was designed for the auto-stereoscopic display C-i by SeeReal [See08] featuring interleaved columns for left-eye/right-eye information, it is not limited to such configurations only: virtually all types of stereo-rendering (including anaglyph, time-multiplexed, etc.) can be implemented. The basic idea of "StereoMaker" is to grab the current camera settings and replace the single rendering by shifting its position slightly for two-eye sight, and render both views into an offscreen buffer (i.e., texture) first. The final onscreen rendering step is then performed by a custom shader that assembles the image depending on the display's layout; in the aforementioned setup using columns from both renderings alternatingly.

6.3 Implementation

The following paragraphs summarize several features of the framework's implementation, and discuss special functionality or enhancements. After an overview of the general architecture and basic entities, the representation and handling of volume data, as well as important aspects of GPU programming are going to be addressed. In these sections, the two version of CASCADA are discussed separately, whereas the subsequent description of internal shader handling is mostly similar for both versions. Further concepts such as the plugin system, former approaches to application programming, or the external editor "Fountain" are shortly outlined at the end of this section.

6.3.1 General information

Many concepts of CASCADA 1 were already described in the preceding chapters, particularly in chapter 5. As most of the implementation details are also relevant for the second version, these are going to be shortly reviewed in this section.

Practically all data in CASCADA is based on custom fundamental types. Inspired by SIMD-like[3] vector types used in shading languages, they are also implemented in software by means of template classes: `BaseVec{1|2|3|4}<T>` are the base classes. For convenience, typical types are pre-defined, e.g., `Vec3f` (three floats), `Vec4ui` (four unsigned int), or `Vec2b` (two booleans). Conversion between these types is provided by the tool class `TypeConversion`.

Later in CASCADA 1, the concept of *variants* has been implemented for manipulating objects of different types in a uniform manner. That is, the class `Variant` realizes a data type that can hold data of various kind, but only one at a time, to avoid internal type conversion. In contrast to the basic `union` type provided in C-languages, both the actual data and additional information about the type are stored, as well as according methods are provided for correct data access. This concept is extensively used in the core of CASCADA 2 (fig. 6.2), however by resorting to the implementation provided by the Boost library [Boo08]. In addition to the

---

[3] The support of native SIMD operations is left as future work, as the focus for CASCADA has been the utilization of the GPU. Therefore, the CPU performance has to be considered suboptimal, especially on modern processors.

basic concept and highly optimized code, the library also implements the visitor pattern and supports recursive types; see the Boost documentation for further information.

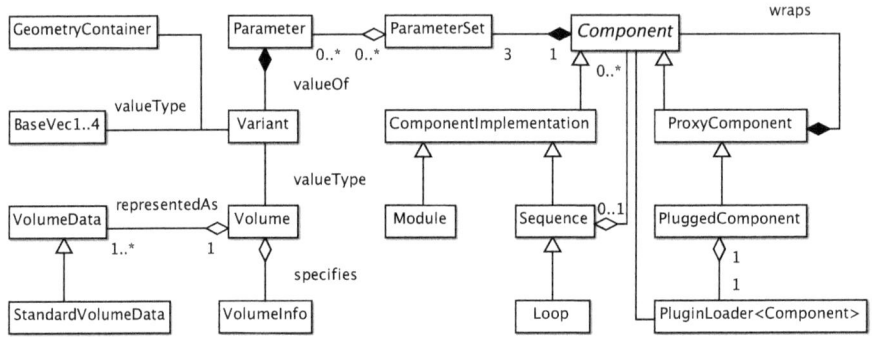

Figure 6.2: Simplified class diagram of CASCADA 2's core package.

As lots of memory has to be allocated and shared among multiple "owners" in a system for volume data processing and rendering, the possibility of programming errors due to extensive memory handling is increased considerably. To reduce this complexity, the idea of *smart pointers* provides means to automatically keep track of unused objects. Thus, the framework uses Boost's implementation (`shared_ptr` template) for practically all heap-allocated objects.

In addition to Boost, "TinyXML" [TBE08] is integrated as another external library for XML support. It is a lightweight C++ XML parser that provides all required functionality, such as parsing, editing, and writing data to XML files. In contrast to CASCADA 1, where XML files have been used only for defining parts of the user interface and basic shader functions, the second version of the framework features persistence for practically all classes. Therefore, an `XMLHelper` class disassembles the according objects that provide a `toXML()` implementation, and writes the whole structure to a file. Deserialization as the inverse process is realized by the factory method pattern: `ComponentFactory` creates the according objects.

Finally, `Component`s represent any kind of computation and are thus the main building blocks of applications that use the `CascadaCore` library. As outlined in section 5.2, a component manages the input parameters needed to perform the computation, and provides its results as output parameters, both with the same interface via `ParameterSet`. Objects of this class store the input and output parameters and provide according access methods, as well as local parameters for the component's name or activation state, for example.

`Component` is an abstract base class: components can be hierarchical, since there are composite and leaf implementations of `Component`, according to the composite design pattern. As illustrated in figure 6.2, the leaf is `Module`, while the composite implementations are currently `Sequence` and `Loop`. In addition to the actual realizations of `Component` – which are subclasses of `ComponentImplementation` – there is also `ProxyComponent`. It

6.3.2 Volume representation

One of the "first class citizens" in CASCADA is the class `Volume`. From the very beginning of the framework, data has been represented as three-dimensional regular grid.[4] While the data acquired by medical imaging procedures is usually organized as a series of two-dimensional slices or images, representing the data volumetrically is natural and often advantageous for visualization and processing purposes, as shown in chapter 3. Although there exist multi-dimensional formats (e.g., DTI), all of the volume data considered here consist of scalar values; vector information such as gradients is either computed on-the-fly or handled separately. Depending on the specific acquisition method and configuration, the voxels' layout, coordinate systems, and other properties are usually given by meta-information (e.g., DICOM header), or defined by the global setup; see also section 2.2.

As already mentioned in preceding chapters, the utilization of graphics hardware – especially through the use of graphics APIs – requires special attention for an efficient handling of large amounts of data. Thus, lots of researchers have addressed this topic and proposed various approaches to achieve optimal performance for practically all hardware generations; see Engel et al. [EHK+06] and Akenine-Möller et al. [AMHH08] for further information and references. While the contributions and concepts in the course of this thesis have been implemented with attention to good performance, the focus has not been on highly advanced optimizations, as they tend to become obsolete with subsequent driver versions or hardware generations. Furthermore, the implementation of the CUDA API allowed to overcome several restrictions of graphics interfaces.

CASCADA 1

There are different volume implementations for software and hardware, of course, but the representations are practically identical. All classes are implemented as templates, therefore providing compile-time support for different types of data, including conversions between internal formats. Volume data for CPU usage (class `Volume<T>`) consists basically of a linear array and additional property information, such as pixel dimensions or origin. Special operators for convenient element access, methods for editing sub-regions or computing statistical information (min/max, histograms, etc.) are provided as well.

This thesis focuses on the utilization of graphics hardware for processing and displaying volume data, so textures are the workhorse for GPU representation and are thus comprised of graphics-oriented data types. The most common (and backward compatible) format is RGBA:

---

[4]In CASCADA 1 there also exists a class `Array`, which has turned out to be redundant in practice: two-dimensional data can be also regarded as volume consisting of one slice.

here, every data element in the texture consists of four individual values. Shader languages provide dedicated operators for accessing these channels efficiently, and many essential GPU techniques required the RGBA format at the time of development.[5] Yet another advantage of this format is an improved utilization of graphics memory, especially if RGBA textures are a must. Instead of leaving channels unused, the scalar data can be packed by rearranging the data: in CASCADA 1 four successive slices of the scalar volume (e.g. four DICOM slices) are combined into one RGBA slice, as illustrated in figure 6.3.

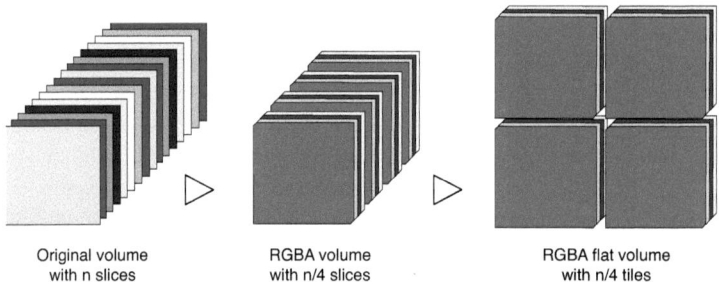

Original volume with n slices　　　RGBA volume with n/4 slices　　　RGBA flat volume with n/4 tiles

Figure 6.3: Main representation of volumes in CASCADA 1: the scalar volume is packed into RGBA channels, and finally spread into a tiled two-dimensional RGBA texture.

In addition to the equivalents of volumes and two-dimensional arrays, GLTexture3D<T> and GLTexture2D<T>, respectively, the system also uses the two-dimensional representation of volumetric data denoted as "flat-3D", GLTextureFlat3D<T> in CASCADA 1. This workaround originally introduced by Harris et al. [HBSL03] to overcome the rudimental support of three-dimensional textures back then has turned out to be very efficient. As a matter of fact, accessing the flat-3D texture has better performance than the direct three-dimensional texture fetch for nearest neighbor interpolation – despite the conversion from native 3D texture coordinates to the two-dimensional address (Langs and Biedermann [LB07]). This is mainly due to the two-dimensional memory layout of graphics hardware. The principle of flat-3D textures is also depicted in figure 6.3.

All specialized versions of GPU data share an abstract class GLTexture, that contains all common information such as texture IDs, fields for OpenGL format definitions, etc. Consequently, the (instantiable) subclasses contain pointers to the according data containers and provide dedicated methods, depending on the particular type: for example, GLTexture3D<float> references to a Volume<float>, or a GLTextureFlat3D<Vec3i> contains both a Volume<Vec3i> and an additional Array<Vec3i> as temporary memory for conversion. Finally, the GPU equivalents provide means for transferring the data between host and graphics memory, as well as efficient methods for (partial) updating and reloading.

At run-time, multiple representations have to be handled and synchronized: for example, the data set initially loaded from a file (CPU volume) is visualized on the GPU, and processed

---

[5]Most notably is the render-to-texture feature, that has been usable for RGB or RGBA formats only. Also, these formats are a direct realization of the SIMD concept that has been the predominant paradigm of GPU architectures for many years and are therefore very efficient.

6.3. IMPLEMENTATION

by various shaders. Hence, subsequent processing steps on the CPU require a data transfer from GPU memory back to the host. Above that, the processing (and visualization) of compressed data introduced in chapter 4 was implemented using a specialization of the standard volume, CompressedVolume. In addition to the inherited functionality, it contains the different coefficient lists and maps, as well as means for multi-level compression. Therefore, the aforementioned handling of different representations applies to compressed volume data, as well as to other possible features and formats (e.g., bricked volumes, time-varying data). In CASCADA 1, the class AbstractVolume is used in conjunction with the observer pattern for this book-keeping, whereas the second version makes use of a custom type information system, which is going to be outlined in the next paragraph.

CASCADA 2

The second version of the framework features a completely reworked representation of volume data. In CASCADA 1, all volume data, i.e., both meta-information and the data itself, are contained in a single class. Although several variants of one volume are possible through the common (abstract) base class UniformData, sharing information about their properties or internal data becomes cumbersome and memory-inefficient. Hence, the classes are separated in CASCADA 2, as depicted in figure 6.4: Volume contains a named list of VolumeData to model one or multiple representations, as well as an instance of VolumeInfo for meta-information.

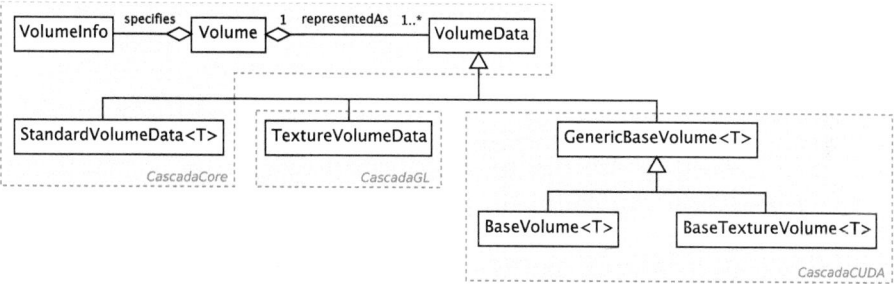

Figure 6.4: Simplified class diagram of CASCADA 2's volume representation in the different packages.

Volume is the main class used as a Parameter value to pass volumes between components, as indicated in figure 6.2. Different data representations are implemented by subclassing VolumeData in order to store the actual volume data and provide dedicated access methods, operators, etc. A specific volume data representation can be obtained using the template method getVolumeData(). For a Volume object, there has to be at least one instance of a data representation. That is, if a volume does not have a specific representation (e.g., StandardVolumeData<T>), the method will try to create one via conversion from another representation; or returning the existing instance otherwise. Both Volume and VolumeData implement routines to allow this behaviour. Most notably, VolumeData has a `getType()` method to query run-time type information; therefore, all of its subclasses must have a static `TYPE()` method. The conversion process itself is available after registering converter functions (implemented by the subclasses) using a global macro called once during initialization.

In addition to specializations within `CascadaCore`, figure 6.4 also contains subclasses in the `CascadaGL` and `CascadaCUDA` packages, respectively. As will be described below, an additional infrastructure was needed for efficient access to the graphics API within CUDA.

6.3.3 Rendering system

The rendering infrastructure has been an integral part of many visual computing approaches that were already discussed in chapter 3. In addition, its object-oriented aspects were addressed in section 5.2 and 5.3, respectively, so that this section is limited to implementation details as well as related topics.

CASCADA 1

As previously introduced, the rendering system in CASCADA follows a multi-level approach. That is, a sequence consists of multiple passes, that are in turn built from (shader) programs. Figures 5.3 and 5.4 on page 148 et seq. depict the structure, with and without taking the composite pattern into account, respectively. The sequences derive from a common base class, `CommonSequence`, which defines the input and output data and the executing device (i.e., CPU or GPU). Subclasses for the different platforms provide further details, such as the contained components, parameters, or timers. CPU and GPU implementations can be used interchangeably, as shown in section 3.1.3. This set of functionality is supplemented with classes representing condition and state information in order to implement dynamic, data-dependent loops, complex processes controllable by external events, etc.

For hardware implementations, `GLRenderPasses` contained in a `GLRenderSequence` – both subclasses of `GLRenderComponent` – are further separated into onscreen and offscreen variants. While the former is the default type and uses the visible framebuffer for rendering geometry (and thus executing the shader programs), `GLOffscreenRenderPass` is more complex. In addition to the `FramebufferObject` employed for convenient use of offscreen facilities and related entities, a `GLTexture` object is used as render target. Due to the object-oriented structure, using the texture's content for subsequent passes is straightforward, regardless of CPU or GPU implementations.

CASCADA 2

The rendering functionality in the second framework version has been outsourced into a separate package. This allows the use of `CascadaCore` as an individual library, if no utilization of graphics hardware is required at all. On the other hand, `CascadaGL` provides the infrastructure to use shader programs for both visualization and computation purposes, and can be regarded as an extended implementation of the core library for graphics hardware.

6.3. IMPLEMENTATION

This is shown in figure 6.5: `RenderPass` derives from `Module` and implements an adapted execution method, as well as means for persistently storing the object to XML. It is also supple-

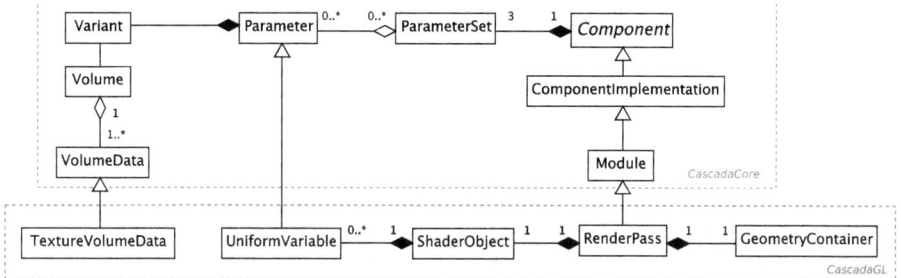

Figure 6.5: Overview of the `CascadaGL` package of CASCADA 2 as simplified class diagram.

mented by the `ShaderObject` that represents shader programs and associated parameters via `UniformVariable`; further details on shaders are given below. As for all GPU implementations, the shaders are assigned to geometry collectively stored in `GeometryContainer` to initiate and control shader program execution. Finally, `TextureVolumeData` provides means for representing volume data in graphics memory by deriving the general base class `VolumeData`. Of course, the structure is designed for further specializations such as compressed data, flat3D layout, hierarchical representations, etc.

In addition to the graphics package, Christian Feinen has designed and implemented a first version of `CascadaCUDA` in his thesis [Fei09]. The idea has been to follow the concepts of the core library, as well as establishing the CUDA package similar to `CascadaGL`.

On the one hand, this similarity can be found in respective specializations of core classes such as `ExecutionPass`, `KernelParameter`, or `KernelObject`, depicted in figure 6.6. On the other hand, CUDA's architecture differs for purely non-graphics usage and graphics applications, respectively. While there are practically no restrictions with respect to memory handling, data formats, or thread communication for the former (see section 1.2.4), not all buffers or functions can be used directly with the OpenGL API. Therefore, an additional layer for the representation of volume data by the class `GenericBaseVolume` was required, mainly to avoid severe performance loss for extra device–to–host data transfers that would be needed otherwise.

Two other concepts conclude this overview of CASCADA's CUDA interface. Firstly, `CUDAPluginInterface` defines the structure of plugins to be used with the CUDA system. It consists of numerous (function-)macros that allow the communication between CUDA implementations and the central entity `KernelObject`, considering the fact that CUDA kernels are implemented using external files (`*.cu` extension), which require additional pre-compilation steps. Thus, the interface can be regarded as the equivalent of `ShaderObjects`'s functionality described in the next section. Secondly, the tool class `CardProperties` provides information about the underlying hardware. This is particularly useful for an efficient

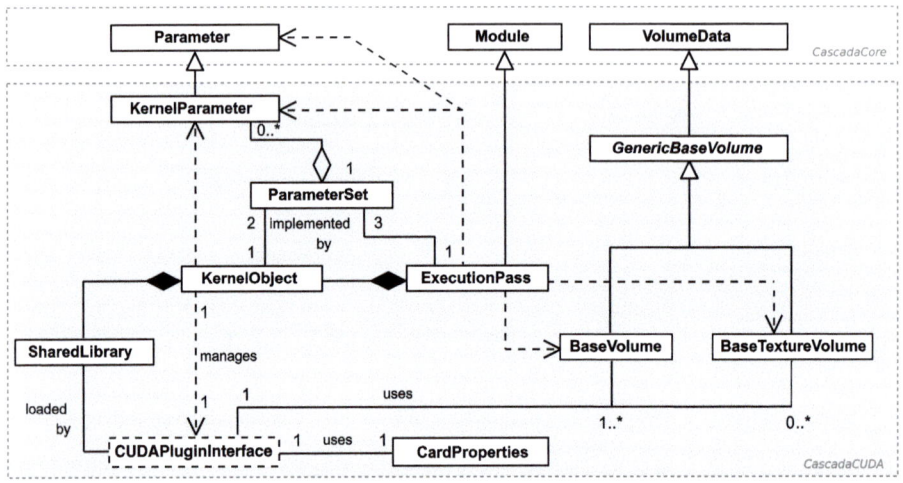

Figure 6.6: Overview of the `CascadaCUDA` package of CASCADA 2 as simplified class diagram. (Image based on Feinen [Fei09])

CUDA implementation, as lots of parameters such as the optimal number of threads, grid size, etc. directly correspond to the capabilities of the available hardware.

6.3.4 Shader handling

Modularization

As mentioned above, CASCADA uses GLSL as shading language. This results in several shader files usually for all different types of shaders (i.e., vertex/fragment/geometry programs). In section 5.2, the extension of object-oriented concepts to shader programming was discussed in detail, where modularization played an important role. Therefore, the handling of shader files has been realized by defining small, incomplete shader code sections that are assembled to functional units as needed. Unfortunately, GLSL has not provided any `include`-mechanism until the release of version 3.0, so that a custom implementation was needed. While the initial approach used concatenated strings for multiple shader fragments – and thus required an application-controlled shader assembly –, the current version supports `include` by means of shader code parsing. This enables a direct combination of code fragments within the shaders, resulting in improved maintainability, and the possibility of changes during application run-time.

Parsing the shader code has been an important feature already in early versions of the framework to handle `uniform` parameters. Custom delimiters are used for parameter specification and (optional) initialization using comments, thus not affecting any functionality or performance. Listing 6.1 shows an example for such an initialization in CASCADA 1:

6.3. IMPLEMENTATION

```
1  // initializing common texture parameters and shader-specific data
2
3  uniform vec3 texelOffsets;    /*/ global texelOffsets /*/
4  uniform sampler2D inputTexture; /*/ local gaussTex /*/
5  uniform float kernel[27];     /*/ local gaussian /*/
6  uniform vec4 chWeights;       /*/ local ( 1.0, 0.5, 0.5, 0.0 ) /*/
7
8  void main()
9  {
10    \\ some code...
11 }
```

Listing 6.1: Direct initialization of uniform parameters within shader code.

Extensions

During the implementation of more advanced and computationally expensive operations, some optimizations have been necessary to maintain reasonable performance. Extensive optimization is common for both shader and GPGPU programming – but at the same time very dependent on hardware details and driver versions. Therefore, only a few general techniques have been applied, such as the so-called *early z-culling* that is provided by all Shader Model 3.0 compliant hardware.

The key motivation is the fact that most GPGPU implementations utilize the fragment shader because of its high computational performance. However, these programs are usually rather complex, so executing them for all pixels (i.e., regardless of their contribution to the result) can lead to a considerable loss of performance. Basically two approaches are possible to overcome this problem. Firstly, static regions-of-interest can be realized by drawing geometry only where shaders should be executed (e.g., by drawing multiple lines instead of a single large quad), thus effectively controlling the computation domain. Secondly, depth testing can be exploited to select only "valid" fragments to avoid unnecessary utilization of the pixel pipeline. This technique is needed for dynamic, i.e., data-dependent shader executions and requires an additional shader for evaluating the particular condition. If the condition is met (i.e., subsequent computations should be performed), the current fragment is discarded; or drawn otherwise, respectively. The actual computation is then initiated by geometry drawn at a different depth, thus leading to the early culling of the fragments where the previous shader did not remove the pixels.

The second procedure requires some additional API calls and application setup, but the intermediate shader is much cheaper than the actual computations, and thus compensates for the overhead in most cases.[6] Further details on the technique, as well as a discussion of hardware-related effects can be found in Harris and Buck [HB05] and Leung et al. [LNM06], respectively.

---

[6] By using geometry shaders and features such as "transform feedback", more flexible and efficient approaches would be possible with latest graphics hardware.

Another technique for efficient shader–application communication is *occlusion querying*. Here, appropriate API calls are needed during rendering for specifying counters and enabling/disabling counting mechanisms. This can be reduced to a simple method call on the `RenderPass` object by means of object-orientation. See listing 7.1 on page 187 for an example, or again Harris and Buck [HB05] for further information.

6.3.5 Application programming

This section will address the integration of the framework's components to be used as application. Of course, this can only be a short outline as the variety of applications and optionally used libraries is virtually unlimited. After the discussion of basic concepts in CASCADA 1, the second part of this section outlines both the plugin system and the external editor of CASCADA 2.

CASCADA 1

As mentioned before, the first version of the framework did not separate between library and application, which led to a tight coupling of various parts of the code. However, the concept of managers as building blocks of the application has been a rather powerful, yet suboptimal feature from a software-engineering point of view. Following the singleton pattern (see section 5.4.1), each of the following facilities makes up the application's functionality and is accessible from all components of the framework:

VolumeManager Handling of volume representations by maintaining a named list of `AbstractVolume` and several convenience functions. Via multiple inheritance, it also implements the subject of the observer pattern.

ShaderManager Administration of both `GLShaderProgram` and `GLRender-Sequence`, in addition to a `ParameterSet` for global parameters. It resembles the observer in the respective pattern.

HardwareManager This unit is a collection of tools and functions for querying hardware states and capabilities, as well as handles for external devices (Phantom, SpaceNavigator; see section 6.2.3).

GUIManager The central unit containing the entry point for the application loop, and initializes all other units, including the GUI.

Although this centralized approach has been straightforward at the beginning, it has not scaled well with the framework's complexity. Also, the coupling of code has become an additional burden for maintenance, compilation time, and debugging, so that a complete redesign and the development of CASCADA 2 has become necessary. However, the first

6.3. IMPLEMENTATION 175

version consists of approximately 37,000 lines of code[7] and provides lots of algorithms, shader programs and infrastructure; thus, both versions are still going to coexist for a while.

During the development of CASCADA 1 with several contributions from student projects and theses, the graphical user interface based on Qt 4 has also been extended. This will be described in the context of the "LiverGPU" project in section 7.1.3, with further images shown in figure 1.10 on page 29. Based on the aforementioned `GUIManager`, an XML file specifying the application's feature set is parsed and according widgets are created by the `GUIFactory`. This allows the convenient integration of functionality for different purposes, but is not as powerful as a true plugin system described in the next section.

CASCADA 2

In section 5.4.2 the plugin concept was introduced, with according references to the classes in CASCADA 2. Therefore, the following paragraphs shortly describe the process of plugin creation and usage from an implementational point of view. The section concludes with technical information about the current state of the visual editor "Fountain" that has been developed for creating applications based on the second version of CASCADA.

A plugin library is created by implementing a class that derives a base class known inside the core application. Typically, a `Component` plugin is implemented by subclassing `Module`; note the resemblance to specializations in `CascadaGL` or `CascadaCUDA`, respectively. By means of an additional macro, the custom class is converted into a valid `Component` plugin across all supported platforms.

Once the plugin has been created, the `PluginLoader` can create instances of a given base class using code from a `SharedLibrary` at run-time. This wrapper class hides the different functions needed on each platform and provides a common interface to shared libraries (.dll, .so, or .dylib, depending on the platform). A template parameter specifies the type of the object to be created in the loader. Destruction of the plugin is performed analogously; listing 6.2 summarizes the concepts.

In addition to standard approaches for application programming, the modular design of CASCADA 2 allows the rapid development of applications by means of a visual editor – an approach used by many systems. In the context of medical image processing and visualization, MeVisLab [MeV07] is a well-known and widely used example; see also section 2.4. The editor "Fountain" is still in an early stage of development, but documents the benefits of CASCADA 2 quite well.

Based on a simple Qt user interface, every `Component` is represented by an according visual item. Each of these `ComponentItems` (or specializations thereof) maintain input and output parameters. The communication between these parameters is modeled by `ConnectionItems`, as already described in section 5.2.3. Depending on the type of the

---

[7]including all shader files; measured using David A. Wheeler's SLOCCount http://www.dwheeler.com/sloccount/ (last visit Mar 11 2009)

```
1  // derive from core class
2  class MyComponent : public Module
3  {
4    // ...
5  };
6
7  // turn into Component plugin
8  CASCADA_PLUGIN( Component, MyComponent );
9
10 // create component from dll-file
11 PluginLoader< Component > pluginLoader( "Plugin.dll" );
12 Component * component = pluginLoader.createInstance();
13
14 // destroy after use
15 pluginLoader.deleteInstance( component );
```

Listing 6.2: Pseudo code for the usage of the plugin system in CASCADA 2.

parameter, there exist different views to edit the respective values. These concepts are depicted in the screenshot of a simple test setup in figure 6.7.

Although the range of functions of CASCADA 2 is currently still rather limited, its design and concepts provide an extensible basis for further development. The building blocks of the library, as well as a basic version of the editor are planned to be published as open source in the near future.

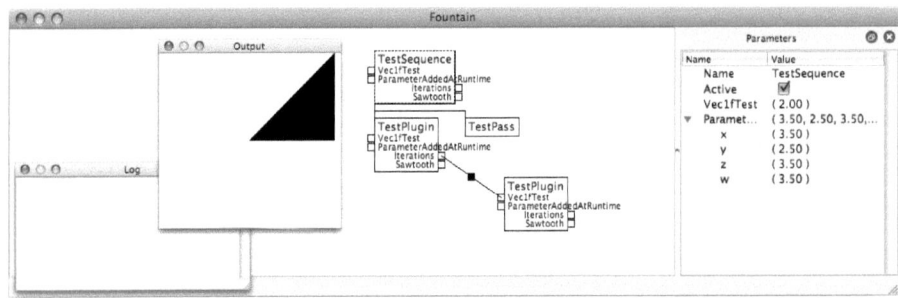

Figure 6.7: Screenshot of an early version of "Fountain"

CHAPTER 7

Projects

In the preceding chapter, the framework CASCADA has been described from a technical point of view. Based upon the concepts from part two of this thesis, both the first and second version of the system integrated several of these approaches. Although most of these contributions have also considered realistic scenarios and applications in the medical context of this thesis, this chapter focuses on prototypes and implementations for clinical projects. In the first section, the project "LiverGPU" will be described, that has actually been the foundation for CASCADA. Therefore, the different stages of the development, as well as a detailed evaluation of the results are provided.

The project described in the second part of this chapter covers a wider range of platforms and a larger period of time, and is still in the process of further development and research. Here, the results of mostly collaborative work is presented based on different publications. While being diverse in the medical configuration, both projects have the quantification of anatomical structures by using visual computing approaches in common to realize computer assistance for the assessment of medical data in clinical practice.

7.1 LiverGPU

During the course of post-graduate research, a collaborative project with the Centre for Image Analysis at Uppsala University was organized in 2006. The clinical partner from Uppsala's University Hospital, Department of Oncology, Radiology and Clinical Immunology, Section of Radiology, provided a self-contained topic of direct relevance, as well as data sets including manual segmentations. In addition to do research in an image processing environment with considerable medical background, the motivation for this three-month visit was also to establish the basis for a programming framework using graphics hardware.

At the radiology department of Uppsala University studies have been conducted that include imaging and spectroscopy based liver investigations. Spectroscopy of the liver allows accurate determination of relative fat content, while MR imaging allows the assessment of liver volume. Today, there is no method available for automated liver volume determination from MRI volumes at the department. Investigating the possibility of segmenting the liver (semi-)automatically in these MRI data sets has been of high interest. The project included the

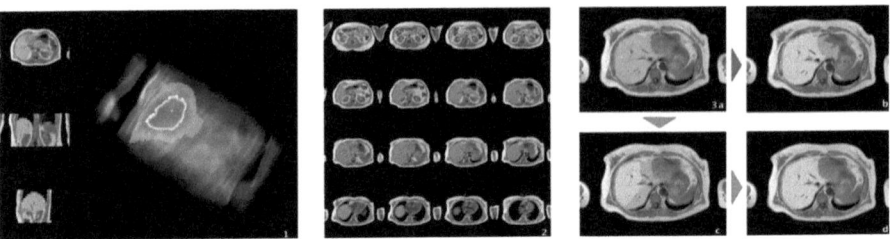

Figure 7.1: GPU-based liver segmentation (1) in low-resolution MRI volume data sets (2). Direct interaction with the visualization guides the segmentation process (3a-d).

creation and validation of an image analysis algorithm implemented on graphics hardware for direct visualization, interaction, and improved overall performance. As the data sets have a considerably lower resolution in z-direction than in xy-direction – due to the fast imaging protocol for breathold acquisitions – slice-oriented approaches might be preferable. In total, 51 MRI liver data sets have been available that were acquired using the same MR protocol, and for which manual segmentations exist. The data sets are of 256×256 axial resolution, with 16-22 slices, each with 16 bit data. This results in rather anisotropic spatial resolutions of $1.7 \times 1.7 \times 10/12/13$ mm.

The following sections will summarize existing work that was related to GPU-based segmentation back then. Subsequently, the different development stages and prototypes will be outlined, with a focus on GPU-based computing and performance results in the project's context.[1] The section will conclude with a summary and possible extensions.

7.1.1 Related Work

There exists a wealth of segmentation approaches for medical data sets, especially for main organs, vascular structures, etc. Some of these methods have been mentioned already in the introductory part of this thesis, as well as in chapter 3 with respect to utilizing graphics hardware. In the context of the liver project and the implementations developed therein, the work by Sherbondy et al. [SHN03] was the most relevant and provided some key techniques that are worth discussing. There are more advanced algorithms available on graphics hardware nowadays, such as level sets or other model-based approaches. However, given the settings of the project (time, available data and hardware, etc.) and the intention to build a general-purpose GPU framework, seeded region growing has been considered as an appropriate candidate. In section 3.2.2 the highly interactive, region growing based approach recently presented by Chen et al. [CSS08] has been mentioned as an application that exploits state-of-the-art graphics hardware, which is also closely related to this work. The following paragraphs shortly summarize contributions relevant for the collaborative

---

[1] Details on the framework itself will only be provided as long as they differ from CASCADA as presented before.

7.1. LIVERGPU

GPU-oriented project, in order to provide a background for the subsequent development stages and discussions.

Seeded Region Growing The region growing algorithm applied in this project is based on the method proposed by Adams and Bischof [AB94]. Their segmentation algorithm does not require extensive parameter settings, but the manual placement of so-called seeds. These sets of pixels influence both the spatial information and the growing process in that the seeds' intensities usually define the initial parameters. While the authors describe their algorithm for two-dimensional intensity images, Justice et al. [JSS$^+$97] have extended the approach to 3D data sets, especially for medical applications. The basic idea of the seeded region growing algorithm is to iteratively expand the initial set of regions by evaluating certain criteria for the elements to be added. In the original contribution, this criterion is realized as the difference of intensity values between the element in question and the mean of the already segmented region; the criterion can therefore be regarded as static. This requires the definition of a threshold in order to merge or reject the new elements. These candidates are direct neighbors of the current region in order to maintain connected regions, where the definition of neighborhood may depend on the image's dimension and structure, or some other criterion.

Lin et al. [LJT01] have proposed an interesting extension in that their approach is completely parameter-free: no explicit seeds need to be placed by the user. In addition to the original algorithm, their workflow includes anisotropic filtering as preprocess. Although they are able to achieve good visual results, both the details of the underlying algorithm and the validation of the segmentation results are not clear or even missing.

Segmentation of medical images using adaptive region growing Pohle and Tönnies [PT01] proposed an automatic adaptation of the homogeneity criterion, as well as an extension of the original approach towards volume data sets and different modalities. The idea is to initialize the region growing with the criterion learned from a preceding step that uses the same seed. Therefore, estimates based on both the mean value and standard deviation are iteratively computed. This search for a model of regions is performed randomly and incorporates the image formation process. That is, variations due to noise (i.e., standard deviation), partial volume effect, or shading effects in MR data are taken into account. By means of additional weights that depend on the iteration count, they are able to achieve robust and good results, even in difficult settings.

Fast Volume Segmentation With Simultaneous Visualization Using Programmable Graphics Hardware In 2003, Sherbondy et al. [SHN03] proposed to utilize graphics hardware for segmentation procedures on CT data. This work is quite fundamental in that it provides various techniques for processing volume data on the rather limited graphics hardware available at that time. In their implementation, the input volume is represented as three-dimensional texture containing 32-bit floating point values, where each element encodes both the CT data and seed information. Consequently, the raw data and number of seeds per voxel is limited to 16 bit each. After an optional smoothing step, the seeds are placed into the volume by user-specified locations in cross-sectional views. As the authors use a specific graphics card (ATI Radeon 9800 Pro), both the rendering and processing can be performed directly in native 3D textures.[2] This allows for a true three-dimensional realization of the region growing algorithm, which is in their case based on simplified Perona-Malik diffusion computations [PM90]. In order to limit the subsequent operations to voxels that are potential candidates for region growing, another rendering pass is used to set up a computational mask. This technique has been introduced by Purcell et al. in their graphics hardware implementation of ray tracing (see [OLG+07] for additional information) and prevents fragments from being generated on modern graphics hardware ("early z-cull", see section 6.3.4). After the region growing process for the current iteration step has finished, the volume is updated for the next iteration. The performance penalty for the additional direct visualization of the (intermediate) results is very low and they achieve a complete segmentation of anatomical structures in a few seconds. However, due to the limited video memory in older graphics hardware and the fact that a copy of the volume is needed for reading/writing, their data sets are relatively small.

7.1.2 Prototypes

In the preceding section, different contributions based on region growing as well as an early GPU implementation have been reviewed. Given the settings and requirements of the project, the implemented algorithms and concepts are a combination and adaptation of these approaches. For example, most of the 3D algorithms assume that voxels are (almost) isotropic. In this project, however, the slice distance is almost an order of magnitude larger than the in-slice voxel size, thus requiring additional weights or purely 2D-based approaches. During the three months, two different prototypes ("MRILiver") have been developed with only few existing functionality from external code and libraries. The final application "LiverGPU" has been the base for subsequent work, and has ultimately led to the development of CASCADA. In the following sections, main development steps, technical features, as well as results will be presented and discussed.

Prototype 1

Starting with the first prototype, different essential functionality and classes were implemented. In addition to the representation of the volume data by means of basic vector classes and tool functions, a simple infrastructure for using the graphics hardware was established. Due to the fact that three different systems with all three operating systems and both Nvidia and ATI graphics cards (consumer and workstation class) were available, all implementations were realized as cross-platform C++ programs using GLSL shader programs. In addition to getting in-depth knowledge of the details, the reasons for a self-written platform were the

---

[2]This feature has not been available on Nvidia-based graphics hardware until Shader Model 3.0; see section 1.1 for details.

7.1. LiverGPU

limited capabilities of available GPU programming systems back then. The only alternative considered was Sh [MT04], but was excluded due to different reasons; see also section 5.1.2.

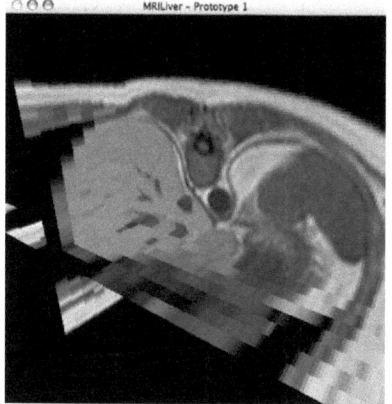

(a) MPR-like visualization of the volume and manual segmentation

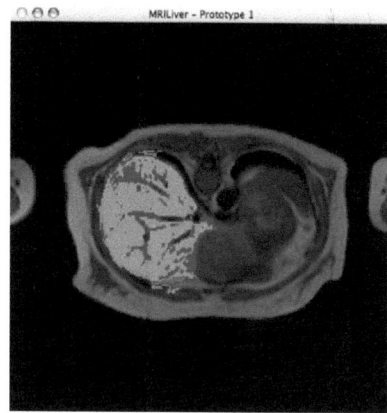

(b) First GPU-implementation of region growing

Figure 7.2: Screenshots of the first prototype

MPR volume rendering was implemented first using shader programs, including simple tone-mapping for the 16 bit data. As shown in figure 7.2(a), the original volume data is overlaid with the corresponding manual segmentation. Because of the strong anisotropy of the voxels no interpolation is used for the textures, as can be seen in the screen capture as well. In the second image of figure 7.2, the very first implementation of simplified region growing using shaders is depicted. Although leakages are easily noticeable, the focus was on implementing such iterative algorithms on graphics hardware only. Therefore, a simple abstraction for the low-level API calls was established and extended since then.[3]

Prototype 2

The second prototype started by reimplementing the test system from the preceding version in a completely object-oriented manner. While some of the basic classes only had to be improved slightly, the focus was on providing a sophisticated infrastructure for using the graphics hardware, both for rendering and non-graphics purposes. This includes platform-independent wrapping of API calls, representation of simple geometry, texture, shader program, and parameter handling, etc. Especially the texture handling and representation became rather involved, as rendering to an offscreen buffer was limited to two-dimensional textures at that time. Therefore, "flat-3D textures" were implemented in addition to native 2D/3D textures. In combination with shader code fragments, these textures can be used

---

[3] As described in section 1.2, such non-graphics implementations typically use offscreen render targets. Further details can be found in chapter 6.

as their 3D counterparts; the address translation is hidden from the user. The layout of the flat-3D texture in the application is depicted in figure 7.3(a).

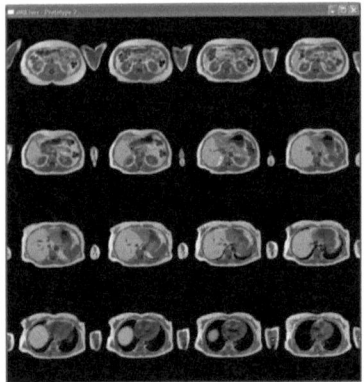 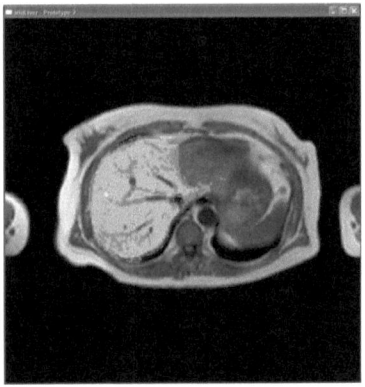

(a) Visualization of the flat 3D representation of the volume.

(b) Some internal improvements on the region growing algoritm

Figure 7.3: Screenshots of second prototype

Only few improvements were done regarding the segmentation algorithm. In addition to changing the orientation of the data to the standard view used in many clinical applications (axial-caudal), the acquisition of samples from the selected seed point (yellow dot in figure 7.3(b)) was implemented. This allows the immediate adaptation of region growing parameters to the data set by averaging multiple samples around the seed point(s), as well as the generation of internal information (e.g., gradients) on-the-fly.

Results

Both the performance of the visualization and the combined region growing/visualization have been clearly real-time. Depending on the driver settings, frame rates of over 1000 fps have been achieved for rendering only; region growing has been in the range of 240 fps – 30fps, and 700 fps – 150 fps, on ATI and Nvidia hardware, respectively.[4] All of the measurements have been performed on 512×512 rendering viewports (up to 1280×1280 for offscreen passes, respectively), using 16 bit floating point RGBA textures.

In terms of programming, the main problems during the six week development phase have been cross-vendor graphics driver issues and limitations due to older APIs. For example, OpenGL 1.5 does only support power-of-two-dimension textures natively and thus requires additional handling (padding etc.) for an odd number of slices. Also, the mechanisms for error checking of shader code are limited and – especially for cross-vendor GPU programming – introduce inconsistencies, incorrect shader code, etc. Being forced to use two-dimensional

---

[4]The decreasing performance is due to the increasing number of fragments being processed as the region grows (i.e., the bounding box expands)

RGBA textures as render targets introduced considerable overhead. Nevertheless, the performance still has been competitive, if not superior to native 3D implementations (as shown in Langs and Biedermann [LB07], for example).

7.1.3 Final version

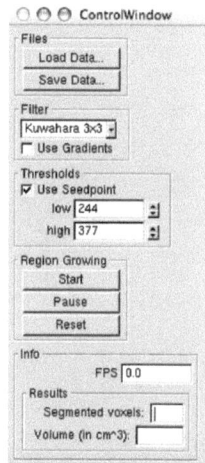

The final version of "LiverGPU" reflects several changes and can be subdivided into two phases. Firstly, the segmentation and interaction functionality of the preceding prototype was extended in order to improve the segmentation results. In addition to the concept of blockers (see below and also section 3.2.2), several preprocessing filters were implemented. Among initial tests with simple mean and Gaussian kernels, the 2D/3D-Kuwahara filter [KHEK76] and two-dimensional anistropic diffusion [PM90] were implemented, depending on the GPU's capabilities. At the end of the project abroad, the application utilized a very simple and limited user interface using GLUI[5], as depicted in figure 7.4. In addition to the 3D standard view, three orthogonal views for the main anatomical axes were provided. Also, the visualization was extended to integrate the segmented volume into the original volume by means of direct volume rendering.

Figure 7.4: GLUI

In the subsequent development phase of the application, lots of enhancements during the "MedGPU" students' project extended the system. While several details of the underlying concepts were presented in the preceding chapter already, the main change visible for the user has been the Qt-based interface. As shown in figure 7.5(a), dialog boxes, menu bar, etc. have greatly simplified the application and more adaptable to the user's needs.

Interactive mode While the introduction of concepts for interacting with algorithms in section 3.2.2 was limited to two-dimensional visualization, it is desirable to interact with the volume rendering in 3D. Therefore, different techniques were implemented. The first method was to compute the 3D position of the mouse by inverting the OpenGL projection step. The utility package GLU provides the function `gluUnProject` that transforms window coordinates back into object coordinates. While the x- and y-component of the current window coordinate are at hand, the z-coordinate has to be determined by reading the depth buffer of the current rendering. This results in correct values for MPR rendering, but is not directly applicable for volume raycasting: here, the depth buffer contains the bounding box's values, instead of the structure being rendered. Although this problem can be alleviated by explicitly writing depth values during integration along the viewing ray in the fragment shader (e.g. Kratz et al. [KSFB06]), such an extension was not implemented.

---

[5]`http://www.cs.unc.edu/~rademach/glui`

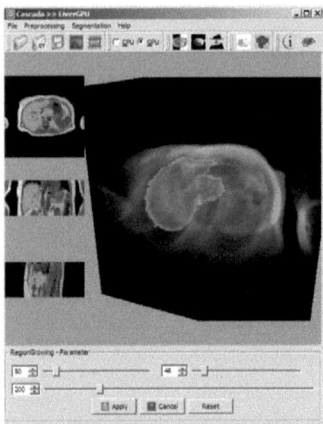 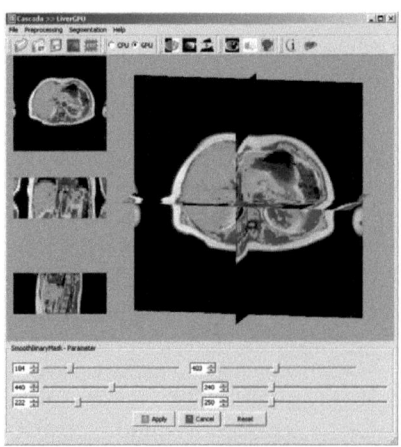

(a) Perspective DVR mode with segmentation result

(b) Applying the SmoothThreshold operation for pre-selection

Figure 7.5: Screenshots of the current version of "LiverGPU", as a specialized application built from CASCADA 1.

Extensions   As already mentioned before, several enhancements of the underlying concepts and algorithms were made, especially for the region growing procedure. Firstly, an extension of global thresholding has been implemented. This "Smooth Threshold" operation classifies all voxels that are within a value range of interest. By using a combination of smoothstep functions[6], different intervals of the data set's value range can be selected, as depicted in figure 7.5(b). Being a simple global operation this pre-selection can be computed in one pass for the whole volume. The region to be determined by the subsequent segmentation algorithm is a subset of these voxels. Therefore, "early z-culling" can exploit this information in order to restrict the subsequent expensive operations to this set of voxels. Hence, in the case of the region growing algorithm, not all voxels of the data set have to be evaluated which results in a significant speedup of the process. Note that this approach is a simplified version of the computation masks used in the system proposed by Sherbondy et al. [SHN03]. They update the mask per iteration, thus being more effective on the one hand, but more expensive on the other hand.

The second extension has been on the region growing step itself. As in Sherbondy's approach, "LiverGPU" evaluates the direct neighbors of the current region for being added. That is, a simple $3 \times 3 \times 3$ dilation is performed, with a certain threshold or weight for the differently connected neighbors. While this leads to reasonably good results and is simple and fast to compute, one can think of extending the dilation mask to more complex structuring elements, as they are used in image morphology. This task is rather challenging in terms of efficient and backward-compatible GPU implementation and it would not lead to an

---

[6]The smoothstep function implements cubic interpolation for $x \in [a, b]$, clamp otherwise.

7.1. LiverGPU

improvement for the data at hand. Due to the clear anisotropy and low resolution, larger and more complex masks are hard to determine without introducing additional errors.

In addition to the iterative algorithms, occlusion queries as described in section 6.3.4 were also employed. Here, it was used twofold: firstly, for an automatic termination of the segmentation after the iterative process had converged; secondly, for computing the number of segmented voxels, thus realizing volumetry. Both applications of this method contribute to the reduction of data transfer, as the calculations can be performed directly on the GPU. In addition to the occlusion query itself, a so-called discarding shader is needed to separate the elements to be counted from the whole rendering content. The code in listing 7.1 summarizes the steps that are needed for computing the segmented volume, as well as shows the use of object-oriented concepts.[7]

```
// setup region growing
m_rg = createRenderPass( "RegionGrowing" );

// segments counting, with active occlusion querying
m_count = createRenderPass( "CountSegmentedFrags" );
m_count->setQuerying( true );

// ...

// init counter
GLuint segcount = 0;

// iteration
while( !m_rg->hasConverged() )
{
    // region growing
    m_rg->execute();

    // count segmented voxels only
    m_count->execute();
    segcount = m_count->getRenderedFragmentsCount();

    // ...
}
```

Listing 7.1: Simplified code showing the setup and execution of volume computation for region growing by means of shader programs and occlusion queries.

Results

As already mentioned in the introduction of the "LiverGPU" project, the clinical partners have provided manual segmentations for all 51 MRI data sets. These segmentations are represented as binary volumes with the same format and properties and thus allow an easy and direct comparison with the algorithms' segmentation results. In section 2.1.3, different approaches for assessing and validating the results have been discussed. Although these computations

---

[7]Note that this resembles a GPU version of the software volumetry implementation denoted in the last step of the case study in figure 5.5 on page 150.

could have been implemented as shaders (i.e., within "LiverGPU"), MeVisLab [MeV07] has been used as an external tool for analyzing the results, in order to avoid implementation any errors or bias.

The segmentations of the liver data sets were created by a single operator only, but will be assumed as ground truth data in the following comparison. Also, the focus will be on the segmentation quality of the system, both for automatic[8] application and direct interaction using the techniques described before. The time required to complete the task for one data set is, as expected, of different orders of magnitude: while the fully manual segmentation by a medical expert requires several minutes, the automatic algorithm takes less than ten seconds after setting the seed point. Interactive correction has been limited to one minute for the evaluation, respectively.

Segmentation quality The quality of the automatic segmentation was evaluated for all 51 data sets first. Therefore, each volume was loaded and segmented, without additional preprocessing or normalization[9]. One or multiple seed points were specified by clicking into a representative region of liver tissue in the default axial view. Although the current version of the application is able to further accelerate subsequent computations defining an additional volume-of-interest, this step was omitted for the rather small data sets. Also, the aforementioned pre-selection was not used, as this would introduce another variable and complicate the comparison of the procedures. The user-definable thresholds for lower and upper deviation, and the gradient weight, respectively, were changed similarly for the same data sets, if necessary at all.

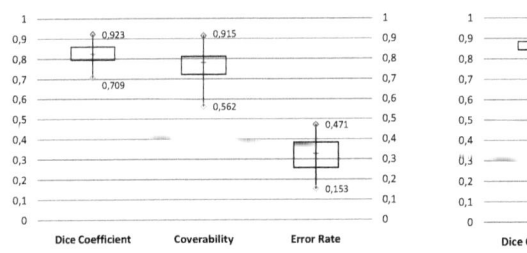
(a) Results without manual interaction

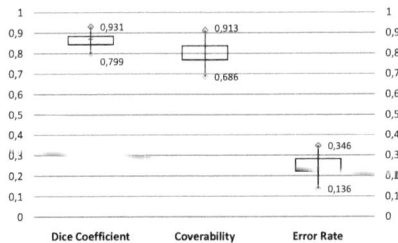
(b) Results with interaction (time-limited)

Figure 7.6: Summary diagrams showing the segmentation results without (a) and with (b) manual interaction; depicted are the minimum, maximum, and the main quartiles (first, median, and third).

As can be seen in figures 7.6 and 7.7, the results without any local interaction vary in the range from 0.709 to 0.923 for the Dice coefficient, and approximately 0.35 for both the

---

[8]This still requires the manual specification of the seed point, of course, but with default algorithm settings (thresholds etc.) else.
[9]Some data sets suffered from slight MRI shading artefacts as well as some general difference in the value ranges (i.e., brightness). However, partial volume effects and other impairments due to the low resolution had more influence on the results.

7.1. LiverGPU

coverability and error rate. By interacting locally with the region growing procedure, the results are improved on average by approximately 10% for the Dice coefficient, and around 15% for the coverability/error rate, respectively. Although the coverability was lower for some data sets, the error rate was decreased for practially all segmentations.

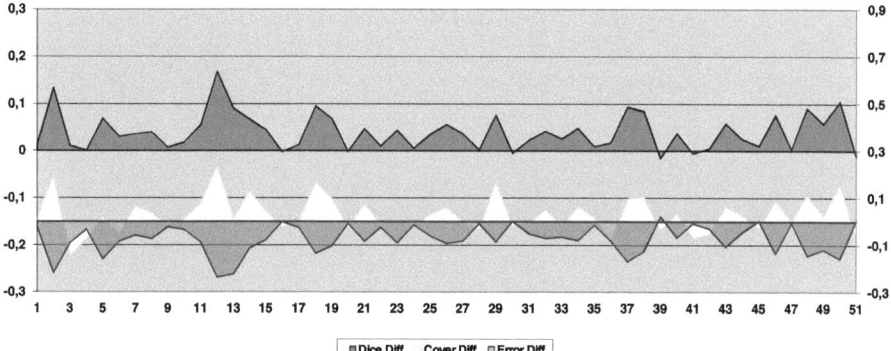

Figure 7.7: The upper graph depicts the changes for the Dice coefficient (left scale), the lower graphs show the differences (right scale) for the coverability (yellow) and the error (red), repectively.

Preprocessing During additional experiments, the application of preprocessing algorithms was not able to improve the results significantly. This is mainly due to the coarse resolution and resulting degradations such as partial volume effects of the data sets, where the region growing procedure cannot benefit from edge-preserving algorithms.

On the other hand, using gradients as an additional delineation metric has shown a clear impact on the results. While simply using the absolute value of the three-dimensional gradient introduces a considerable error due to the strong anisotropy, the gradient vector has to account for the different resolution. Hence, the inter-slice gradient has to be reduced, where the ratio of voxel sizes provides a sufficient measure. Although there are more advanced gradient computation methods available, central differencing has proven to be a very fast and sufficiently exact approximation in this case.

Discussion The segmentation results were enhanced by interacting locally with the iterative region growing. However, there are several ways to extend the approach and further improve the process. As mentioned in the introduction of this section, the approach by Pohle and Tönnies [PT01] seems to be capable of improving the parameter setting. Although the thresholds are already adapted to a considerable number of samples in the vicinity of the seed point(s), this approach is more subject to outliers due to ambiguous interaction.[10] In addition, the region growing algorithm used in the presented GPU implementation does

---

[10] For example, setting the seed point too close to a boundary might introduce non-representative values.

not evaluate potential candidates in the neighborhood based on the current region's mean value, but on two thresholds. This limits the adaptability of the algorithm during iteration on the one hand, but allows a considerably faster execution on the GPU – especially on the hardware available at the time of the project. In addition, experiments using a CPU reference implementation with the given data sets have indicated that the mean of the region during the iterative process varies only slightly and would not be advantageous for this kind of application.

7.2 ARCADE

This research project is part of the MTI Mittelrhein[11] and a collaboration of the Central Medical Facility of the German Armed Forces in Koblenz, the University of Applied Sciences in Remagen, and the Institute for Computational Visualistics at the University of Koblenz-Landau. The objective of this project is to improve the assessment of aortic aneurysms based on CT scans.[12] Quantifying this potentially lethal vascular disease by traditional means requires high efforts for exact and robust results, especially for long-term monitoring or already implanted prostheses. The developed software allows an interactive 3D analysis of the vascular structures by utilizing modern graphics hardware and direct volume visualization, in order to calculate the parameters for endovascular repair. Various software platforms were used for the initial phase of the project, while the current implementation is planned as a plugin for the DICOM/PACS software "OsiriX" [Osi], supplemented by different components of CASCADA.

The remainder of this section is structured as follows. After an introduction to the medical context, current assessment and therapy methods will be described. As the focus of the project is on improving the assessment by means of image processing and visualization methods, different approaches and their results – if already available – will be presented and discussed.

7.2.1 Medical background

Epidemiology

Aortic aneurysms are one of many vascular diseases especially in industrial countries with a considerable lethal risk. The prevalence of abdominal aneurysms is estimated at 3-8%, predominantly among men older than approximately 60 years [FWBL05, SLD05]. The aorta itself runs as largest and most important artery of the human body from the heart through

---

[11] http://www.mti-mittelrhein.de
[12] The acronym "ARCADE" stands for: Aneurysm Repair by Computer Assisted Delineation and Evaluation

the thorax into the abdomen, where it forks into the lower extremities, and supplies the regions directly and indirectly with oxygen-rich blood. A destabilized aortic wall leads to the dilation of the aorta due to the blood pressure. This process is initially caused by proteolytic activity with subsequent elastin fibre degradation [MEW⁺94, Bla99]. Continuous blood pressure on the weakened aorta leads to aneurysm growth and, if not treated, the patient is at a steadily increasing risk of a rupture resulting in high mortality (80-90%). Of course, degeneration affects other sections of the aortic wall as well. Strained parts such as the aortic arch, thoracical and abdominal section are primarily subject to the development of aneurysms. Abdominal aortic aneurysms (AAA) are in the abdominal section of the aorta, usually starting below the renal arteries down to the iliacal bifurcation (see figure 7.8).

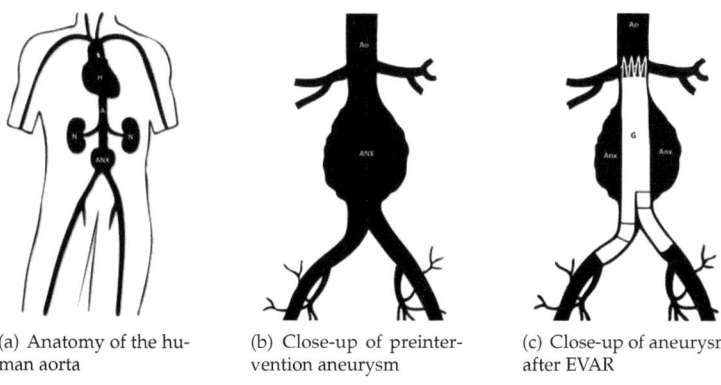

(a) Anatomy of the human aorta

(b) Close-up of preintervention aneurysm

(c) Close-up of aneurysm after EVAR

Figure 7.8: Depictions of aortic aneurysms. (Images courtesy of R. Wickenhöfer)

In order to assess such an aneurysm once it has been detected, measuring the maximum diameter of the dilated aorta is an established method for different imaging modalities. With diameters exceeding a certain threshold and/or growth rate (usually 50 millimeters [SLD05] or 10 millimeters per year) an intervention is required. This also applies to postoperative assessment in order to monitor implants that have been placed via endovascular procedures.

While this evaluation seems to be a straightforward and fast approach, measuring the diameter is not a very robust method, as is discussed for example in the context of endovascular repair by Wever et al. [WBME00]. Firstly, finding the correct plane for the actual measurement by means of multi-planar reformation (MPR) is often an error-prone and tedious step. Due to considerable interobserver variability, the measured value deviates from the real maximal diameter, as has been investigated by Diehm et al. [DKG⁺07]. This becomes critical for long-term screenings, where the patients' anatomy is subject to changes, and the examiner is usually not the same person. Secondly, one-dimensional parameters such as the diameter do neither account for the different types of aneurysms, nor for the potential implant's structure. This often leads to diagnostic ambiguities that need further investigation. While early volumetric approaches as Baskin et al. [BKS⁺96] provide an improved assessment of the anatomy, they are still used to measure only one-dimensional parameters such as lengths or diameters.

Classification and assessment

The assessment of aneurysms can be divided into three different stages: the first, potentially incidental examination, the preintervention assessment, and postintervention imaging ("follow-up" monitoring). The most common situation is where the patient suffers from diffuse pain in the abdominal region that can emanate into the back, groin, legs etc., depending on the aneurysm's location. Except for incidental cases, where CT scans are acquired for other reasons, ultrasound imaging is usually the modality used in the first place. If the examiner finds indications for an aneurysm, as depicted in figure 7.9(a), the dilation is usually gauged using measurement tools of the ultrasound system.

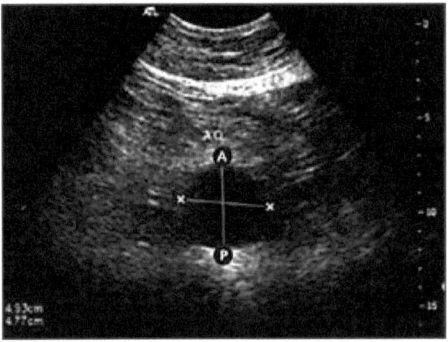

(a) Ultrasound of AAA, including measurements. (Image courtesy of Upchurch et al.)

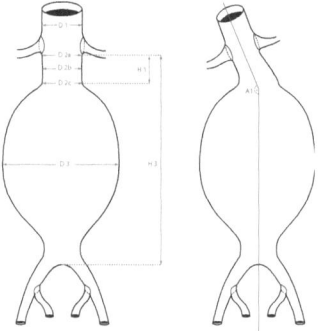

(b) Typical length and angular parameters for AAA assessment.

Figure 7.9: Assessment methods for AAA: ultrasound measurement (a), and standardized parameters (b).

Depending on the stage of the dilation and other factors such as clearness of results, additional examinations have to be performed. Usually CT scans (including bolus-triggered application of contrast agent) are acquired due to their high image resolution. For potential preintervention situations, i.e., where no metal implants are present, MRI has been proposed as a less invasive alternative. As mentioned before, an intervention is required if the maximal diameter of the aneurysm exceeds a certain limit. If the diameter is below the threshold but considered aneurysmal (i.e., 30-50 mm), an increasing growth rate over time also indicates an intervention. The maximal diameter represents one of multiple measurements that are usually performed for aneurysm assessment. Figure 7.9(b) illustrates the parameters following the EUROSTAR[13] registry program. In this case the acquired image data is reviewed for operation planning and prosthesis specification. Improving this process, especially for endovascular procedures (see next section), by means of software assistance is the project's objective and will be addressed in the subsequent sections.

---

[13] European Collaborators on Stent/graft Techniques for aortic Aneurysm Repair

From the technical point of view, there are differences for the processing of pre- and postintervention situations. While for the former practically all mentioned imaging modalities are applicable (if there are no contraindications, such as earlier implants), the latter require some attention. If the intervention involved the placement of metallic structures (e.g., endograft material, surgical clips), the images will contain artefacts: in CT data, metal appears at maximum density with streaks and other ringing artefacts; in ultrasound images, typical effects are resonance, or comet tile artefact; for MRI imaging, the presence of metal is usually a contraindication. In addition, for follow-up routines the whole imaging protocol has to be the same to allow a proper comparison of the data sets.

As will be described in the remainder of this chapter, the assessment of aneurysms is typically a highly manual and thus variable process. This is mainly due to the fact that a one-dimensional parameter (i.e., the maximum diameter) has to be measured within a three-dimensional structure. Although there are commercial software components available for analyzing vascular structures semi-automatically, the usability, stability, and overall performance of the tools often falls short of expectations – especially in clinical practice.

Surgical treatment of abdominal aneuryms, especially endovascular repair requires the assessment of several properties of the infrarenal aortic section. In addition to the aforementioned diameter, the length of both the proximal and distal aortic neck is of vital interest for robust stent-graft placement. If the neck is too short, the implant will be at risk of migration due to the continuing longitudinal blood pressure. This extends to adjacent or branching vessel structures, e.g., the renal arteries for fenestrated implants (f-EVAR). Also, the iliac arteries have to be examined to ensure a sufficient minimal diameter (in order to allow EVAR device application) which includes the consideration of possible calcifications, thrombi, and other impairments. Further parameters are the angulation of the aortic neck, as proposed by Filis et al. [FARZ03], as well as their discussion of the arteries' tortuosity to ensure proper graft placement at all.

Therapies

Once an abdominal aortic aneurysm has been detected and intervention is required, basically two surgical procedures are available: open surgical repair (OSR), and endovascular aneurysm/aortic repair (EVAR).[14]

Open surgery The conventional method is practically always possible, but represents a rather invasive procedure. The abdominal cavity is opened from the epigastric region to the hypogastrium first. After freeing the aorta from occluding structures (i.e., intestines), the vessel is disconnected from blood circulation above and below the arterial dilation and opened longitudinally. Then the prosthesis, an artificial fabric hose, is connected to both ends of the aorta. Depending on the location of the aneuryms, the implant is either a tube or, for iliacal aneuryms, Y-shaped. Finally, thrombotic residues are removed from the vascular

---

[14]Usually the therapies described here are also applicable to other aortic sections (e.g., for thoracic aneurysms), the discussion will be limited to abdominal aneurysms.

wall, before it is wrapped around the prothesis to support the implant as well as protect surrounding organs.

EVAR Contrary to the conventional procedure, endovascular aneurysm repair is a minimally-invasive method. In addition to the pre-intervention image data, the procedure is guided by X-ray fluoroscopy. Through small incisions in the femoral arteries, vascular sheaths are placed first. After the proper placement of guidewires and catheters, the tightly folded endograft (also called stent-graft) is moved into the final location. Several angiography images ensure the position intraoperatively, and the main part of the endograft is eventually unfolded and "modelled" onto the vascular wall. Finally, the complete prosthesis is assembled from an additional endograft "leg", that is positioned in the iliacal section. As for the open surgery, the placed endograft excludes the aneurysm from the blood pressure by providing an artificial lumen; the remaining, outer blood will thrombose over time. Figure 7.10 illustrates the situation.

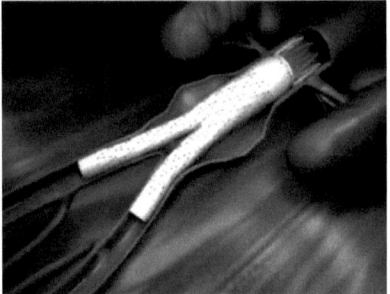

Figure 7.10: Endograft for AAA treatment. (Image courtesy of Cook Medical Inc.)

Discussion Although the EVAR method seems advantageous, there are several issues. Firstly, the minimally-invasive method is only applicable to approximately 30% of the patients due to morphological characteristics (e.g., aortic structure, minimum diameter, calcifications, etc.), and functional configuration (kidney function, contrast agent compatibility, etc.).[15] In addition, the method requires a regular follow-up protocol to ensure stable positioning and rule out any type of leakage. Finally, the EVAR procedure is on average twice as expensive as conventional open surgery, mainly due to the very expensive stent-graft prosthesis and post-intervention surveillance.

7.2.2 Approaches

This section describes several approaches that were proposed during the first research phases of the project. While the first focuses on the (semi-)automatic guidance of manual measurements, the subsequent contribution discusses the complete determination of relevant parameters, making explicit use of graphics hardware.

Automatic Path Reconstruction of Aortic Aneurysms in Postintervention CTA Images

There are two different therapies for abdominal aortic aneurysms, as outlined in the preceding section. However, EVAR procedures are not always applicable and the analysis and

---

[15] Based on statistical information and limitations of current endograft technology.

7.2. ARCADE

correlation of follow-up image data is a challenging and time-consuming task due to the manual process and long time between the different acquisitions. The following approach proposed by Schmitt et al. [SRW08] strives to automate the specification of planes orthogonal to the aortic path, and thus accelerating the whole procedure.

Introduction While there exist several methods for the pre-operative aneurysm segmentation (e.g., Olabarriaga et al. [ORF$^+$05] or de Bruijne et al. [dBvGVN04]), follow-up analysis and quantification is usually performed manually today. During the detection of effects caused by the implant (e.g., leakage of contrast agent), the maximum diameter as the main parameter is examined. For an exact measurement, however, it is essential to have a cross-sectional slice orthogonal to the aortic path. In addition to this challenging task, the determination of the largest global diameter is also a highly manual process.

In the following workflow, the user specifies only start and end point of the region to be analyzed. The centerline of the aorta is then automatically computed by means of three-dimensional segmentation methods and graph-based algorithms. Based on this centerline, the volume data set can be reformatted in arbitrary directions, so that correct cross-sections can be provided, as well as a normalized section along the path (i.e., curved MPR). This allows the examination of the overall shape of the aneurysm, in addition to a single diameter.

Methods After the user selected the region-of-interest [16] (usually from renal arteries to the aortic bifurcation or iliac arteries), an edge-preserving noise reduction filter is applied. Although advanced algorithms such as anistropic diffusion might achieve better results in general, the subsequent steps are less sensitive to noise. Another disadvantage of complex algorithms is the setting of (multiple) parameters, which is contrary to the goal of minimal user interaction and manual steps. Thus, in order to automate this process a three-dimensional extension of the Kuwahara-Nagao filter [KHEK76] is used here as a parameter-free algorithm.

The segmentation is performed by means of the 3D-CSC algorithm developed by Sturm et al. [Stu04, PSW05]. This method is based on a hierarchical cell structure that segments arbitrary volume data sets into regions of homogeneous values. The threshold needed for segmenting the aortic lumen can be usually determined by the user's initial input. In order to classify the segmented regions, the data set's histogram is computed and divided into five classes based on the k-Harmonic-Means algorithm proposed by Zhang et al. [ZHD01]. These clusters represent the different tissue or material types: air, fat tissue, blood vessels (without contrast agent), contrasted blood, bone/metal. The resulting thresholds thus enable the classification of the CSC segments into these classes. As there might occur small inclusions of different classes due to noise or local artefacts which can deteriorate the centerline computation, a neighborhood analysis detects and removes such elements.

Based on the classification of every voxel in the data set, a binary volume can be created: the contrasted lumen is designated as foreground, all other voxels as background. Then a

---

[16]This step is optional, as usually the acquired data is limited in axial direction to the interest region anyway. However, the amount of computation can be reduced considerably by defining the ROI in sagittal/coronal direction.

distance transform on this three-dimensional data set is performed, with special attention to the usually anisotropic voxel size. There exist several algorithms for this procedure, where the methods proposed by Meijster et al. [MRH00] offers the best performance and flexibility for software implementations, the approach by Cuntz and Kolb [CK07] for GPU systems, respectively.

After this distance transform the centerline is determined. Therefore, a directed, weighted graph is created, where all voxels within the lumen resemble nodes. For every node there exist 26 neighboring nodes in 3D. Let d_{max} be the global maximum of the distance transform of lumen voxels. The weight of one edge in the graph is then computed by the difference of d_{max} and the current voxel's value that resembles the target node of this edge. Hence, edges that lead to outer voxels (nodes) are assigned a higher weight than inward edges. This results in a centerline by means of a Dijkstra-based shortest-path search between the initially specified start and end point. In order to smooth the centerline, a Gaussian kernel is applied to the line and ultimately leads to a less noisy path. Based on this curve it is straightforward to create two-dimensional cross-sections as well as sections along the whole curve (i.e., curved MPR). The whole process is summarized in the diagram in figure 7.11.

Results The presented method has been tested on ten pre- and post-intervention data sets of different patients, with the pre-operative data being as suited for examination as post-operative data. Figure 7.12(a) depicts a cross-section of the aorta in axial direction. Due to the non-orthogonal slice orientation and the resulting distortion, the aorta appears to be of elliptical shape. The correct, undistorted cross-section with the slice orientation computed by the determined centerline is shown in figure 7.12(b). The subsequent images 7.12(c) and 7.12(d) depict the path of the aortic centerline as white line, and a longitudinal section of the aorta based on a curved MPR, respectively.[17]

Discussion The proposed method is able to analyze CTA data sets of the human abdominal region robustly, in order to provide visualizations for improved and more reliable measurements. Firstly, the quantification of the aneurysm's diameter requires less interaction, and the automatic computation of the slice orientation allows stable results. Secondly, the longitudinal section view enables the assessment of changes at global scale.

While the aforementioned implementation is based on several tools and applications, the integration of the whole workflow into one platform is of interest. In addition to this software engineering task, the next step is the integration and extension of graphics hardware accelerated computations, as indicated by the tagged processing items in figure 7.11. Many of the computationally expensive procedures would benefit from GPU implementations, as shown in chapter 3. From a medical point of view, deriving novel parameters to better describe aneurysms, as well as the extension of such algorithms to adjacent sections of the aorta or other vascular systems (e.g., cerebral arteries) is also of interest.

---

[17]The implementation and images are based on a modified version of the MPRPath module in MeVis-Lab [MeV07]; see also Boskamp et al. [BRL+04].

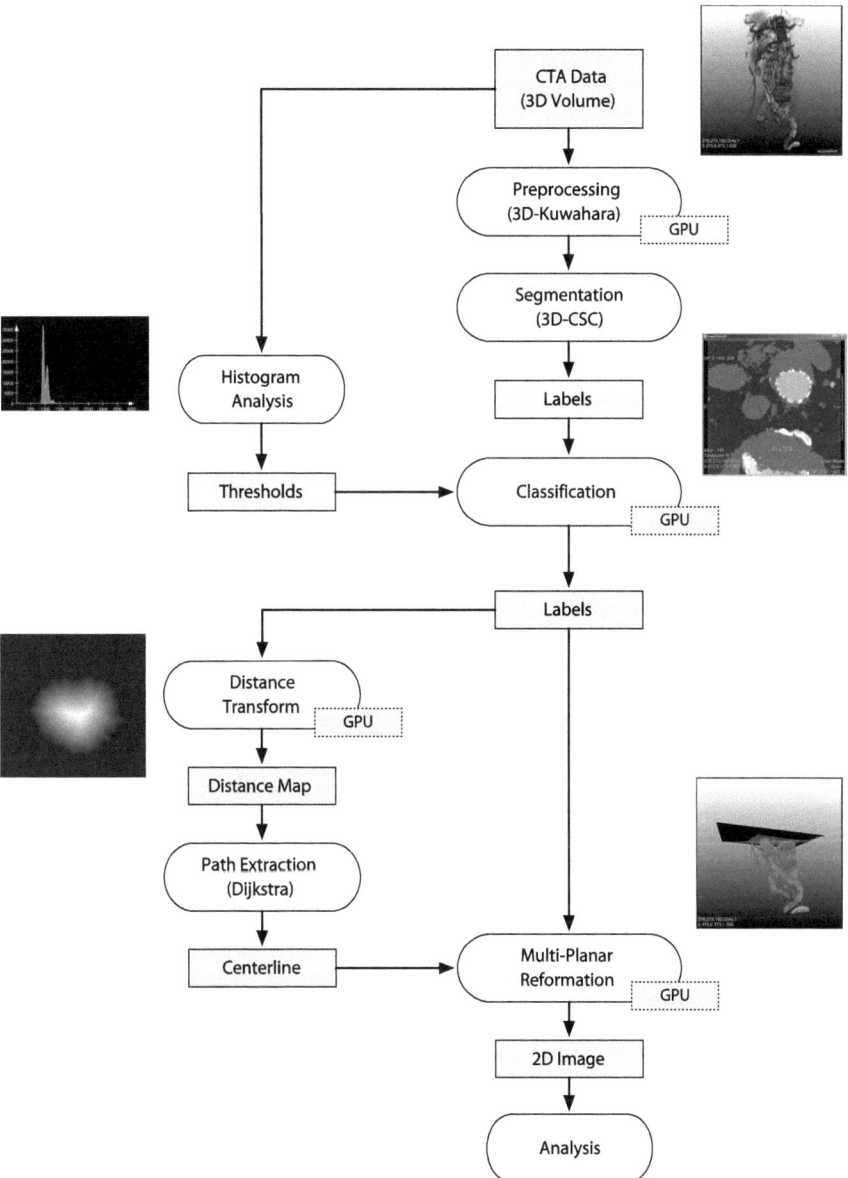

Figure 7.11: Flow chart depicting the processing steps in [SRW08] with possible extensions to GPU implementations.

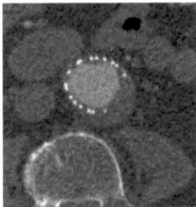 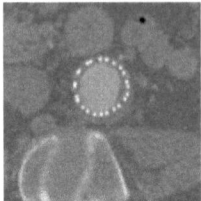  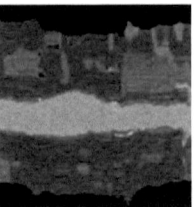

(a) Axial cross-section of the aorta.   (b) Orthogonal cross-section of the aorta.   (c) 3D path of the aorta (white curve)   (d) Longitudinal cut of aortic section.

Figure 7.12: Different views of the analyzed aortic section.

Visualization-based 3D Segmentation and Quantification of Abdominal Aortic Aneurysms

The preceding approach has focused on supporting the assessment of length parameters by automatically determining cross-sectional images. Although this allows a more stable measurement of the aneurysm's diameter, it requires some user interaction as well as the use of multiple systems. As already indicated in the diagram in figure 7.11 on page 197, several processing steps can be performed on the graphics hardware. This would accelerate computationally expensive tasks on the one hand, and support the further integration of the toolchain into one platform on the other hand. An attempt to combine the processing and visualization for abdominal aneurysms will be presented in the following paragraphs and is based on Raspe et al. [RWS07].

Introduction As described before, the diagnosis of (abdominal) aortic aneurysms is usually based on measurements in two-dimensional images, both for pre- and postintervention assessment. Therefore, a considerable amount of manual interaction is needed to select a specific slice from a whole three-dimensional data set. This volumetric nature, however, lends itself to use other, preferably three-dimensional parameters and additional visualization techniques. However, performing advanced computations on such volume data sets is complex and time-consuming, and usually does not go well with the requirements of clinical workflows.

Therefore, this approach proposes the utilization of programmable graphics hardware for the processing and quantification of aneurysms. As shown in chapter 3, various applications benefit from the computational performance of modern GPUs widely available in commodity systems today.

Related Work The segmentation and quantification of vascular structures has been covered in numerous contributions. For a broader overview of such algorithms in the general case, the reader is referred to Preim and Bartz [PB07] and the references therein, as only a few will be mentioned here. The following approaches can be divided into two categories:

- model-based methods (deformable objects, active shape models (ASM))
- combinations of morphological and intensity-based operations

All systems work semi-automatically, i.e., the user has to specify at least the region of interest; often further parameters have to be set. De Bruijne et al. [dBvGVN04] utilize algorithms that are based on ASMs, but have been extended by non-linear parameters for aneurysm segmentation. Subasic et al. [SKLS02] evaluate two different ASM methods with respect to user interaction and segmentation results.

The approach by Boskamp et al. [BRL$^+$04] represents the second category in that they do not employ shape models. In their method, several region growing iterations are analyzed (see section 3.2.2 for additional information on this aspect) and serve as input for a skeletonization of the vascular structure. The resulting path is used for a multiplanar reformation, and watershed segmentation on these slice images allow for the quantification of the volume.[18] Bodur et al. [BGS$^+$07] perform similar steps, but build a distance graph upon a directly computed centerline instead. This is also used for the computation of two-dimensional sections along the path, where these cross-sectional images are analyzed by algorithms based on the circumference of the aortic section.

Material The approach proposed in this work was realized using different platforms and applications that will be outlined shortly. The underlying data have resolutions of 512×512 (0.34 − 0.71 mm), with the number of slices ranging from 61 to 325 (2 − 0.5 mm, resp.). Six patients have already undergone endovascular surgery, whereas the remaining 14 data sets show pre-intervention anatomy. For all acquisitions contrast agent was used. In addition to the framework CASCADA developed in the course of this thesis, the plug-in oriented library "KIPL" (Image Recognition Working Group, University of Koblenz-Landau), and "MeVisLab" [MeV07] was used.

Approach Based on the short review of related work in the preceding paragraph, the approach outlined here can be categorized as a region-based method with additional hierarchical information. With respect to the cited contributions, the approach by Boskamp et al. [BRL$^+$04] is most similar. Here, however, the GPU is explicitly utilized for different computation steps.

The incorporation of a multi-resolution method is motivated by the following facts. Firstly, as this implementation is based on graphics hardware, different resolutions of the data set can be efficiently computed, especially if standard linear interpolation is sufficient. The second reason is the fact that for discrete models, geometric information such as gradients is limited by the grid size. By reducing the resolution incrementally and interpolating the data, however, smooth gradients can be achieved (see figure 7.13). This allows for a better and more global characterization of the structure's surface.

The acquired image data (here: CTA images) are loaded into the application and represented as volume. The additional reduction of artefacts from metallic structures in post-intervention data will not be addressed here; see Yu et al. [YZB$^+$07] for reference, for example. Starting at that point, the remaining steps are:

---

[18] Note that this approach was used in the approach presented in the preceding section.

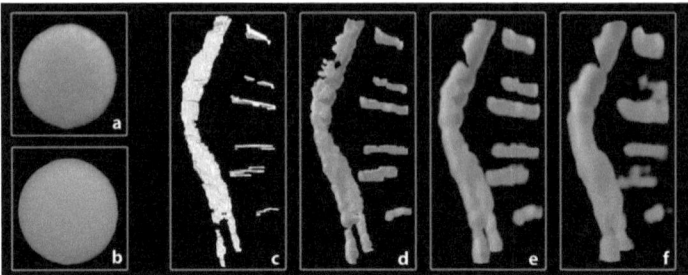

Figure 7.13: Smoothing gradient information (here: color-coded) by resampling in different resolution levels. Sphere (a), factor 2 (b); segmented structure from AAA data set (c), factor 2, 4, and 8, resp. (d-f)

1. Selection of region-of-interest (usually from renal arteries to the bifurcation or iliac arteries)

2. Computation of multi-resolution information (factor 2-4)

3. Gradient computation (central differencing or 3D Sobel)

   - Direct region growing. (Aortic lumen with the contrast agent is trivial. For aneurysm/thrombotic tissue the additional resolutions are used for weighting the growing process)
   - Thresholding (binary, interval/multilevel): results in coarse representation of the (contrasted) volume

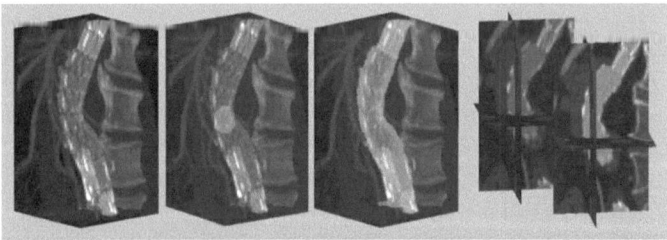

Figure 7.14: Segmenting the aorta lumen using GPU-based region growing with simultaneous volume rendering (MIP). from left to right: initial data set, after 3 iterations, after 94 iterations (converged), additional MPR visualization

The good results of the region growing method (see figures 7.14 and 7.15) with respect to robustness, performance, and segmentation results support this type of algorithm, especially for GPU implementations. In addition to this variant, further steps for the quantification of cross-sectional diameters are:

7.2. ARCADE

4. Determination of the centerline by skeletonization using the hit-miss operator or distance transform

5. Creation of cross-sectional images orthogonal to centerline

6. Detection and quantification of aortic sections using circular shapes

The last step is based on the assumption that orthogonal cross-sections contain mainly circular (or elliptical) shapes, as can be seen in figures 7.12(a) and 7.12(b) on page 198. In case of interrupted or strongly deviating shapes, e.g., due to imaging artefacts or irregular tissue structures, these effects are in most cases limited to few slices and/or voxels. Despite these deteriorations, the hierarchical approach in combination with robust algorithms such as the Hough transform compensate for these local effects.

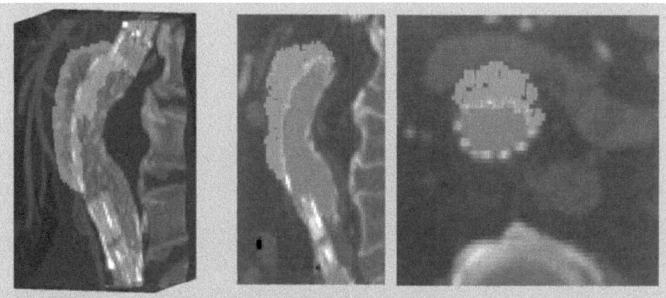

Figure 7.15: GPU-based region growing segmentation of the thrombotic aneurysm (converged after 73 iterations). from left to right: MIP rendering, sagittal-/axial view; note the separation from structures with equal gray value

Discussion As shown in the preceding section, modern graphics hardware is not only suited for visualizing medical data in real-time. It also allows the fast processing of the data, as well as the direct interaction with the algorithms, as discussed in chapter 3. Especially the segmentation based on region growing for abdominal aortic aneurysms has been improved by means of the hierarchical approach. Instead of being sensitive to local deteriorations, the global information enhanced this rather simple algorithm considerably. In addition, the hardware implementation of certain computations clearly reduced the run-time.

The aforementioned concepts have been preliminary steps towards an extended assessment of abdominal aortic aneurysms. The utilization of graphics hardware has to be compared to established methods in terms of performance and quality. In particular, the segmentation quality will be evaluated on a larger set of example data and manual segmentations performed by experts.

7.2.3 Resume

The contributions in this project about the assessment of abdominal aortic aneurysms pursued two different directions. Firstly, the procedure of measuring the diameter (and other parameters) is supported by an automated determination of the cross-sectional plane. Although this still requires the manual assessment of the diameter(s), the whole process is clearly accelerated and reduces the results' variability due to stable plane derivation. Secondly, the overall assessment of the lumen and aneurysm by means of segmentation methods. As outlined in the introductory part of this thesis, as well as the preceding discussions, there is a large amount of efficent algorithms available. Due to the utilization of graphics hardware and its interactive visualization possibilities, preferably region/volume-based methods have been used in the early stage of the project. It was also shown that GPU implementations could be easily integrated by using the framework CASCADA.

In addition, first approaches towards a segmentation based on level sets and extended gradient information (e.g., gradient vector flow [XP97]) have been followed and will be the focus of subsequent research – especially in combination with GPU implementations. Moreover, the extension to other modalities or dimensions (e.g., the aforementioned 4D data sets), as well as the adaptability of the methods to adjacent structures (i.e., thoracic/iliac aorta, etc.) are of interest. As a matter of course, the approaches presented in the preceding sections and for upcoming work require further evaluation and thorough comparison with procedures in clinical practice.

CHAPTER 8

CONCLUSION

This chapter concludes the thesis by summarizing the contributions and applications described in part two and three, respectively, in the first section. Subsequent remarks propose the establishment of a classification to assess and rate the performance of a hardware implementation for the given configuration and data at hand during run-time. This is not limited to a decision between CPU and GPU implementations, but also extends to the notion of compression computing. As such a system for decision finding can be arbitrarily complex and would be beyond the scope of this work, the concepts are only outlined theoretically. Prospects to further extensions and trends in both graphics systems and medical imaging will round off the thesis.

8.1 Summary

The goal of this work has been to establish methods and applications to use graphics hardware conveniently for the processing and visualization of medical (volume) data as basis for diagnosis assistance. While the latter has been the focus of intensive research for many years, the combination of both techniques provides various benefits. As shown in the context of "visual computing" approaches, not only the acceleration of computationally expensive tasks is a clear advantage of employing hardware implementations. In addition, the inherent visualization capabilities at real-time performance allow the direct interaction with processes, parameters, or local properties.

Interactive visualization of computations

Different approaches, such as the extension of edge-preserving filtering to three-dimensional video sequences or the comparison of tone-mapping procedures for improving the visualization of medical image data with varying dynamical range were discussed at the beginning of chapter 3 to emphasize the high potential of GPU-based implementations. This led to the evaluation of implementation variants in order to optimize the computation intensity, that is, the ratio of arithmetic operations to memory transfers. Supporting the use of the GPU for as much consecutive computations as possible is one of the key features of the developed framework CASCADA.

As already mentioned before, extending state-of-the-art volume rendering techniques such as ray casting provides powerful and flexible methods for interacting with the visualization. The concept of "ray textures" introduced in section 3.2.1 allows various possibilities to control rendering parameters locally. Moreover, this approach is not dependent of the specific ray casting implementation and thus integrates well with software implementations, acceleration techniques, etc.

Compression Computing

However, one of the main problems with using the graphics hardware for processing large amounts of data is the limited bandwidth and size of (graphics) memory. Whereas the processing and visualization of data too large to fit into the graphics memory can be alleviated or bypassed by divide-and-conquer strategies (e.g., bricking or hierarchical approaches), the relatively low transfer rate between host and graphics memory is still an issue. On the other hand, data compression is an established approach used in virtually all fields of information technology. Although this allows the reduction of the data at almost arbitrary levels – depending on the specific quality requirements – accessing the data for purposes other than storage requires decompression.

Hence, in chapter 4 the concept of data processing within the compression domain is presented and evaluated in the context of medical volume data. In addition to the discussion of compression procedures suited for the task, different topics regarding implementation, visual quality, performance, and possible extensions are addressed. In spite of the moderate results, combining this approach with the aforementioned concatenation of GPU-based computations is certain to break even for practical applications – let alone further optimizations of the prototypical implementation.

Object-oriented GPU Programming

Yet another aspect is the creation of GPU implementations itself. Many authors have proposed approaches to abstract from the intricate hardware details, as is extensively discussed in section 5.1. However, these systems are either limited to certain applications (e.g., traditional graphics rendering), or too abstract to map further development of the GPU's architecture, or require the use of inflexible programming constructs or systems. Although this situation is going to improve with dedicated general purpose APIs such as Nvidia's CUDA that also alleviate several programming limitations due to hardware restrictions, established methods from software engineering are still hard to apply.

Therefore, the introduction of object-orientation and hierarchical concepts to (traditional) GPU programming is the very basis of CASCADA. The framework provides a view to hardware implementation more problem- or workflow-driven than previous approaches, which has several advantages: the implementation's layout is natural in that it strives to follow the problem's structure; existing functionality is easy to maintain and can be reused; technical advancements such as CUDA can be integrated straightforwardly, while maintaining abstraction from low-level details.

Applications

In chapter 7, two projects are described that make use of several concepts mentioned above. The medical background for both projects is the assessment of anatomical structures by means of preprocessing and segmenting volume data for diagnosis assistance. While the final version of the "LiverGPU" application uses a subset of CASCADA 1, the still ongoing project "ARCADE" utilizes various systems in combination with core functionality of CASCADA. As shown in section 6.2 there have been additional projects and extensions to the framework. In a nutshell, the different projects have demonstrated that the framework and its underlying theoretical concepts allow the utilization of graphics hardware for non-graphics applications to improve the overall performance and interactivity – also in collaboration with other systems.

8.2 Prospects

The following paragraphs will discuss current trends that have been touched on throughout the thesis as well as refer to topics that are subject to further research. While the first section takes up the idea of assessing the performance of GPU computations in more detail, the remaining two sections reconsider recent developments and eventually conclude this thesis.

8.2.1 Classification of computations

As shown in section 3.1.3, utilizing the graphics hardware is not always beneficial. There are several factors that affect the overall performance of such implementations, aside from the underlying hardware generation: type and characteristics of the algorithm, properties of the data, etc. It would be therefore of high interest to *forecast the potential benefit* of a GPU implementation based on some generalized criteria. This extends to the direct processing of compressed data, as introduced in chapter 4, whether an additional benefit with respect to memory and/or computation efficiency is possible.

In order to assess the performance gain of GPU algorithms over software implementations different approaches are imaginable. Software engineering problems, for example, require an evaluation of development cycles, code complexity, maintainability, or simply the number of developer hours. Although there exist different measures such as the COCOMO standard[1] or the (debatable) unit SLOC[2], these are obviously more difficult to apply to graphics hardware programming – if relevant at all. Firstly, the code length of shader programs is often much more important due to technical restrictions of the hardware or performance reasons. Secondly, some operations can be hardly applied to other contexts (e.g., swizzling

---

[1] for more information see http://sunset.usc.edu/research/COCOMOII/, last visit December 10, 2008

[2] SLOC = source lines of code

or interpolated texture fetch) or are of very different complexity (e.g., simple addition vs. computing a reciprocal).

Another approach would be to benchmark the algorithms in question on current graphics platforms and compare it with standardized software implementations like sorting algorithms, BLAS routines[3], etc. Using such information is, however, rather unstable due to a large number of factors that might affect the result: driver version, operating system, data layout, to mention only a few. Above that, such implementations are usually subject to change because of the rapid technical advances of graphics hardware today.

As discussed in chapter 5, programming GPUs does not employ high-level programming paradigms like object-orientation yet. While several authors have proposed to utilize concepts from object-oriented programming or meta-languages such as "Sh" [MQP02], application code controlling the GPU shader programs is often written in plain C, especially in programs using the lately introduced GPGPU interfaces.

So, if GPU programming is not suitable for standard software assessment, how can a classification be accomplished? Basic algorithms – no matter the language they are implemented in – are usually qualified by their big O notation which is the de-facto standard for specifying the computational complexity of functions with respect to input data. Although this measure could be applied to shader programs in principle as well, it would be too coarse, however: different kinds of data representations, the complex architecture of modern graphics hardware, etc. are not covered (sufficiently) by the notational model. In addition, not only the single program plays an important role for the algorithmic complexity, but much more how often it is executed: fragment programs, for example, are executed lots of million times per second with numerous execution units in parallel.

Therefore, one approach would be to *analyze the system beforehand* with different types of data sets and algorithms. This preparation step is commonly used during installation of software components such as libraries, modules, or drivers and is often referred to as "configure step".[4] There are some means for querying the current GPUs configuration, but they highly depend on the graphics driver, the graphics API used (i.e., OpenGL, DirectX, etc.), and the operating system itself.

The benefit of using such a configuration step is to rate the graphics hardware at hand and decide during run-time whether utilizing the GPU would improve the overall performance. This approach would be twofold: the platform has to be rated as well as the algorithm itself. The former can be queried using dedicated API tools (see the `CascadaCUDA` implementation in section 6.3.3), for example. However, assessing the implemented functionality (i.e., the particular preprocessing sequence or computation/visualization procedure) is not as straightforward. Although different computational complexities can be identified for algorithms, e.g. for image preprocessing as in section 2.3.1, this is practically impossible for all kinds of applications.

---

[3]BLAS = Basic linear algebra subprograms

[4]Depending on the operating system this is hidden from the user or directly controllable with the well-known `configure; make; make install` command on UNIX systems.

As shown in section 3.1.3, the data transfer plays an important role for GPU algorithms and their potential benefit. While the pure computation can be several orders of magnitude faster using hardware implementations, frequent data transfer can negate the overall performance gain. As the bandwidth between host and graphics memory is still a technological issue, the system can overcome this by concatenating multiple computation steps on the graphics hardware; hence the concepts in CASCADA. Simply said, the more (computationally expensive) operations are performed on the GPU, the less important the time-consuming transfer becomes; see Buck [Buc05, BFH$^+$04] for this "arithmetic intensity". Additionally, if intermediate results should be displayed during execution a hardware implementation will be the preferable option in almost all cases, because the data has to be transferred to video memory for display anyway.

Especially compression techniques contribute to reducing the amount of data to be transferred. As discussed in chapter 4, performing computations also in the compression domain can further increase the benefit of GPU implementations. Such a classification scheme is already prepared in CASCADA 2 and will be pursued in subsequent research, as well as the extension of compression computing.

8.2.2 Graphics systems

In the fundamentals part as well as in chapter 5 the role of the recently introduced programming interfaces (i.e., Nvidia CUDA and OpenCL) was addressed. During the course of this thesis, CUDA has become the major platform for practically all kinds of GPGPU implementations. In combination with the latest generation of graphics hardware or dedicated visual computing systems, many compute-intense applications have been accelerated by multiple orders of magnitude. Although real-time applications are appealing from a computer graphics perspective, offline computations benefit even more from these rapid advancements – not only because of the direct visualization capabilities addressed in part two of the thesis.

On the other hand, there are active developments towards an "xPU", that is, the fusion of dedicated (graphics) processors with the standard processing unit. This trend is a rather logical consequence of current advances: while GPUs become more versatile and programmable, main processors consist of an increasing number of cores. The most prominent and capable candidate that has been introduced recently is Intel's Larrabee. Its architecture can be mainly regarded as a combination of a multi-core CPU and a GPU, with adoptions from both worlds. As it uses the instructions set of standard processors, programming is supposed to be as flexible and universal as software implementations today. Although it is supposed to be available not before 2010, first prototypes already indicate competitive, if not superior performance especially for "number crunching" applications due to the large vector units. More details can be found in Seiler et al. [SCS$^+$08] and, of course, upcoming developments of these systems.

8.2.3 Medical imaging

In functional imaging the anatomical context is of great importance due to the low spatial resolution provided by the complex acquisition procedure. Therefore, additional information is generated by means of combining functional and morphological imaging, as addressed in section 2.1.1. In the past, the patient has been examined by both conventional CT and PET or SPECT separately; merging the acquired data has been a very challenging task. On the one hand, patient movement cannot be avoided due to the time between both scans. On the other hand, the different modalities acquire data at different resolutions, value ranges, etc. Thus, aligning one data set onto the other is a very time-consuming task – if possible at all. Although intensive research has proposed lots of approaches to perform this registration algorithmically, such procedures achieve either incorrect results or are not compatible with clinical workflows regarding time and costs.

A few years ago, devices have become available that combine these modalities; SPECT/CT or PET/CT are typical examples. These systems feature both acquisition facilities in one device, thus reducing the motion artefacts and overall scanning time to a minimum. The workstations' software already performs the matching of the different data sets, as the geometrical configuration of the device is known. In addition, using the higher resolution of the CT scanner, the reconstruction quality of the functional imaging can be improved as well. This results in most cases in near-optimal registrations, and often justifies the disadvantages of such approaches (increased radiation exposure, very high costs of devices, etc.).

MRI-based modalities are even more advantageous in that they allow the acquisition of multiple information "in-place". That is, except for numerical inaccuracies during reconstruction, for each position in space different data can be measured by simply altering the protocol, whereas the aforementioned devices consist of separate parts. Recent developments take the benefits of nuclear imaging even further and combine PET devices with MRI – which is very challenging with respect to manufacturing parts that are both compatible with the strong magnetic field, and do not deteriorate quality by introducing (unknown) inhomogenities.

Managing large data sets from these acquisition systems is another challenging task, especially considering the interactive exploration of such multi-modal information. Another example are dual-source CTs that use an additional x-ray source for a second imaging process (section 2.1.1). Following the trends of earlier developments, multiple sources seem probable and may extend the benefits of dual-source systems.[5] This results in even more image data being acquired, especially regarding the additional advances in spatial and/or temporal resolution. Therefore, the utilization of graphics hardware for both visualization *and* computation, as well as the integration of compression techniques represent key supplements for future developments.

---

[5]Note that CT-based imaging is always connected with (high) radiation exposure where such multi-source systems add another complexity to controlling the acquisition process.

APPENDIX

PUBLICATIONS

[ERS08]   Marius Erdt, Matthias Raspe, and Michael Suehling. Automatic Hepatic Vessel Segmentation using Graphics Hardware. In Takeyoshi Dohi, Ichiro Sakuma, and Hongen Liao, editors, *4th International Workshop on Medical Imaging and Augmented Reality*, volume 5128 of *Lecture Notes in Computer Science*, pages 403–412. Springer, 8 2008.

[LB07]   Andreas Langs and Matthias Biedermann. Filtering Video Volumes Using the Graphics Hardware. In Bjarne K. Ersbøll and Kim Steenstrup Pedersen, editors, *SCIA*, volume 4522 of *Lecture Notes in Computer Science*, pages 878–887. Springer, 2007.

[RLM08]   Matthias Raspe, Guido Lorenz, and Stefan Müller. Evaluating the Performance of Processing Medical Volume Data on Graphics Hardware. In T. Tolxdorff, J. Braun, T.M. Deserno, H. Handels, A. Horsch, and H.-P. Meinzer, editors, *Bildverarbeitung für die Medizin 2008*, Informatik aktuell, pages 427–431. Springer, 4 2008.

[RLP08]   Matthias Raspe, Guido Lorenz, and Stephan Palmer. Hierarchical and Object-Oriented GPU Programming. In *Computer Graphics International Conference*, pages 333–337, 6 2008.

[RM07]   Matthias Raspe and Stefan Müller. Using a GPU-based Framework for Interactive Tone Mapping of Medical Volume Data. In Anders Hast, editor, *SIGRAD 2007. The Annual SIGRAD Conference, Special Theme: Computer Graphics in Healthcare*, pages 3–10. Linköping University Electronic Press, Linköpings universitet, 11 2007.

[RM08]   Matthias Raspe and Stefan Müller. Controlling GPU-based Volume Rendering using Ray Textures. In Vaclav Skala, editor, *International Conference in Central Europe on Computer Graphics, Visualization and Computer Vision*, pages 277–283, 2 2008.

[RRRP08] Christian Rieder, Felix Ritter, Matthias Raspe, and Heinz-Otto Peitgen. Interactive Visualization of Multimodal Volume Data for Neurosurgical Tumor Treatment. *Computer Graphics Forum (Special Issue on Eurographics Symposium on Visualization)*, 27(3):1055–1062, 2008.

[RWS07]   Matthias Raspe, Ralph Wickenhöfer, and Frank Schmitt. Visualisierungsgestützte 3D-Segmentierung und Quantifizierung von Bauchaortenaneurysmen. In *6.*

Jahrestagung der Deutschen Gesellschaft für Computer- und Roboterassistierte Chirurgie, CURAC, pages 197–200, 2007.

[SRW08] Frank Schmitt, Matthias Raspe, and Ralph Wickenhöfer. Automatische Rekonstruktion des Verlaufs aneurysmatischer Aorten in postoperativen CTA-Bildern. In T. Tolxdorff, J. Braun, T.M. Deserno, H. Handels, A. Horsch, and H.-P. Meinzer, editors, *Bildverarbeitung für die Medizin 2008*, Informatik aktuell, pages 382–386. Springer Verlag, 2008.

Bibliography

[AB94]   R. Adams and L. Bischof. Seeded region growing. *Pattern Analysis and Machine Intelligence, IEEE Transactions on*, 16(6):641–647, 1994.

[AMHH08] Tomas Akenine-Möller, Eric Haines, and Natty Hoffman. *Real-Time Rendering 3rd Edition*. A. K. Peters, Ltd., Natick, MA, USA, 2008. website: http://www.realtimerendering.com/.

[AW90]   Gregory D. Abram and Turner Whitted. Building Block Shaders. In *SIGGRAPH '90: Proceedings of the 17th annual conference on Computer graphics and interactive techniques*, pages 283–288, New York, NY, USA, 1990. ACM.

[Bar00]   Danny Barash. Bilateral Filtering and Anisotropic Diffusion: Towards a Unified Viewpoint. *Third International Conference on Scale-Space and Morphology*, pages 273–280, 2000.

[BB03]   Michael Bender and Manfred Brill. *Computergrafik*. Carl Hanser Verlag München Wien, 2003.

[BFH+04] Ian Buck, Tim Foley, Daniel Horn, Jeremy Sugerman, Kayvon Fatahalian, Mike Houston, and Pat Hanrahan. Brook for GPUs: Stream Computing on Graphics Hardware. In *SIGGRAPH '04: ACM SIGGRAPH 2004 Papers*, pages 777–786, New York, NY, USA, 2004. ACM.

[BG05]   Stefan Bruckner and Meister Eduard Gröller. VolumeShop: An Interactive System for Direct Volume Illustration. In H. Rushmeier C. T. Silva, E. Gröller, editor, *Proceedings of IEEE Visualization 2005*, pages 671–678, October 2005.

[BGS+07] Osman Bodur, Leo Grady, Arthur Stillman, Randolph Setser, Gareth Funka-Lea, and Thomas O'Donnell. Semi-Automatic Aortic Aneurysm Analysis. In *Medical Imaging 2007: Physiology, Function, and Structure from Medical Images. Edited by Manduca, Armando; Hu, Xiaoping P.. Proceedings of the SPIE, Volume 6511, pp. 65111G (2007).*, volume 6511 of *Presented at the Society of Photo-Optical Instrumentation Engine*, March 2007.

[BH93]   Michael F. Barnsley and Lyman P. Hurd. *Fractal Image Compression*. A. K. Peters, Ltd., Natick, MA, USA, 1993.

[BKS+96]   Kevin M. Baskin, Catherine A. Kusnick, Susanne Shamsolkottabi, Elvira V. Lang, J. D. Corson, William Stanford, Brad H. Thompson, and Eric A. Hoffman. Volumetric analysis of abdominal aortic aneurysm. volume 2709, pages 323–337. SPIE, 1996.

[Bla99]   James F. Blanchard. Epidemiology of Abdominal Aortic Aneurysms. *Epidemiol Rev*, 21(2):207–221, 1999.

[Bow00]   Kevin W. Bowyer. Validation of Medical Image Analysis Techniques. In Milan Sonka and J. Michael Fitzpatrick, editors, *Handbook of Medical Imaging, Volume 2: Medical Image Processing and Analysis*, chapter 10, pages 567–607. SPIE–The International Society for Optical Engineering, 2000.

[Bra03]   Andrew P. Bradley. Shift-invariance in the Discrete Wavelet Transform. In *Digital Image Computing: Techniques and Applications (DICTA'03)*, pages 29–38. CSIRO Publishing, 12 2003.

[BRL+04]   T. Boskamp, D. Rinck, F. Link, B. Kümmerlen, G. Stamm, and P. Mildenberger. New Vessel Analysis Tool for Morphometric Quantification and Visualization of Vessels in CT and MR Imaging Data Sets. *Radiographics: a review publication of the Radiological Society of North America, Inc*, 24(1):287–297, 2004.

[Bru08]   Stefan Bruckner. *Interactive Illustrative Volume Visualization*. PhD thesis, Institute of Computer Graphics and Algorithms, Vienna University of Technology, Favoritenstrasse 9-11/186, A-1040 Vienna, Austria, 3 2008.

[BSC+06]   Dirk Bartz, Benjamin Schnaidt, Jirko Cernik, Ludwig Gauckler, Jan Fischer, and Angel del Río. Volumetric High Dynamic Range Windowing for Better Data Representation. In *Afrigaph '06: Proceedings of the 4th international conference on Computer graphics, virtual reality, visualisation and interaction in Africa*, pages 137–144, New York, NY, USA, 2006. ACM.

[Buc05]   Ian Buck. *Stream Computing on Graphics Hardware*. PhD thesis, Stanford University, Stanford, CA, USA, 2005. Pat Hanrahan (advisor).

[BUW+07]   Ingmar Bitter, Robert Van Uitert, Ivo Wolf, Luis Ibáñez, and Jan-Martin Kuhnigk. Comparison of Four Freely Available Frameworks for Image Processing and Visualization That Use ITK. *IEEE Transactions on Visualization and Computer Graphics*, 13(3):483–493, 2007.

[CK07]   Nicolas Cuntz and Andreas Kolb. Fast Hierarchical 3D Distance Transforms on the GPU. In *Eurographics 2007*, pages 93–96, 2007.

[CMS99]   Stuart K. Card, Jock D. Mackinlay, and Ben Shneiderman. *Readings in Information Visualization: Using Vision to Think*. Morgan Kaufmann, 1999.

[Coo84]	Robert L. Cook. Shade Trees. In *SIGGRAPH '84: Proceedings of the 11th annual conference on Computer graphics and interactive techniques*, pages 223–231, New York, NY, USA, 1984. ACM.
[CORG93]	Pamela C. Cosman, Karen L. Oehler, Eve A. Riskin, and Robert M. Gray. Using Vector Quantization for Image Processing. In *Proceedings of the IEEE '93*, volume 81, pages 1326–1341, Washington, DC, USA, 1993. IEEE Computer Society.
[CSS08]	Hungi-Li Jason Chen, Faramarz F. Samavati, and Mario Costa Sousa. GPU-based point radiation for interactive volume sculpting and segmentation. *Vis. Comput.*, 24(7):689–698, 2008.
[dBvGVN04]	Marleen de Bruijne, Bram van Ginneken, Max A. Viergever, and Wiro J. Niessen. Interactive segmentation of abdominal aortic aneurysms in CTA images. *Medical Image Analysis*, 8:127–138, 2004.
[DC03]	Gareth Daniel and Min Chen. Visualising Video Sequences Using Direct Volume Rendering. In *Vision, Video, and Graphics (VVG 2003)*, pages 103–110, 2003.
[DHK07]	Atam P. Dhawan, H. K. Huang, and Dae-Shik Kim. *Principles and Recent Advances in Medical Imaging and Image Analysis*. World Scientific Publishers Inc., 2007.
[Die05]	Christian Dietz. Design eines Interfaces mit effizienter visueller Rückkopplung zur Anwendung in chirurgischer Navigation von Hüfttotalendoprothesen, 2005. *Diplomarbeit*, Universität Koblenz-Landau, FB4 D 855 CV.
[DKG+07]	Nicolas Diehm, Ralph Kickuth, Brigitta Gahl, Dai-Do Do, Jörg Schmidli, Henning Rattunde, Iris Baumgartner, and Florian Dick. Intraobserver and interobserver variability of 64-row computed tomography abdominal aortic aneurysm neck measurements. *J Vasc Surg.*, 45(2):263–268, 2007.
[DL95]	Andrew Dorrell and David Lowe. Fast Image Operations in Wavelet Spaces. In *Digital Image Computing, Techniques and Applications*, Brisbane, Australia, 1995. Australian Pattern Recognition Society.
[DM97]	Paul E. Debevec and Jitendra Malik. Recovering high dynamic range radiance maps from photographs. In *ACM SIGGRAPH Conference Proceedings*, pages 369–378, August 1997.
[DMAC03]	Frederic Drago, Karol Myszkowski, Thomas Annen, and Norishige Chiba. Adaptive Logarithmic Mapping For Displaying High Contrast Scenes. In Pere Brunet and Dieter W. Fellner, editors, *Proc. of EUROGRAPHICS 2003*, volume 22 of *Computer Graphics Forum*, pages 419–426, Granada, Spain, 2003. Blackwell.

[EE02] Klaus Engel and Thomas Ertl. Interactive High-Quality Volume Rendering with Flexible Consumer Graphics Hardware, 2002.

[EHK+06] Klaus Engel, Markus Hadwiger, Joe M. Kniss, Christof Rezk-Salama, and Daniel Weiskopf. *Real-Time Volume Graphics*. A K Peters, 2006. http://www.real-time-volume-graphics.org, last visit Feb 14 2009.

[Err05] Ugo Erra. Toward Real Time Fractal Compression Using Graphics Hardware. In *ISVC '05: Proceedings of the International Symposium on Visual Computing*, volume 3804, pages 723–728, 2005.

[EWE04] Mike Eissele, Daniel Weiskopf, and Thomas Ertl. The G2-Buffer Framework. In *Proceedings of SimVis*, pages 287–298, 2004.

[FAM+05] Nathaniel Fout, Hiroshi Akiba, Kwan-Liu Ma, Aaron E. Lefohn, and Joe Kniss. High-Quality Rendering of Compressed Volume Data Formats. In Ken Brodlie, David J. Duke, and Kenneth I. Joy, editors, *EuroVis*, pages 77–84. Eurographics Association, 2005.

[FARZ03] K.A. Filis, Fr.R. Arko, G.D. Robin, and Chr. K. Zarins. Three-dimensional CT evaluation for Endovascular abdominal aortic aneurysm repair. Quantitative assessment of the infrarenal aortic neck. *Acta chir. Belg.*, (1):81–86, 2003.

[Fei09] Christian Feinen. Integration von CUDA in ein GPU-Framework anhand einer Beispielanwendung, 2009. *Studienarbeit*, Universität Koblenz-Landau.

[FHCRM00] J. Michael Fitzpatrick, Derek L. G. Hill, and Jr. Calvin R. Maurer. Image Registration. In Milan Sonka and J. Michael Fitzpatrick, editors, *Handbook of Medical Imaging, Volume 2: Medical Image Processing and Analysis*, chapter 8, pages 449–513. SPIE–The International Society for Optical Engineering, 2000.

[FK03] Randima Fernando and Mark J. Kilgard. *The Cg Tutorial – The Definite Guide to Programmable Real-Time Graphics*. Addison-Wesley, 2003. http://www.nvidia.com/object/cg_toolkit.html.

[FM07] Nathaniel Fout and Kwan-Liu Ma. Transform Coding for Hardware-accelerated Volume Rendering. *IEEE Transactions on Visualization and Computer Graphics*, 13(6):1600–1607, 2007.

[FNVV98] Alejandro F. Frangi, Wiro J. Niessen, Koen L. Vincken, and Max A. Viergever. Multiscale Vessel Enhancement Filtering. In William M. Wells, Alan C. F. Colchester, and Scott L. Delp, editors, *Medical Image Computing and Computer-Assisted Intervention – MICCAI'98, First International Conference, Cambridge, MA, USA, October 11-13, 1998, Proceedings*, volume 1496 of *LNCS*, pages 130–137. Springer, 1998.

[FUS+98] Alexandre X. Falcão, Jayaram K. Udupa, Supun Samarasekera, Shoba Sharma, Bruce Elliot Hirsch, and Roberto de Alencar Lotufo. User-Steered Image Segmentation Paradigms: Live Wire and Live Lane. *Graphical Models and Image Processing*, 60(4):233–260, 1998.

[FWBL05] Craig Fleming, Evelyn Whitlock, Tracy Beil, and Frank Lederle. Primary Care Screening for Abdominal Aortic Aneurysm. Technical report, Oregon Evidence-based Practice Center, Portland, Oregon, February 2005. Prepared for Agency for Healthcare Research and Quality, U.S. Department of Health and Human Services.

[GEA96] Roberto Grosso, Thomas Ertl, and Joachim Aschoff. Efficient Data Structures for Volume Rendering of Wavelet-Compressed Data. In N.M. Thalmann and V. Skala, editors, *WSCG '96 - The Fourth International Conference in Central Europe on Computer Graphics and Visualization*, volume I, pages 103–112, University of West Bohemia, Plzen, 1996.

[GG92] Allen Gersho and Robert M. Gray. *Vector Quantization and Signal Compression*. Kluwer Academic Publishers, 1992.

[GHJV95] Erich Gamma, Richard Helm, Ralph Johnson, and John M. Vlissides. *Design Patterns: Elements of Reusable Object-Oriented Software*. Addison-Wesley Professional, 1995.

[Gra84] Robert M. Gray. Vector Quantization. *ASSP Magazine, IEEE*, 1:4–29, 1984.

[Gro94] Markus Groß. *Visual Computing: Integration of Computer Graphics, Visual Perception and Imaging*. Springer, 1994.

[GS04] S. Guthe and W. Strasser. Advanced Techniques for High-Quality Multi Resolution Volume Rendering. *Computers & Graphics*, 28(1):51–58, February 2004.

[GWGS02] Stefan Guthe, Michael Wand, Julius Gonser, and Wolfgang Strasser. Interactive Rendering of Large Volume Data Sets. In *VIS '02: Proceedings of the conference on Visualization '02*, pages 53–60, Washington, DC, USA, 2002. IEEE Computer Society.

[GWWH03] Nolan Goodnight, Rui Wang, Cliff Woolley, and Greg Humphreys. Interactive Time-Dependent Tone Mapping Using Programmable Graphics Hardware. In *Proceedings of the 14th Eurographics workshop on Rendering*, pages 26–37. Eurographics Association, 2003.

[Háj02] Juraj Hájek. Timespace Reconstruction of Videosequences. In *6th Central European Seminar on Computer Graphics (CESCG)*, 2002.

[Har04]   Mark J. Harris. Fast Fluid Dynamics Simulation on the GPU. In Randima Fernando, editor, *GPU Gems, Programming Techniques, Tips, and Tricks for Real-Time Graphics*, chapter 38, pages 637–665. Addison-Wesley, 2004.

[Har05]   Mark Harris. Mapping Computational Concepts to GPUs. In Matt Pharr and Randima Fernando, editors, *GPU Gems 2: Programming Techniques for High-Performance Graphics and General-Purpose Computation*, chapter 31, pages 493–508. Addison Wesley, 2005.

[HB05]   Mark Harris and Ian Buck. Flow-Control Challenges. In Matt Pharr and Randima Fernando, editors, *GPU Gems 2: Programming Techniques for High-Performance Graphics and General-Purpose Computation*, chapter 34, pages 547–555. Addison Wesley, 2005.

[HBSL03]   Mark J. Harris, William V. Baxter, Thorsten Scheuermann, and Anselmo Lastra. Simulation of Cloud Dynamics on Graphics Hardware. In *HWWS '03: Proceedings of the ACM SIGGRAPH/EUROGRAPHICS conference on Graphics hardware*, pages 92–101, 2003.

[HE99]   Matthias Hopf and Thomas Ertl. Hardware-Based Wavelet Transformations. In *Workshop of Vision, Modelling, and Visualization (VMV '99)*, pages 317–328. infix, 1999.

[Höl08]   Thomas Höllt. Direct Processing of Compressed Volume Data, 2008. *Diplomarbeit*, Universität Koblenz-Landau, FB4 D 1096 CV.

[HSO07]   Mark Harris, Shubhabrata Sengupta, and John D. Owens. Parallel Prefix Sum (Scan) with CUDA. In Hubert Nguyen, editor, *GPU Gems 3*, chapter 39, pages 851–876. Addison Wesley, August 2007.

[HZG08]   Qiming Hou, Kun Zhou, and Baining Guo. BSGP: Bulk-Synchronous GPU Programming. In *SIGGRAPH '08: ACM SIGGRAPH 2008 papers*, pages 1–12, New York, NY, USA, 2008. ACM.

[IKLH04]   Milan Ikits, Joe Kniss, Aaron Lefohn, and Charles Hansen. Volume Rendering Techniques. In Randima Fernando, editor, *GPU Gems, Programming Techniques, Tips, and Tricks for Real-Time Graphics*, chapter 39, pages 667–692. Addison-Wesley, 2004.

[Jäh93]   Bernd Jähne. *Spatio-Temporal Image Processing: Theory and Scientific Applications*, volume 751 of *Lecture Notes in Computer Science*. Springer, 1993.

[Jäh97]   Bernd Jähne. *Digitale Bildverarbeitung*. Springer-Verlag Berlin Heidelberg New York, 1997.

Bibliography 217

[Jan07]   Thomas Jansen. *GPU++ - An Embedded GPU Development System for General-Purpose Computations*. Dissertation, Technische Universität München, München, 2007.

[JSS+97] R K Justice, E M Stokeley, J S Strobel, R E Ideker, and W M Smith. Medical image segmentation using 3-D seeded region growing. In *In Proceedings of SPIE: Image Processing*, volume 3034, pages 900–910, 1997.

[KBF+08] Jan Klein, Dirk Bartz, Ola Friman, Markus Hadwiger, Bernhard Preim, Felix Ritter, Anna Vilanova, and Gabriel Zachmann. Advanced Algorithms in Medical Computer Graphics. In *Annex to the Conference Proceedings of EUROGRAPHICS*, pages 25–44, Hersonissos, Greece, 2008. Eurographics Association.

[KBH04]   Florian Kainz, Rod Bogart, and Drew Hess. The OpenEXR Image File Format. In Randima Fernando, editor, *GPU Gems, Programming Techniques, Tips, and Tricks for Real-Time Graphics*, chapter 26, pages 425–444. Addison-Wesley, 2004. http://www.openexr.com (last visit Mar 5 2009).

[KDR+06] Alexander Köhn, Johann Drexl, Felix Ritter, M. König, and Heinz-Otto Peitgen. GPU Accelerated Image Registration in Two and Three Dimensions. In *Bildverarbeitung für die Medizin 2006*, pages 261–265. Springer, 2006.

[KFDB07] Philippe Komma, Jan Fischer, Frank Duffner, and Dirk Bartz. Lossless Volume Data Compression Schemes. In *Simulation und Visualisierung (SimVis 2007)*, pages 169–182, 2007.

[KHEK76] M. Kuwahara, K. Hachimura, S. Eiho, and M. Kinoshita. Processing of bi-angiocardiographic images. *Digital Processing of Biomedical Images, K. Preston and M. Onoe*, pages 187–202, 1976.

[KLF05]   J.M. Kniss, A.E. Lefohn, and N. Fout. Deferred Filtering: Rendering from Difficult Data Formats. In Matt Pharr and Randima Fernando, editors, *GPU Gems 2: Programming Techniques for High-Performance Graphics and General-Purpose Computation*, chapter 41, pages 669–677. Addison Wesley, 2005.

[Kra02]   Rüdiger Kramme. *Medizintechnik: Verfahren- Systeme- Informationsverarbeitung*. Springer, 2nd edition, 2002.

[KSFB06] Andrea Kratz, Rainer Splechtna, Anton L. Fuhrmann, and Katja Bühler. GPU-Based High-Quality Hardware Volume Rendering For Virtual Environments. In *International Workshop on Augmented Environments for Medical Imaging and Computer Aided Surgery*, 2006.

[Kuc07]   Roland Kuck. Object-Oriented Shader Design. In J. Sochor P. Cignoni, editor, *Proceedings of Eurographics 2007*, pages 65–68. Eurographics, The Eurographics Association, September 2007.

[KW03a]   Jens Krüger and Rüdiger Westermann. Acceleration Techniques for GPU-based Volume Rendering. In *Proceedings of IEEE Visualization 2003*, pages 287–292, 2003.

[KW03b]   Jens Krüger and Rüdiger Westermann. Linear Algebra Operators for GPU Implementation of Numerical Algorithms. *ACM Transactions on Graphics (TOG)*, 22(3):908–916, 2003.

[LC87]   William E. Lorensen and Harvey E. Cline. Marching Cubes: A High Resolution 3D Surface Construction Algorithm. *SIGGRAPH Comput. Graph.*, 21(4):163–169, 1987.

[Lev90]   Marc Levoy. Efficient Ray Tracing of Volume Data. *ACM Trans. Graph.*, 9(3):245–261, 1990.

[LJT01]   Zheng Lin, Jesse Jin, and Hugues Talbot. Unseeded Region Growing for 3D Image Segmentation. In *VIP '00: Selected papers from the Pan-Sydney workshop on Visualisation*, pages 31–37, Darlinghurst, Australia, Australia, 2001. Australian Computer Society, Inc.

[LKS+06]   Aaron Lefohn, Joe M. Kniss, Robert Strzodka, Shubhabrata Sengupta, and John D. Owens. Glift: Generic, efficient, random-access gpu data structures. *ACM Transactions on Graphics*, 25(1):60–99, January 2006.

[LNM06]   Warren Leung, Neophytos Neophytou, and Klaus Mueller. SIMD-Aware Ray-Casting. In *Eurographics / IEEE VGTC Workshop on Volume Graphics*, pages 59–62, July 2006.

[LOPR97]   Thomas Lehmann, Walter Oberschelp, Erich Pelikan, and Rudolf Repges. *Bildverarbeitung für die Medizin*. Springer, Berlin, 1997.

[LWP+06]   Patric Ljung, C. Winskog, Anders Persson, Claes Lundström, and Anders Ynnerman. Full Body Virtual Autopsies using a State-of-the-art Volume Rendering Pipeline. *IEEE Transactions on Visualization and Computer Graphics*, 12(5):869–876, 2006.

[MAB+97]   Joe Marks, Brad Andalman, Paul A. Beardsley, William T. Freeman, S. Gibson, Jessica K. Hodgins, T. Kang, Brian Mirtich, Hanspeter Pfister, Wheeler Ruml, Kathy Ryall, J. Seims, and Stuart M. Shieber. Design Galleries: A General Approach to Setting Parameters for Computer Graphics and Animation. In *SIGGRAPH '97: Proceedings of the 24th annual conference on Computer graphics and interactive techniques*, pages 389–400, 1997.

[Mal99]   Stéphane Mallat. *A Wavelet Tour of Signal Processing (Wavelet Analysis & Its Applications)*. Academic Press, 2nd edition, September 1999.

[Mar06] Michelle Kristin Martin. Gegenüberstellung herkömmlicher Shader-Hochsprachen und der Metasprache Sh bei der GPU Programmierung, 2006. *Studienarbeit*, Universität Koblenz-Landau, FB4 S 1016 CV.

[McG05] Morgan McGuire. The supershader. In Wolfgang Engel, editor, *ShaderX^4*, chapter 8.1, pages 485–498. Charles River Media, 2005.

[MEW$^+$94] S.T. MacSweeney, M. Ellis, P.C. Worrell, R.M. Greenhalgh, and J.T. Powell. Smoking and growth rate of small abdominal aortic aneurysms. *The Lancet*, 344(8923):651–652, 1994.

[MMBU92] E. N. Mortensen, B. S. Morse, W. A. Barrett, and J. K. Udupa. Adaptive Boundary Detection Using 'Live-Wire' Two-Dimensional Dynamic Programming. In *IEEE Proceedings of Computers in Cardiology (CIC '92)*, pages 635–638, 10 1992.

[MMG07] Muhammad Muddassir Malik, Torsten Möller, and Meister Eduard Gröller. Feature Peeling. In *Proceedings of Graphics Interface 2007*, pages 273–280, May 2007.

[MQP02] Michael D. McCool, Zheng Qin, and Tiberiu S. Popa. Shader Metaprogramming. In *HWWS '02: Proceedings of the ACM SIGGRAPH/EUROGRAPHICS conference on Graphics hardware*, pages 57–68, Aire-la-Ville, Switzerland, 2002. Eurographics Association.

[MRH00] A. Meijster, J. Roerdink, and W. Hesselink. A general algorithm for computing distance transforms in linear time. In *Mathematical Morphology and its Applications to Image and Signal Processing*, pages 331–340. Kluwer, 2000.

[MSPK06] Morgan McGuire, George Stathis, Hanspeter Pfister, and Shriram Krishnamurthi. Abstract Shade Trees. In *I3D '06: Proceedings of the 2006 symposium on Interactive 3D graphics and games*, pages 79–86, New York, NY, USA, 2006. ACM.

[MT04] Michael McCool and Stefanus Du Toit. *Metaprogramming GPUs with Sh*. AK Peters Ltd, 2004.

[MTP$^+$04] Michael McCool, Stefanus Du Toit, Tiberiu Popa, Bryan Chan, and Kevin Moule. Shader Algebra. In *SIGGRAPH '04: ACM SIGGRAPH 2004 Papers*, pages 787–795, New York, NY, USA, 2004. ACM.

[Mur93] Shigeru Muraki. Volume Data and Wavelet Transforms. *Computer Graphics and Applications*, 13(4), 1993.

[MV98] J. B. A. Maintz and M. A. Viergever. A Survey of Medical Image Registration. *Med Image Anal*, 2(1):1–36, March 1998.

[NH92] Paul Ning and Lambertus Hesselink. Vector Quantization for Volume Rendering. In *VVS '92: Proceedings of the 1992 workshop on Volume visualization*, pages 69–74, New York, NY, USA, 1992. ACM.

[OHL+08] John D. Owens, Mike Houston, David Luebke, Simon Green, John E. Stone, and James C. Phillips. GPU Computing. *Proceedings of the IEEE*, 96(5):879–899, May 2008.

[OLG+07] John D. Owens, David Luebke, Naga Govindaraju, Mark Harris, Jens Krüger, Aaron E. Lefohn, and Timothy J. Purcell. A Survey of General-Purpose Computation on Graphics Hardware. *Computer Graphics Forum*, 26(1):80–113, 2007.

[Ope00] OpenGL Architecture Review Board. *The Official OpenGL Library. OpenGL Programming Guide & Reference Manual, Version 1.2*. Addison-Wesley, 3rd edition, 2000. http://www.opengl.org.

[ORF+05] Silvia D. Olabarriaga, Jean-Michel Rouet, Maxim Fradkin, Marcel Breeuwer, and Wiro J. Niessen. Segmentation of Thrombus in Abdominal Aortic Aneurysms From CTA With Nonparametric Statistical Grey Level Appearance Modeling. *MedImg*, 24(4):477–485, April 2005.

[Pal08] Stephan Palmer. Ein modulares Shaderframework für Volumenrendering, 2008. *Diplomarbeit*, Universität Koblenz-Landau, FB4 D 1072 CV.

[PB07] Bernhard Preim and Dirk Bartz. *Visualization in Medicine: Theory, Algorithms, and Applications (The Morgan Kaufmann Series in Computer Graphics)*. Morgan Kaufmann Publishers Inc., San Francisco, CA, USA, 2007.

[PM90] Pietro Perona and Jitendra Malik. Scale-Space and Edge Detection Using Anisotropic Diffusion. *IEEE Trans. Pattern Anal. Mach. Intell.*, 12(7):629–639, July 1990.

[PSW05] Lutz Priese, Patrick Sturm, and Haojun Wang. Hierarchical Cell Structures for Segmentation of Voxel Images. In *Image Analysis: 14th Scandinavian Conference, SCIA 2005, Joensuu, Finland, June 19-22, 2005.*, LNCS 3540, pages 6–16. Springer Verlag, 2005.

[PT01] Regina Pohle and Klaus D. Tönnies. Segmentation of Medical Images using Adaptive Region Growing. In *Proceedings of SPIE (Medical Imaging 2001)*, volume 4322, pages 1337–1346, San Diego, 2001.

[PvV05] T.Q. Pham and L.J. van Vliet. Separable Bilateral Filtering for Fast Video Preprocessing. In *ICME 2005: IEEE International Conference on Multimedia & Expo, 2005*, pages 1–4, Washington, DC, USA, 2005. IEEE Computer Society.

[RBE08] F. Rößler, R. P. Botchen, and T. Ertl. Dynamic Shader Generation for Flexible Multi-Volume Visualization. In *Proceedings of IEEE Pacific Visualization Symposium 2008 (PacificVis '08)*, pages 17–24, 2008.

[RC98] Jon K. Rogers and Pamela C. Cosman. Robust Wavelet Zerotree Image Compression with Fixed-Length Packetization. In *DCC '98: Proceedings of the Conference on Data Compression*, pages 418–427, Washington, DC, USA, 1998. IEEE Computer Society.

[RD05] Erik Reinhard and Kate Devlin. Dynamic Range Reduction Inspired by Photoreceptor Physiology. *IEEE Transactions on Visualization and Computer Graphics*, 11(1):13–24, 2005.

[Ros05] Randi J. Rost. *OpenGL(R) Shading Language*. Addison-Wesley Professional, 2nd edition, 2005.

[RSK06] Christof Rezk-Salama and Andreas Kolb. Opacity Peeling for Direct Volume Rendering. *Computer Graphics Forum (Proc. Eurographics)*, 25(3):597–606, 2006.

[RSKK06] Christof Rezk-Salama, Maik Keller, and Peter Kohlmann. High-Level User Interfaces for Transfer Function Design with Semantics. *IEEE Trans. on Visualization and Computer Graphics (Proc. IEEE Visualization)*, 11(5):1021–1028, 2006.

[RSSF02] Erik Reinhard, Michael Stark, Peter Shirley, and James Ferwerda. Photographic Tone Reproduction for Digital Images. *ACM Trans. Graph.*, 21(3):267–276, 2002.

[RWPD05] Erik Reinhard, Greg Ward, Sumanta Pattanaik, and Paul E. Debevec. *High Dynamic Range Imaging – Acquisition, Display, and Image-Based Lighting*. Morgan Kaufmann, November 2005.

[Sch96] Peter Schröder. Wavelets in Computer Graphics. In *Proceedings of the IEEE*, volume 84, pages 615–625, 1996.

[Sch05] Henning Scharsach. Advanced GPU Raycasting. In *Proceedings of CESCG 2005*, pages 69–76, 2005.

[SCS+08] Larry Seiler, Doug Carmean, Eric Sprangle, Tom Forsyth, Michael Abrash, Pradeep Dubey, Stephen Junkins, Adam Lake, Jeremy Sugerman, Robert Cavin, Roger Espasa, Ed Grochowski, Toni Juan, and Pat Hanrahan. Larrabee: A Many-Core x86 Architecture for Visual Computing. *ACM Trans. Graph.*, 27(3):1–15, August 2008.

[SHB99] Milan Sonka, Vaclav Hlavac, and Roger Boyle. *Image Processing, Analysis, and Machine Vision*. Thomson-Engineering, 2nd edition, September 1999.

[She92] Mark J. Shensa. The Discrete Wavelet Transform: Wedding the À Trous and Mallat Algorithms. *IEEE Transactions on Acoustics, Speech, and Signal Processing*, 40(10):2464–2482, 1992.

[Shn83] Ben Shneiderman. Direct Manipulation. A Step Beyond Programming Languages. *IEEE Transactions on Computers*, 16(8):57–69, August 1983.

[SHN03]   Anthony Sherbondy, Mike Houston, and Sandy Napel. Fast Volume Segmentation With Simultaneous Visualization Using Programmable Graphics Hardware. In *VIS '03: Proceedings of the 14th IEEE Visualization 2003 (VIS'03)*, pages 171–176, Washington, DC, USA, 2003. IEEE Computer Society.

[SHN+05]   Henning Scharsach, Markus Hadwiger, André Neubauer, Stefan Wolfsberger, and Katja Bühler. Perspective Isosurface and Direct Volume Rendering for Virtual Endoscopy Applications. In *Proceedings of EuroVis/IEEE-VGTC Symposium on Visualization 2006*, 2005.

[SKE07]   M. Strengert, T. Klein, and T. Ertl. A Hardware-Aware Debugger for the OpenGL Shading Language. In *Proceedings of the ACM SIGGRAPH/EUROGRAPHICS conference on Graphics Hardware*, pages 81–88. Eurographics Association, 2007.

[SKLS02]   Marko Subasic, Domagoj Kovacevic, Sven Loncaric, and Erich Sorantin. Segmentation of Abdominal Aortic Aneurysm using Deformable Models. In *Proceedings of East-West-Vision 2002*, pages 61–66, 2002.

[SLD05]   Natzi Sakalihasan, Raymond Limet, and Olivier Defawe. Abdominal aortic aneurysm. *The Lancet*, 365(9470):1577–1589, 2005.

[SML04]   Will Schroeder, Ken Martin, and Bill Lorensen. *The Visualization Toolkit: An Object-Oriented Approach to 3-D Graphics*. Kitware, Inc., 3 edition, December 2004.

[SOB05]   Zein Salah, Jasmina Orman, and Dirk Bartz. Live-Wire Revisited. In Hans-Peter Meinzer, Heinz Handels, Alexander Horsch, and Thomas Tolxdorff, editors, *Bildverarbeitung für die Medizin*, Informatik Aktuell, pages 158–162. Springer, 2005.

[SPSP02]   Dirk Selle, Bernhard Preim, Andrea Schenk, and Heinz-Otto Peitgen. Analysis of Vasculature for Liver Surgery Planning. *IEEE Trans. Med. Imaging*, 21(8), 2002.

[SR93]   Brian C. Smith and Lawrence A. Rowe. Algorithms for manipulating compressed images. *Computer Graphics and Applications*, 13(5):34–42, 1993.

[SR96]   Brian C. Smith and Lawrence A. Rowe. Compressed domain processing of jpeg-encoded images. *Real-Time Imaging*, 2:3–17, 1996.

[SS96]   Bo Shen and Ishwar K. Sethi. Convolution-based edge detection for image/video in block dct domain. *Journal of Visual Communications and Image Representation*, 1996.

[Str01]   Z. R. Struzik. Oversampling the Haar Wavelet Transform. Technical Report INS-R0102, CWI, Amsterdam, The Netherlands, March 2001.

[Stu04]   Patrick Sturm. 3D-Color-Structure-Code - Segmentation by Using a New Non-Plainness Island Hierarchy. In *IEEE International Conference on Image Processing*, pages 953–956. IEEE Signal Processing Society, IEEE Signal Processing Society, 10 2004. 0-7803-8555-1 (ISBN), ICIP 2004, Singapore.

[Sue02]   Paul Suetens. *Fundamentals of Medical Imaging*. Cambridge University Press, 2002.

[SW03]   Jens Schneider and Rüdiger Westermann. Compression Domain Volume Rendering. In *VIS '03: Proceedings of the 14th IEEE Visualization 2003 (VIS'03)*, pages 293–300, Washington, DC, USA, 2003. IEEE Computer Society.

[SXMOO08]   Sanjiv S. Samant, Junyi Xia, Pinar Muyan-Özçelik, and John D. Owens. High performance computing for deformable image registration: Towards a new paradigm in adaptive radiotherapy. *Medical Physics*, 35(8):3546–3553, 2008.

[TD07]   Matthias Trapp and Jürgen Döllner. Automated Combination of Real-Time Shader Programs. In J. Sochor P. Cignoni, editor, *Proceedings of Eurographics 2007*, pages 53–56. Eurographics, The Eurographics Association, September 2007.

[TM98]   C. Tomasi and R. Manduchi. Bilateral Filtering for Gray and Color Images. In *ICCV '98: Proceedings of the Sixth International Conference on Computer Vision*, pages 839–846, Washington, DC, USA, 1998. IEEE Computer Society.

[TPO06]   David Tarditi, Sidd Puri, and Jose Oglesby. Accelerator: Using Data Parallelism to Program GPUs for General-Purpose Uses. *SIGARCH Comput. Archit. News*, 34(5):325–335, 2006.

[ULZ$^+$06] Jayaram K. Udupa, Vicki R. Leblanc, Ying Zhuge, Celina Imielinska, Hilary Schmidt, Leanne M. Currie, Bruce E. Hirsch, and James Woodburn. A Framework for Evaluating Image Segmentation Algorithms. *Computerized Medical Imaging and Graphics*, 30(2):75–87, March 2006.

[USB92]   J. K. Udupa, S. Samarasekera, and W. A. Barrett. Boundary detection via dynamic programming. In R. A. Robb, editor, *Society of Photo-Optical Instrumentation Engineers (SPIE) Conference Series*, volume 1808 of *Presented at the Society of Photo-Optical Instrumentation Engineers (SPIE) Conference*, pages 33–39, September 1992.

[Val05]   Oscar Valero. On banach fixed point theorems for partial metric spaces. *Applied General Topology*, 6:229–240, 2005.

[VKG04]   Ivan Viola, Armin Kanitsar, and Meister Eduard Gröller. Importance-Driven Volume Rendering. In *Proceedings of IEEE Visualization 2004*, pages 139–145. H. Rushmeier, G. Turk, J. van Wijk, October 2004.

[VWE05]   Joachim E. Vollrath, Daniel Weiskopf, and Thomas Ertl. A Generic Software Framework for the GPU Volume Rendering Pipeline. In *Vision, Modeling, and Visualization VMV '05 Conference Proceedings,*, pages 391–398, 2005.

[Wal91]   Gregory K. Wallace. The jpeg still picture compression standard. *Commun. ACM*, 34(4):30–44, 1991.

[WBME00]   J.J. Wever, J.D. Blankensteijn, WP Th. M Mali, and B.C. Eikelboom. Maximal aneurysm diameter follow-up is inadequate after endovascular abdominal aortic aneurysm repair. *Eur J Vasc Endovasc Surg.*, 20(2):177–182, 2000.

[WBSS04]   Zhou Wang, Alan C. Bovik, Hamid R. Sheikh, and Eero P. Simoncelli. Image Quality Assessment: from Error Visibility to Structural Similarity. *IEEE Transactions on Image Processing*, 13(4):600–612, 2004.

[WEE03]   Daniel Weiskopf, Klaus Engel, and Thomas Ertl. Interactive Clipping Techniques for Texture-Based Volume Visualization and Volume Shading. *IEEE Transactions on Visualization and Computer Graphics*, 9(3):298–312, 2003.

[Wes94]   Rüdiger Westermann. A Multiresolution Framework for Volume Rendering. In *VVS '94: Proceedings of the 1994 symposium on Volume visualization*, pages 51–58, New York, NY, USA, 1994. ACM.

[Wes95]   Rüdiger Westermann. Compression Domain Rendering of Time-Resolved Volume Data. In *VIS '95: Proceedings of the 6th conference on Visualization '95*, pages 168–175, Washington, DC, USA, 1995. IEEE Computer Society.

[Wet07]   Martin Wetzke. *BASICS Bildgebende Verfahren*. Urban & Fischer bei Elsevier, 2007.

[WLHW07]   T. T. Wong, C. S. Leung, P. A. Heng, and J. Wang. Discrete Wavelet Transform on Consumer-Level Graphics Hardware. In *IEEE Transactions on Multimedia*, volume 9, pages 668–673. IEEE Computer Society, 4 2007.

[Wri04]   Helen Wright. Putting Visualization First in Computational Steering. In SJ Cox, editor, *Proceedings of UK e-Science All Hands Meeting, AHM2004*, pages 326–331, 2004.

[XP97]   Chenyang Xu and Jerry L. Prince. Gradient Vector Flow: A New External Force for Snakes. *Computer Vision and Pattern Recognition, IEEE Computer Society Conference on*, 0:66–71, June 1997.

[YNCP06]   Xiaoru Yuan, Minh X. Nguyen, Baoquan Chen, and David H. Porter. HDR VolVis: High Dynamic Range Volume Visualization. *IEEE Trans Vis Comput Graph*, 12(4):433–445, 2006.

[YZB+07]   H. Yu, K. Zeng, D.K. Bharkhada, G. Wang, M.T. Madsen, O. Saba, B. Policeni, M.A. Howard, and W.R. Smoker. A segmentation-based method for metal artifact reduction. *Acad Radiol.*, 14(4):495–504, 2007.

[ZHD01]   Bin Zhang, Meichun Hsu, and Umeshwar Dayal. K-Harmonic Means - A Spatial Clustering Algorithm with Boosting. In *TSDM '00: Proceedings of the First International Workshop on Temporal, Spatial, and Spatio-Temporal Data Mining-Revised Papers*, volume 2007/2001 of *Lecture Notes in Computer Science*, pages 31–45, London, UK, 2001. Springer-Verlag.

[ZHWG08]   Kun Zhou, Qiming Hou, Rui Wang, and Baining Guo. Real-Time KD-Tree Construction on Graphics Hardware. *ACM Trans. Graph.*, 27(5):1–11, 2008.

Web-based References

[3Dc08] SpaceNavigator. website, 2008. `http://www.3dconnexion.de/3dmouse/spacenavigator.php` (last visit March 5, 2009).

[Ble01] Guy E. Blelloch. Introduction to Data Compression, 2001. `http://www.cs.cmu.edu/afs/cs/project/pscico-guyb/realworld/www/compression.pdf`, last visit January 5, 2009.

[Boo08] Boost – C++ Libraries. website, 2008. Boost Version 1.37, `http://www.boost.org`, last visit January 10, 2009.

[Bro07] Brook+ SC07 BOF Session. PDF, 2007. `http://ati.amd.com/technology/streamcomputing/AMD-Brookplus.pdf` (last visit March 12 2009).

[CMa08] CMake – Cross Platform Make. website, 2008. `http://www.cmake.org`, last visit March 8 2009.

[IM08] Milan Ikits and Marcelo Magallon. OpenGL Extension Wranger. website, 2008. `http://glew.sourceforge.net`, last visit March 12 2009.

[JPGa] The JPEG standard. website. Joint Photographic Experts Group, `http://jpeg.org/jpeg/index.html`.

[JPGb] The JPEG 2000 standard. website. Joint Photographic Experts Group, `http://jpeg.org/jpeg2000/index.html`.

[Khr] OpenCL – The open standard for parallel programming of heterogeneous systems. website. Khronos Group, `http://www.khronos.org/opencl/`, last visit January 13 2009.

[MeV07] MeVis. MeVisLab: A Development Environment for Medical Image Processing and Visualization, 2007. `http://www.mevislab.de`, last visit February 5 2009.

[Mic08] Microsoft. Direct3D 11, Technical Preview. website, November 2008. Microsoft Corporation, `http://msdn.microsoft.com/en-us/xna/bb896684.aspx`, last visit January 13, 2009.

[OMP]   OpenMP Application Program Interface. website. OpenMP Architecture Review Board, http://www.openmp.org/mp-documents/spec30.pdf, last visit December 29, 2008.

[Osi]   Osirix medical imaging software and DICOM sample image sets. website. http://www.osirix-viewer.com and http://pubimage.hcuge.ch:8080/ (last visit June 23 2008).

[See08] PHANTOM Omni Haptic Device. website, 2008. http://www.seereal.com (last visit March 8, 2009).

[Sen07] PHANTOM Omni Haptic Device. website, 2007. http://www.sensable.com/haptic-phantom-omni.htm (last visit March 5, 2009).

[SIG]   SIGGRAPH Los Angeles 2008 - OpenGL BOF slides. website. Khronos Group, http://www.khronos.org/library/detail/2008_siggraph_opengl_bof_slides/, last visit September 23, 2008.

[TBE08] Lee Thomason, Yves Berquin, and Andrew Ellerton. TinyXML Documentation. website, 2008. http://www.grinninglizard.com/tinyxmldocs (last visit Mar 10, 2009).

Die VDM Verlagsservicegesellschaft sucht für wissenschaftliche Verlage abgeschlossene und herausragende

Dissertationen, Habilitationen, Diplomarbeiten, Master Theses, Magisterarbeiten usw.

für die kostenlose Publikation als Fachbuch.

Sie verfügen über eine Arbeit, die hohen inhaltlichen und formalen Ansprüchen genügt, und haben Interesse an einer honorarvergüteten Publikation?

Dann senden Sie bitte erste Informationen über sich und Ihre Arbeit per Email an *info@vdm-vsg.de*.

Sie erhalten kurzfristig unser Feedback!

VDM Verlagsservicegesellschaft mbH
Dudweiler Landstr. 99   Telefon   +49 681 3720 174
D - 66123 Saarbrücken   Fax   +49 681 3720 1749
www.vdm-vsg.de

Die VDM Verlagsservicegesellschaft mbH vertritt

Printed by Books on Demand GmbH, Norderstedt / Germany